CW00515012

THE BOY ON THE TRAIN

A Father and Son's Kindertransport Story

Gerry Hahlo

Copyright © Gerry Hahlo
All rights reserved

No part of this publication may be reproduced, distributed or transmitted in any form or by any means, including photocopying, recording, or other electronic or mechanical methods, without the prior written permission of the author.

Every effort has been made to trace copyright holders and obtain permission to reproduce images. Please get in touch with any information relating to any image or rights holder.

For permissions and other enquires, contact boyonthetrain@outlook.com

First edition, January 2022

Any proceeds from the sale of this book are donated to The Wiener Holocaust Library in London

Cover background image: reverse side of Dieter's birth announcement postcard, 1926
Front cover photo: Georg and Dieter, c 1931
Back cover photos: Georg Hahlo, 1922; Dieter Hahlo, 1938

CONTENTS

INTRODUCTION

I have always taken pride in my name. My family name, not my given name and definitely not my second given name, come to that. The family name was a point of difference, a name with a story, which I often embellished, such that I struggled to separate fact from fiction. When young, I told friends that the name was invented by the five heads of the family using their initials when they were forced, by Napoleon who had sequestered Prussia, to adopt second names, which had previously not been the practice in the region. There was also a story about family disgrace, someone being hanged and the family deciding to move on from this by inventing a new name. This fanciful fabrication landed me in hot water during my French A-Level oral exam. In the weeks before we rehearsed feverishly the answers to standard questions about visiting France and holidays in general. Instead, I was asked about the origins of my name and embarked on a stuttering story about someone being hanged that was well beyond my capabilities. I burbled away, wishing I had never started the tale and realising that the required answer had been simply: 'It's German.'

Another claim enthusiastically developed by me is that everyone with this name is related in some way to us. This may be true, at least the theory has not been disproved yet. My father came up with something even more outlandish. When Frida Kahlo came to prominence in the UK, helped by a theatre production in which my brother Richard played, he developed the theory that Kahlo was derived from Hahlo and that she too was part of our family tree. This one has not been disproved either, but seems to be lying fallow and is unlikely to be resurrected.

Why does a name matter? It is a sign that binds a group of people together. Family ties unite, in most cases, and create support and emotional bonds. Blood is thicker than water they say. And when you have a distinctive name, perhaps it unites more strongly?

The name is unusual, even in Germany. In March 2020 I visited the family's home town of Oldenburg. It is a prosperous, comfortable town of around 150,000 inhabitants, not too big and not too small to keep its people busy and fulfilled. I was directed to the town archives to see what records of the family's business and life could be uncovered. I wrote down my name and the archivist, who would have been born in the 1950s, immediately said 'Ah, that is a well-known family here in Oldenburg.'

This memoir is a tribute to two generations who were pivotal in ensuring that our name survived, in Britain at least. The story focuses on Georg Hahlo, my grandfather, and Dieter Hahlo, his son and my father. It is thanks to their bravery and endurance, their forbearance of emotional and physical hardships, that I am here now and able to write this, and perhaps that you are able to read it too. Many of us Hahlos and related people in England are alive due to their will to survive. Without them and their sacrifices, we would not exist. And that, to my mind, deserves a fitting tribute.

The story focuses on two men because their accounts are the most complete. It's a masculine perspective and experience, which is not to diminish the hardships endured by Ella Hahlo and Ursula Hahlo, wife/mother and daughter/sister respectively of these two men. The two women were reluctant to acknowledge the past, meaning their perspectives are mostly unrecorded and must be imagined. They were emotionally scarred by their experiences and reticence was their way of dealing with the pain. As Virginia Woolf put it, women tend to appear 'as a glimpse in the lives of the great, whisking away into the background, concealing... a wink, a laugh, perhaps a tear'. And women are often hidden from wartime narratives which focus on the derring-do of men, because their roles were much less about external heroism. I don't mean to underappreciate them but I have little material from them or of them. This is not a hagiography of two great men battling against the odds, it is simply the story of how they behaved in extreme circumstances. They could not have done it without the support of Ella and Ursula and that must not be forgotten. Lives that are more domestic, more private, what George Eliot described as a hidden life of 'unrecorded acts', are still filled with emotional drama. I like to think that these two women would be encouraged to hear that what we know of their part in the story is to be heard and appreciated by future generations.

The need to know who we are and how we got here is strong. We ought to feel the pain of our forebears to understand where we came from, to gain a fuller sense of shared history. For me, it is a sense of fulfilment that I didn't know I needed until I contemplated the passing of these two generations and the stories that would have died with them. My father's gradual decline began with a minor stroke in 2000, at which point it seemed that a stopwatch had been started. History was going to escape from us before we had got to grips with it. Someone needed to write it down and ensure it lives on for generations to come. If not now, when? If not me, who?

So the book charts the lives of two key figures in the Hahlo history at pivotal points of that history, people who took extraordinary steps to ensure their own survival and that of others. Plenty of stories have been told from the Nazi era of people who survived and those who did not. Our family is one of the lucky ones, because there are survivors. We will see what Georg and Dieter went through, the turmoil of their times, their bravery, how they managed to keep this branch of the Hahlo family alive.

Writing about family is complicated. We have Georg's and Dieter's recollections, which may or may not be true, many of which needed to be fleshed out, to make sense of them. But this is not a definitive account because it cannot be so. There are too many gaps in what Georg and Dieter chose to record and from what they failed to recall. My interpretation of events and how they might have felt comes from a different era, based on assumptions that are different from those of yesterday. They took risks that are unimaginable to us, their children, grandchildren and great-grandchildren, because we live cosseted lives without any of the evils that confronted them. Who can know how we would have reacted, what we would have done if faced with the horrors of the first half of the twentieth century?

Everyone will have a different perspective of the same events. Biography is a cumulative process. Anyone who wants to tell others the story will be shaped by this telling. I am only helping to unfold what I know; new truths might emerge in the future, as generations build the collective jigsaw of where they come from. My aim is simply to keep alive the family story. It is the only way left of saying thank you to real people we have known and of acknowledging their bravery. It is thanks to them that we can love and nurture new people who will have their own stories and give life to future generations, and thanks to them that the name lives on.

The two primary sources are a series of interviews I conducted with my father and the account written by my grandfather between December 1939 and March 1940 when he was in Bolivia. It seems that Georg Hahlo was blessed with a prodigious memory (he must have had contemporaneous diaries of his wartime exploits, although there is no record of these) and concentrated productivity. I guess that at this time he would have had only the bare scratchings of a life and he must have been lonely, homesick, forlorn and free to concentrate on his most important task: justifying his actions to those who mattered most.

Georg's generation went through the First World War, the revolution of 1918, the rampaging inflation of 1923, the occupation of the Rhineland and total upheaval following the ascent of Hitler in 1933. For Jews and other minorities in Germany, this was the beginning of unspeakable suffering, and of their expulsion from Germany. To have lived through all this filled life to the brim. Georg wrote his account as something to be handed to future generations, for information and as a warning. But mainly it was to provide for his children a lasting memory of their father. He states at the outset:

> 'My experiences, it is true, are no different from those of many thousands of others – indeed, they may even be of lesser value – but they deserve nonetheless to be written down, to teach and warn coming generations and to remind my dear children of their Dad.'

Georg prized loyalty and honour with family at the apex of his values, cherishing his wife and children. All that he treasured, all his plans and dreams, had been shattered. This was his opportunity to put his side of the story and explain to his children how he had striven throughout his life to uphold the values of German society and how those in power had turned on him, forcing his drastic actions. It was his last chance to declare his love and to justify what he had been forced to do. He hoped for forgiveness.

There is a lot he does not say. He does not dwell on the gory reality of war, to protect his children from the horrors he experienced and the ensuing trauma. He doesn't go into detail of life under Nazi rule, the terrors of persecution and its impact on his state of mind. He doesn't say how escapes were arranged. These facts have been lost. Our frustration at missing detail is insignificant when we think what was going through his mind when he wrote; he was faced with an impossible task. We are grateful to have his record of events because it enables us to recognise his exploits and his role as the foundation of a thriving family, a family that he saved from probable extinction.

It seems Georg posted his typescript to his sister's home in London for passing on to his wife and children during the war. There were postal services in both countries at the time. He thought he would never see his children again, hence the dedication that opens the document:

'To my beloved children Ursula and Dieter
In memory of their Dad.

Begun in La Paz on 3rd December 1939.'

NOTES

Our part of the family archive, in hard copy and digitised, will be accessible to view once catalogued at the Wiener Holocaust Library in London, including a typescript of Georg's account in German and an English translation and a hoard of family photos and other documents, some of which are reproduced in this book.

I recorded over fifteen hours of interviews on C90 cassette tapes (remember them?) with my father and with my mother, in less detail. These happened in 2002–3. Transcriptions are available and so are digital audio files of the original recordings, should you want to hear the sound of their voices.

It started as a project around my side of the family's history and I now regret that I did not cast wider, for instance by talking to my father's sister, presupposing that that would have been possible.

Each chapter notes at the start the year(s) and where the main action takes place, although there are multiple locations or journeys in several chapters. Each chapter starts with a direct quotation from my grandfather's memoirs or from my father's recorded recollections, and in one case from my mother's. Quotation marks in the text, unless noted otherwise, signal that the phrases are quotations taken from my grandfather's memoirs or from my parents' remembrances.

Footnotes refer to historical context that can be found at the back, numbered 1 to 25, and which give background and detail to help understand the context of some events and decisions and actions that were taken as a result.

The settings of Georg's war exploits can be determined from the names he uses. Since then villages and territory have changed hands more than once and some names have changed too. Location names in the text are mainly those in use today, and locations are placed in the countries in which they exist today. When the text refers to 'today' it means 2019–20, when the first draft was completed.

Every episode and event in the story are rooted in my grandfather's and my father's first-hand accounts. Sometimes these conflict with public records of dates and numbers and processes. Georg and Dieter contradict themselves and each other. They don't even agree which station Dieter's train to England left from. In some cases I add detail from other people's or historical accounts and sometimes I embellish with imagined scenes and dialogue. In so doing I have, I hope, turned everything into a story, as much as my abilities allow.

In his written account, Georg does not say how he managed to obtain the vital permit to travel which gave him his means of escape. The dialogue in Chapter 17 is based on his recounting of the story subsequently to my father who passed it on to me, with pride in his father's resourcefulness.

There is more detail to uncover and I would be delighted if others had the fortitude to tackle such a task. We don't know much about other strands of family, about the details of Georg's military activity and we have few details of Dieter's journey to England, for example. The answers are out there somewhere if you have the will to find them. I've done my bit, now it's time to pass the baton. Good luck.

Map of Germany

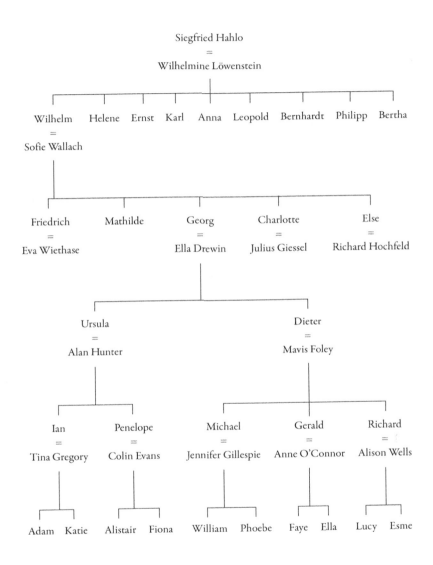

Family Tree

This story is dedicated to

William, Lucy, Phoebe, Esme, Faye and Ella

This is who you are. They did it for you. Long may you prosper.

Prologue

OLDENBURG, GERMANY
NOVEMBER 1938

Dieter had set off for school and the household was settling into its placid rhythm after the whir of breakfast and school uniform. Georg was dressed in his dark, three-piece suit with a tie and had paid attention to his neat, slicked hair. Despite having no work, it was important to fit the respectability of the neighbourhood. His wife, Elli, was in her room readying herself for a round of the usual domestic chores and thinking that later she should go out to queue for household provisions. As new arrivals in the house, she could not expect the maid to get them everything. Or she might bake a cake, everyone liked a cake. On the floor below, Georg's parents were slowly gathering themselves for another day.

Normality was punctured by the shrillness of the doorbell. It was Dieter in a troubled state. When calmed, he garbled that the school appeared to be closed. Pupils were hanging around outside in groups and teachers were not to be seen. He detected tension. Smoke was rising from the junction north of school but Dieter had been too scared to go and see what was going on. He was new to the school and had no friends he could talk to.

Georg grabbed his coat and hat and rushed off in the direction of the plume of smoke. A crowd had gathered and was watching a smouldering building. Acrid smoke curled around them and some had handkerchiefs over their noses but they seemed to be enjoying the spectacle. Fire crews were standing by, chatting, not attempting to douse the flames or to save the valuables and relics within. It was as if the town were at the theatre for an evening of genteel entertainment. Georg recognised a few local officials in the throng, seemingly unperturbed at the destruction of one of the town's landmarks, and was horrified that this could happen in Germany.

He turned his back on the ruined synagogue and half ran, half walked to his Uncle Leopold's apartment on the other side of the old town. There was an air of menace and bands of men were prowling the streets. Several shopfronts had been smashed and items looted but no police were in attendance. No one was attempting to control the mob. He was out of breath by the time he reached the block. The bell was answered by Leopold's housekeeper who delivered the greatest shock of all: Leopold had been arrested and nobody knew where he had been taken.

Georg hurried home and tried to describe the anarchy he had seen without alarming everyone but he could not help infecting the household with his fear. The family looked at each other with anxiety and bewilderment. Words failed them. What did this mean? They soon learned that synagogues throughout the Reich were burning and that many Jewish men had been rounded up and taken away. It was a miracle that their home had been spared a visit from the thugs. Their old neighbour and friend from Hannover called to say that the police had been searching their old block and asking for Georg Hahlo, so he knew that it was only a matter of time before he was tracked down and arrested. There was no time to think and he kissed his wife, son and parents farewell, attempting to assure them that all would be well, and set off briskly for the station, avoiding places where people were congregating. He bought a ticket for the first train he could find. It took him to Hamburg, where he hoped to be safer.

On the train there were other men who had escaped the notice of the police. In Hamburg, there were more. No one had a plan or knew what might happen next. Everywhere Georg saw the effects of anger against Jews and their businesses. He bought a ticket for another train. And then another train and then another. His mind raced. He could not set foot in his own house without fear. How had it come to this?

The trains were cold and uncomfortable. The nights were unbearable and he could not sleep. He lost track of where he had been. It was hard to think clearly but one thought did crystallise as he watched bleak countryside speed past the window. He could not continue life on the run, he had to get his family to safety: they had to leave Germany. He must show the resolve that had enabled him to survive the war. His parents, his darling wife, his adored son Dieter and his much loved and missed daughter Ursula, already in England, depended on him. It was time to act. He decided to marshal his arguments and appeal to authority to allow him, a decorated war hero, to organise the safety of his family. He had fought for Germany and three times he had nearly paid with his life for his loyalty to the fatherland; he was not going to allow the fatherland to ruin him now.

With his mind fixed, he returned to Oldenburg. In the days he had been away, the family had become a wreck of nervousness. Dieter sensed to keep a low profile and not ask too many questions. Georg called his sister Else and her husband Richard in England, imploring him to speak to English contacts and ask whether they would be willing to give a guarantee for a temporary visa to England. It seemed possible. But for this he would need a permit to travel. And permits were only available from the state police.

It was his most audacious gamble yet. He stood before the police building in Oldenburg, feeling as though he were back in the war, under fire from an enemy he could not see. He adjusted his hat, straightened his tie, held his head high. The consequences of failure were unthinkable. It was now or never. He marched in.

If his plan had not paid off, my brothers and I would not be alive today to tell this story.

1

OLDENBURG, GERMANY, 1895

'We children had no contact, not even socially, with Jewish society and were, superficially, brought up as Christians'

My paternal grandfather, Georg Richard Siegfried Hahlo, was born in November 1895, a small boy who would grow into a small man. His diminutive stature, even by the day's standards, would create social and physical challenges which he faced down with the gusto of youth and a drive to succeed, his determination born out of adversity. These attributes were important throughout his life, never more so than when he was faced by the grim resolve of the Nazis to purge their lands of all traces of Jewish life.

We called him Opa, meaning Grandpa, and I remember him as a jovial figure, always wanting to engage with us boys and looking for opportunities for jokes. We met him once in the centre of London when I was aged about 7 and, despite my mother's qualms, he permitted me to walk on the top of the wall of the Victoria Embankment directly above the river, holding his hand. I tottered along, thrilled, even though I was slightly unnerved by the absence of the top of one of his fingers, an old war wound that was not spoken about. Back on the pavement, we were still holding hands as we came to a lamppost. Opa tried to go the other way round it to me but still held on so that we found it impassable. I thought this was hilarious and insisted the ritual be repeated at every lamppost.

He was quite rotund by the time I knew him. He had a smiling, welcoming face and earnest eyes, eager to be embraced by us boys but without hugging, which was not normal in those days. His clothing was standard for a professional man, a drab suit with waistcoat and tie, yet, being foreign, he seemed exotic and it was a wonder to me that this man was my dad's dad. My regret now is that I never thought to ask so many obvious questions. He never wished to inflict us with a sense of the suffering and hardships he had faced in order for us to have the comfortable lives we enjoyed. Now I wish he had.

He had multiple enthusiasms, such as buses, trams and trains, which he passed on to his son. Also for *Kaffee und Kuchen* (coffee and cake), served at 4 o'clock each afternoon. This remains a German institution. His consternation was palpable when I declined cake and preferred tea to coffee. At times he was typically Germanic and could be brusque or forceful, showing the strong personality that lay within his small build. He treasured the remnants of his family and liked to joke and play with us as much as our brief visits allowed. He was jolly, lively and generous, as well as stout, thanks to his love of cake. He hid his sadness at how life had worked out and the emotional impact of having to sever family ties in order to survive.

Georg Hahlo was a small man living in big times. The generation born in Germany towards the end of the nineteenth century experienced a huge and unexpected change of fortune. When he was born in 1895, Germany was carefree. The country had two cultures. One was conservative, authoritarian, business-driven and wary of the working class, especially of trade unions. The other was working class. These people were piling into the cities and powering rapid industrial growth, benefitting themselves and the economy. These were *Gründerzeit* (the good times). Children in Georg's circles were sheltered by their parents, who helped to arrange careers and ensured stability such that their offspring would eventually be able to support them. It was a time of prosperity, growth, security and preordained futures. The politics of the day were largely unimportant. There were those who followed politics as a career or hobby but it was not a daily topic in Georg's family. Discussion related to more parochial matters, such as whether this or that railway line should be built, or whether shops should close at 8 or 9 o'clock in the evening. These were the topics which seemed important at the time, because there were so few other problems that demanded to be solved.

The solidity and confidence of Germany at the time of Georg's birth had been built on its success in the Franco-Prussian war of 1870/71. A coalition of German states led by Prussia had defeated France and created a unified Germany with inordinate belief in its strength and righteousness. The war had marked the end of French hegemony in continental Europe. In Berlin, the Government set about building a huge Victory Column with three segments, to commemorate three wars and three victories versus Denmark, Austria and now France. Cannons seized from the enemy adorned the column in order to ram home the scale of the victories. To this day, on 2 September, the Day of Sedan, there is no school so children can join the celebrations marking the decisive last battle. Up and down the country bells ring, sermons and prayers of thanks are heard in churches, parades congregate, military bands play and patriotic songs are sung.

The newly-unified Germany became an imperial superpower, boasting the most powerful and professional army in the world. The economy boomed, fed by trainloads of bullion from occupied France. Although Britain remained the dominant world power, British involvement in European affairs was limited owing to its focus on colonial empire-building. Anglo-German tension was mitigated by prominent relationships between the two powers, such as the marriage between Princess Victoria, eldest daughter of Queen

Victoria, and Crown Prince Frederick, later Emperor Frederick III.

The first period of the German Empire was a great age of liberal reform. Germany at a stroke acquired uniform legal procedure, coinage and administration. An imperial bank was created, most restrictions on freedom of enterprise and freedom of movement were removed, and limited companies and trade combinations were allowed. Municipal autonomy was established in 1873, freeing towns from the control of large landowners, and developing local government, in which Germany led the world. Freedom of the press was secured in 1874. The German Empire was an industrial, technological and scientific giant, gaining more Nobel Prizes in science than any other country. Thanks to the iron and steel of the Ruhr, Germany had become the greatest industrial power of Europe and the second-largest economy in the world behind the US. The new Germany knew no moderation.

Georg's grandfather, Siegfried Hahlo, had moved to Oldenburg in 1841 and opened a store at Lange Strasse 36 before moving to larger premises at number 60, virtually opposite, in 1870. He had passed the store to his oldest son Wilhelm by the time Georg was born and had moved with his wife a few paces around the corner, to Gaststrasse. There Siegfried and his wife, Wilhelmine, sat quietly, she doing her crochet and needlework by one window while he dozed in his chaise longue by the other window, from where, when awake, he could observe the shoppers and traders milling in the street below. Their rooms were richly decorated with brocaded wallpaper and many ornaments, pictures and other hangings. Tables and drawers were covered with patterned cloth and doilies, which had been hand-sewn by Wilhelmine. Picture frames, chairs, tables and even the barometer were made of dark wood, as was the heavy carved oak chest. Chests such as theirs were typical furniture and likely to have been crafted in the eighteenth century by a workshop in or close to Oldenburg. More intricately carved chests were more expensive and showed the wealth

A drawing of the Hahlo premises around 1900

of the owner. The front panels of the Hahlo chest were richly carved, of course.

Georg's father Wilhelm was the oldest child and took over the business in 1892. It was a prosperous enterprise that made and sold fashions and household linen. Well-to-do women would come to choose materials and have somebody make up dresses and clothes for them. The store was superbly positioned on the main shopping street at a busy junction. Even casual visitors to Oldenburg would find themselves walking past the site many times over the course of a few days. Years later, in the 1960s, Georg and Dieter returned to Oldenburg. It was a bright day so the shop at Lange Strasse 60 had lowered its blinds and they were astonished to see the faded name of Hahlo still visible on the awnings.

Oldenburg, a pretty garden town in northern Germany, was the economic and cultural hub of its small region and a centre of trade. Founded in the twelfth century by the Counts of Oldenburg, its medieval core was razed by fire in 1676. The parks, promenade and neoclassical buildings that exist today date from the end of the eighteenth century, the town having been left unscathed by the Second World War. The Grand Duchy of Oldenburg was a grand duchy within the German Empire and its ruling family, The House of Oldenburg, is still one of Europe's most influential royal houses; the first fourteen persons in the line of succession to the British throne are all patrilineal members of the house, as was Prince Philip. The monarchs occupied Schloss Oldenburg in the centre of the town until 1918, today a museum. The grounds have become a public park, the Schlossgarten, next to it.

The history of Jews in Oldenburg dates back to the fourteenth century. The Grand Duchy was respected for its liberal regime and Jews were well integrated. They were given places of worship and special schooling and many opened businesses following emancipation in 1871, when there were fewer than 200 people in the Jewish community out of a town

The last Grand Duke, Friedrich, 1910

population just under 20,000. Alemannia Judaica, a group researching the history of Jews in Germany, reports that at the start of the twentieth century there were numerous Jewish businesses in Oldenburg that were important for the economic life of the town. It mentions court banker Carl Ballin and his brother, pharmacist Georg Ballin. It says manufacturers of bicycles and musical instruments had an excellent reputation and that the town was notable for its stores selling textiles and clothing and shoes and leather goods: 'successful merchants included Wilhelm Hahlo, the purveyor to the court, and his brother Leopold'.

The family was prominent in the town. There was a big event on 14 July 1912 when the zeppelin Viktoria Luise landed at the racecourse in Ohmstede, a couple of miles to the north. A crowd gathered to watch in wonder and a few eminent citizens were granted seats for its return flight to Hamburg. Before boarding they

Passengers and onlookers and the Viktoria Luise

The Viktoria Luise on her way back to Hamburg

proudly posed for the photographers. The caption to the photo says that among them were: 'Schwartz the bookseller, Lüttichau from the yeast factory, Gellermann of the monastery brewery, Ahlhorn, Hahlo, Stöver and Frühstück'. Once all were safely on board, the great airship rose and set off to the sound of the band playing *Kommt ein Vogel geflogen* (A bird is flying) and the resounding cheers of the crowd. It is not recorded which Hahlo was on board, most probably Georg's father. He will be in the photograph somewhere.

Georg was born, an 'important event' he wryly notes, on 1 November 1895 at home above the store at Lange Strasse 60. Georg was the second son, following his brother Friedrich (Fritz) born

Else, Georg, Lotte. Oldenburg c 1906

January 1891. Two sisters completed the family, Lotte (21 December 1899) and Else (6 April 1903). The second born Mathilde died aged six months in January 1895.

Their parents Wilhelm and Sofie (née Wallach) had married in Mühlhausen on 2 March 1890. The parents and Leopold were baptised as Protestants in the Lutheran church in 1892, the year in which Wilhelm took over the family business. According to German government records, the Wallach family was not of Jewish descent, yet Georg was unsure of this. He ponders in his memoir whether a wave of antisemitism towards the end of the century was the reason for his parents to get baptised, or whether there were practical motivations. The business was enormously important to the family, having been built from scratch to become pre-eminent in the town and, most prestigiously, to be awarded the title 'Purveyor to the Court', the equivalent of a royal warrant. Or perhaps, Georg says, they simply wanted to make life easier for their children. This thinking would have been justifiable given the large Protestant majority in the region.

The scourge of antisemitism was rife around the time of Georg's birth. Significant pogroms had occurred in Russia, Poland and

Sofie and Wilhelm (undated)   *Leopold in 1929*

elsewhere causing Jews to flee westwards as industrialisation and
urbanisation spread across Europe and the old orders were
overturned, most spectacularly in the French Revolution. Between
1880 and 1925, 3.5 million Jews left central and eastern Europe to
work in the new industrial economies but they came to be seen as
destabilisers, working for themselves rather than for the good of the
nation, especially by those not benefiting as much. Historically,
Jewish conversions have been linked to times of political and
economic upheaval, especially among more affluent Jews who had
the most to lose. I imagine that the Hahlos converted to
Protestantism in order to protect their business and to avoid
antisemitism hampering the lives of their children. What is certain
is that Georg's parents had not been devout Jews and easily shed the
rituals of Jewish life. Georg describes a childhood in which the
family had no contact, not even socially, with Jewish society and
were brought up as Christians. Georg's parents showed little
attachment to any religious beliefs, although Georg was baptised

in Oldenburg on 9 January 1896.[1]

Georg tried his hand at genealogy between the wars. Germans were immaculate record keepers, which helped him at the time but would contribute to his downfall later. Georg reports that many Jews tried to find their origins but this was difficult because Jewish families had no definite surnames before the beginning of the nineteenth century. Jews used to adopt the male parent's first name as a surname for the next generation and as a result each successive generation would have a different last name. In 1812 Napoleon occupied much of Prussia and surname adoption was mandated to enable efficient government and taxation, education and military service. Oldenburg was the last principality to complete the process, in 1852. The Napoleonic reforms ended a lot of aristocratic privileges and established equality before the law, including for Jews.

Surnames derived from Hebrew were not permitted. In Germany Jews tended to take or to be issued with German surnames. The most common way was to make permanent the name they already had, often using patronymics: for example, the son of Mendel would take the name Mendelssohn. Otherwise they followed convention by reflecting their location or origins or their trades and occupations. Some Jews picked names they liked. This might explain why many Jewish names are romanticised and celebrate nature such as Apfelbaum, Kirschbaum, Birnbaum and Rosenzweig which mean apple tree, cherry tree, pear tree and rose twig. Others, those with less money, influence or luck, were allocated names by German officials. These often carried a hint of antisemitism, such as Waldlieferant meaning forest supplier or Afterduft, which can translate as anus odour.

It seems that the Hahlo family did not follow a simple course

---

[1] Why did the Hahlo family convert from Judaism? Antisemitism in late nineteenth century Germany. See p250

Wilhelm Hahlo in 1862 (boy standing)

towards acquiring a surname. Georg's parents had a family tree, made around 1900, which names an ancestor Heinemann Salomon born in 1751 in Hannoversch Münden. He married Chale Müller in 1786, and, according to a newspaper announcement, took the name Hahlo in 1808, deriving from his wife's first name Chale. This is mentioned in the book 'History of Oldenburg Jews' in the town archives. Hence Hahlo appears to be an invented name, explaining its rarity. As far as we know, all people bearing the name Hahlo should be able to trace their ancestry back to Heinemann Salomon. The couple had eight children born between 1787 and 1803. All are credited with the name Hahlo, so it is possible that the name was formally adopted before 1808. Their descendants had large families, so that the Hahlo name had branched far and wide over Germany's borders by 1933.

Georg's mother came from the Wallach family who lived in Kassel. Her parents were from a family of manufacturers in Mühlhausen. Georg managed to trace them back as far as the year 1800. Some relatives in the US have since succeeded in building the family tree even further back.

2

OLDENBURG, GERMANY, 1902–14

'Those were the good old days!
Our Sunday outings were so nice!'

Education in Germany was rigorously organised. The *Gymnasium* (high or grammar school) was for the sons of high society, focusing on classic literature and languages and preparing them for university. *Realschule* focused on Mathematics, Physics and modern languages, educating people to become engineers and clerks, jobs that the elites and merchants looked down upon. *Volksschule* (elementary school) was for the working masses, for whom four years of basic education were regarded as sufficient. There were separate schools for girls and universities had begun cautiously to admit women, for whom careers as teachers and nurses stood open, although in general women were expected to stay at home and accept the role of housewife and mother.

Between Easter 1902 and 1905, Georg attended the *Vorschule* (primary school) and after that the Grand-Ducal *Gymnasium*, the oldest school in Oldenburg situated next to the theatre on the edge of the old town. As a pupil he says he 'belonged to the average' but he must have passed an entrance exam because his brother Fritz did not attend. Given his later achievements, this seems to be false modesty but he does say that he had to repeat the fourth year in order to consolidate his knowledge. He certainly did not have

Pupils in a fraternity at Oldenburg Gymnasium, 1895

enthusiasm for his secondary schooling in the traditional style. It was called a Humanistic Gymnasium and emphasised the importance of the civilisations and languages of ancient Greece and Rome. Boys were taught to write in classical Germanic style, called Sütterlin script, a form of historical handwriting that is now almost impossible to decipher. We must be grateful that Georg used a typewriter to record his memoirs. Georg must have stood out in some way because when the family was forced to move back to Oldenburg in 1938,

The Gymnasium in 1880

Dieter attended the same school for two months and was taught by an old teacher, who said 'I hope you will be as good and as clever as your father was.'

Georg claims that few of the boys liked the school, because the teaching was impersonal knowledge-cramming: 'Almost all the teachers were old, with ossified minds, and no understanding of young people.' This shows Georg's independence of spirit and resourcefulness, which he would demonstrate later. He often felt he could manage better without the direction of others. He says that school outings such as hikes and school festivities were unknown, in contrast to the education received by his own children in the 1930s. He recounts: 'There was no personal communication between teachers, parents and pupils. Once when my mother had to see my language teacher for Greek, she felt this to be a sacrificial walk.' Georg confesses that when he is sleeping badly his dreams usually feature 'disagreeable situations' from his schooldays: 'I still hear Professor Frerichs say, in his cynical tone, "Now to be translated with his peculiar elegance by... Hahlo!" '

Georg derived compensation from the strength and unity of the family: he acknowledges the profound love that 'my dear parents' always gave. Their care was appreciated when Georg at the age of 13 had to go through what he describes as a severe ear operation. There are no details although it must have been successful as his memoirs make no reference to hearing difficulties in later life.

Georg highlights his memories of Christmases featuring traditions and ceremony that still live on in Hahlo families. Germany already had a strong Christmas tradition by the time Georg was a child and the country is credited with establishing the custom of a Christmas tree. Germans had hung boughs over their doors and windows to ward off witches, ghosts and malign spirits and in the sixteenth century devout Christians in Germany started to bring trees decorated with lighted candles into their homes. There was no custom in England until 1846 when Queen Victoria and Prince Albert, a German, were sketched standing with their children around a Christmas tree, immediately making trees fashionable.

The Christmas excitement started each year with the German tradition of leaving shoes outside the bedroom door on the night of 5 December, into which St Nicholas would deposit small gifts and treats – if the children had been good. Georg enjoyed a richly decorated tree, with lighted candles and all manner of adornments. Some German families could not do without a Christmas goose, others would go for potato salad with sausages, depending on their wealth. The Hahlos of Oldenburg were affluent and so a goose would be prepared, accompanied by apple and sausage stuffing, red cabbage and potato dumplings. Dessert typically included stollen, a cake of nuts and fruit with tapered ends and a ridge down the centre, symbolising baby Jesus in his swaddling clothes. There were gingerbreads, biscuits and many other goodies to nibble throughout the festive period.

Later, we will hear Dieter's recall of the Christmas festivities of his youth, before the shattering of such joyful memories.

Georg looks back fondly on his family days. His recollections are tinted by the disrupted times in which he wrote his thoughts but the genuine warmth of his memories shines through: 'We always led a sociable and warm-hearted family life.' Regular Sunday trips were enjoyed with his parents or with Leopold, his father's brother, and his family. On other occasions, Georg cycled off with friends to the moor to the south or to the castle at Rastede. To the north of the city was a large lake, Zwischenahn, where Georg loved to sail, as well as to swim. He played tennis but did not participate in sports at school. He found school gymnastics 'tiresome'.

As a Seventh former (Year 11 nowadays) Georg participated enthusiastically in dancing, for which he had lessons. These were the way to mix and flirt with the opposite sex at dance evenings and house balls. He remembers his first girlfriend Else Greve as 'my first true love'. These were harmless and blissful times that he deeply wished his children would be able to enjoy, though it must have been hard for him to envisage how they ever could, at the time he wrote down his recollections.

There was a huge celebration for the golden wedding of Georg's paternal grandparents, Siegfried and Wilhelmine Hahlo, on 1 June 1907. They had nine children, three of whom had already ventured to England or the US. For this special occasion, all had arrived along with their children. Georg was 11 and he loved it. The feast was ten courses of sumptuous-sounding dishes each with specific wines. Nothing quite screams ostentatious wealth as much as this banquet:

Order of courses:

Caviar on a block of ice

~

Queen soup

~

Poached brown trout with butter

~

Veal tenderloin à la mode

~

Roman punch

~

Duck compote and lettuce

~

Asparagus spears with whipped butter

~

Ice cream

~

Butter and cheese

~

Dessert

Queen soup was cream of chicken and Roman punch was wine fortified with honey and spirits. There were of course official portraits taken, including this shot of the 'happy' couple (who look

*Menu card
for golden
wedding
celebrations*

*Golden wedding celebrations. Back: Leopold, Philipp, Bernhardt. Middle: Bertha.
Front: Wilhelm, Karl, Ernst, Anna, Helene. Seated: Wilhelmine and Siegfried*

anything but in the photo) and all their children. The local military band of Oldenburg Infantry Regiment No. 91 serenaded Georg's grandparents to set the seal on the splendour and specialness of the moment. In his memoir, Georg reflects that 'it was almost unbelievable' that in a few short years this would be his regiment as he set off to fight for his country.

Georg's family holidays were major highlights. They went to Wangerooge, an island off the north coast close to Oldenburg, or they went to Mühlhausen, quite a distance to the south. His mother's brothers lived there and from age 10 Georg often spent time there with his brother Fritz. Lovely Aunt Paula did not know what to do with them, and had the idea to buy them a travel pass for the tram. The boys found this exciting because Oldenburg did not have trams. Almost all day long they sailed round and round the town on the trams becoming such a familiar sight that one of the conductors became a friend. Many years later Fritz returned to Mühlhausen and the conductor saw him in the street. He stopped his tram in the middle of its run in order to say hello to Fritz.

In 1912 the family business was sold, it having become apparent that neither Fritz nor Georg would take on the store. Fritz had moved to Manchester and worked in a factory which belonged to some of his father's brothers and sisters. It manufactured packaging, which was the line Fritz followed on his return to Germany. He had good prospects. Georg wanted to go to university. His father probably did not consider that his daughters could take over, so the business was sold at the beginning of the year, making him a wealthy man with enough money to retire at the age of 54. The store was respected in the town and the new owner continued to trade under the S Hahlo name in order to demonstrate continuity of quality and service. This was until he felt forced to disassociate himself from the name in the 1930s.

The family moved to a temporary house at Auguststrasse 2,

The house on Taubenstrasse, in 2020

where they stayed for a year. Meanwhile, Wilhelm supervised the building of the new family home at Taubenstrasse 22, literally Pigeons Street, reflecting its favourable position in the leafier part of town. It was in a newly developed area on the flood plains of the Haaren river. The streets were wide, cobbled avenues of affluent homes, full of trees and spacious properties. It was only ten minutes' walk from the centre but had the feel of a different world, perfect for a well-earned retirement.

Taubenstrasse had on one side high apartment buildings dating from 1910. On the opposite side were the new villas, most with art nouveau elements. Number 22, which would have been well-known to Dieter and his sister, was a vast, opulent house equipped with the comforts of the age. The home was too big for one family and the population register from 1922 records three other names at the address. The Hahlos occupied the top two floors giving Georg his own pad in the attic. This was before central heating. He kept a jug of water and in winter he had to break the ice in order to wash in the mornings. They had a large balcony at the rear surrounded with flowers. They could sit as though outside and yet sheltered. There was a large dining table and when Dieter visited it seemed to him like eating out on holiday. From October 1913, for the next twenty-five years, this house would be the centre of Hahlo family life.

The gun used for the assassination

On 28 June 1914 Gavrilo Princip shot and killed Archduke Franz Ferdinand in Sarajevo. It is widely believed that this was the literal trigger that precipitated the Great War. The story is a lot more complex than that. How could it not be? It's not as if the assassination of Franz Ferdinand would have been a surprise. It was the sixth attempt on his life in total and the second that day. The countries of Europe had long been itching to take Germany down a peg or two. What Princip did was to start a chain of events that led to the outbreak of full-scale European war.

Plans for university were put on hold as Georg embraced the prospect of war. He shared with his family, his friends and the nation the unshakeable belief that Germany would be victorious. The might of their nation had been confirmed by its successes against Austria and France. Now it was even stronger, with a united federation of German states and a military that was regarded as indomitable.

What, as they say, could possibly go wrong?[2]

---

[2] Why was Germany so confident? The Franco-Prussian war 1870–71. See p252

3

LANGEMARCK, BELGIUM, 1914

'We sang: "Oh Germany, highly honoured,
eternal land of loyalty" '

The assassination of Archduke Franz Ferdinand was a turning point.
A dispute between Austria-Hungary and Russia for predominance in
the Balkans seemed likely at first to be confined to that region and
few anticipated that this distant skirmish would precipitate a
disastrous world war fought on many fronts. Indeed, in July 1914
Georg went with his friend Hans Iben to Laboe, a spa town in the
bay of Kiel, to enjoy 'a few marvellous, carefree weeks'. He was 18
and these were the last such weeks he was to know for a long time.

At the end of July they travelled back via Hamburg, where Uncle
Philipp took them to the stock exchange and they sensed that the
business world was seized by great unrest and that disaster was in the
air. Varying rates of industrial development had created inequality
across Europe, leading to social and political tensions. There was
populist, nationalist and racist posturing throughout the continent.
Doom hovered over Europe.

Austria and Hungary had demanded reparations from Serbia
because the assassination had been carried out by Serbian nationalists
protesting against Austrian rule. Serbia refused, confident that Russia

would help them. The inevitable sequence when those countries declared war was that countries in alliance with Russia became involved, primarily France and England. Germany became embroiled because Kaiser Wilhelm II had loyalty to the ruling clans of Austria and Hungary, promising them full military support. Many factors played into the ensuing diplomatic crisis but tensions had long been high and scores had to be settled by countries such as France, still smarting from its defeat by Prussia forty years earlier.

Europe's dreadful fate was decided in a few days. Within four years, 17 million people would be killed and 20 million injured.

Georg and his friends believed that Germany was the most magnificent, strongest and best-ruled nation in the world. Kaiser Wilhelm embodied this power and magnificence. 'Germany, Germany above everything' was their deep, honestly-held conviction. They believed that war had been forced upon them in order to break Germany's supremacy. Thomas Mann's protagonist in Dr Faustus embodied war fever:

'We marched off enthusiastically — filled with the certainty that the hour of Germany's era had come, that history was holding its hand over us, that after Spain, France and England it was now our turn to put our stamp upon the world and lead it.'

Newspapers trumpeted that the country would soon be victorious. Germany had an overwhelming number of troops, unsurpassed military training and modern techniques. It was hard to imagine a prolonged conflict and the German military was eager to strike in order to gain territory. War meant victory and domination.

On Saturday, 1 August 1914, following Russia's mobilisation in support of Serbia, Germany declared war on Russia. Special evening editions of the papers announced general mobilisation, starting on Monday. On the same day the King of the Belgians refused German violation of his country's neutrality, resulting in Germany declaring war on Belgium and France. The British Foreign Secretary Sir Edward Grey knew his country would have to go to war with Germany should Germany invade Belgium. His famous observation, as he looked down The Mall in London from his room in the Foreign Office at dusk, was: 'The lamps are going out all over Europe; we shall not see them lit again in our lifetime.' Everywhere in Germany news of the war aroused great enthusiasm and Oldenburg was no exception. On 3 August alone more than fifty alleged spies were rounded up in the town and arrested on the basis of rumours, showing how heated the mood had become.

Monday 3 August was the day school restarted after the summer holidays. At the beginning of the 1870/71 war, pupils in the top form had taken their exams straightaway in order to join the army as volunteers. The expectation was that this would happen again. The attractions were freedom from the rules of school life and an easier exam. Their first lesson was physics, during which the caretaker appeared and announced that top form pupils should go to assembly at the break, throwing everyone's thoughts into turmoil. The teacher, ever practical, thought that pupils preparing for war should be acquainted with the mathematical formulae pertaining to the bullet. Georg says the 'dear man' was serious, but his discussion of the bullet passed them all by.

At 10 o'clock in the hall it was announced that top formers who wanted to join up as volunteers could take their final exams later that week, merely a German essay and an oral test on the most important subjects. Everybody agreed joyfully. The following lessons were Latin, Greek and History. The teachers, infected by the enthusiasm, discussed which subject each pupil would prefer for their tests, in order to smooth their progress. The boys went straight home with this exciting news, where books were flung into a corner, and everyone took to the streets. The sole topic was infantry, cavalry or artillery.

The military had long held a prominent position in German society. Its officer class was highly influential and its presence was felt everywhere in the running of the unified country. Troops of soldiers parading through the streets were a common sight and military men wore their uniforms off duty as a statement of fashion and of social standing. With the barracks near the old town centre, thousands of soldiers lived in or around Oldenburg and the town resembled an army camp within a few days, which was a matter of pride to local people.

On 4 August Georg and his class had to write, for five hours, their German essay on the subject of the love for one's country and the sacrifice of one's life. The next morning Georg took his oral test. Only one of twenty-five boys did not pass the exams. The successful twenty-four rented a band in the afternoon and with an exaggerated sense of their own importance placed their red school caps on top of walking sticks and paraded around town to symbolise the schooldays they had left behind. They made their way to the barracks of the local Regiment No. 91, expecting to be received as saviours of the nation, but so many volunteers had rushed to the barracks that no more could be accepted. All resources were needed for mobilisation of active regiments and of reservists, which was happening all over Germany. The army expanded from 800,000 soldiers to more than 3 million, mainly reservists plus 185,000 volunteers.

All Georg and his comrades could do was to wait. In the evening, a memorable day was celebrated at a regular haunt. They were no longer schoolboys, they were *muli* (mules), between school and university, between boys and men. The teachers' authority had collapsed and pub visits could not be forbidden. Their parents were happy to turn a blind eye. Despite the great enthusiasm, the farewell party in the Great Hall of the school at the end of the week made Georg sad 'at least for a few minutes'. For the last time they assembled with parents, and listened to words from the headmaster;

for the last time they looked at the school flag with its inscription 'Spirit and strength for science; heart and hand for your country!'

The main worry was how to become a soldier? Some schoolmates travelled away by train having heard that this or that regiment would accept volunteers. Georg's brother Fritz had returned home on one of the last ships between England and Germany, so that he could do his duty for his country. As he could speak English, French and Spanish, he was accepted at the Headquarters of Reserve Infantry Regiment No. 74 as an interpreter, without having to be trained and in the first days of August, he went into the field with them. Records show that Fritz sustained injuries at some point.

On 17 August Georg and a few friends were accepted by Regiment No. 91. The barracks were filled to the brim so they had to live at home. There were thirty squads totalling approximately 600 men organised by height, which meant Georg was in the last squad. He was small, even for the times, scraping in at five foot tall, when the average height for a man at the time was five feet six inches.

At the stores 600 uniforms lay ready: old-style blue ones with red collars, that had been worn before. Georg's squad was last in the queue and had to take what was left, whether it fitted or not. He says 'I just cannot describe how I looked in this outfit.' Sleeves, trousers, boots, everything was miles too big. They looked so comical that even the squad leader agreed it was impossible to go into the street looking as they did. He arranged that they could go home carrying uniforms over their arms. On the way Georg passed an officer and saluted as smartly as he could. The officer laughed, and asked: 'Are you trying to be funny?', which was not a great start. At home the family set to work adjusting the garments. Sister Lotte fetched fire tongs from the kitchen and boiled the filthy headgear before she dared to touch it.

Over the coming days they tried to learn the military steps, to the left, to the right, straight ahead. They learned to salute and how to behave inside and outside barracks. They swore the oath of allegiance to the flag and received their rifles. They had their first shooting exercises and practised movements in open terrain. In a few days useful soldiers were created from 'ridiculous civilians'. Soon Georg moved into the barracks at Pferdemarkt, the large square that had formerly been the horse market. He had to learn the domestic duties of a soldier, such as making the beds, cleaning the rooms and sweeping the yard. His enthusiasm deepened and he focused on every task.

In September recruits were formed into new regiments. Georg went into Reserve Infantry Regiment No. 216 in Osnabrück, not far to the south, where he lodged with a family in the town. They bade farewell to home and parents, still eager to embark on what was clearly now a 'serious matter'. It was no longer tedious training but full-scale exercises involving night marches and much shooting. At first he struggled to cope with carrying sandbags in his knapsack, a rifle and full cartridge pouches, all together a massive weight in relation to his size. His boots caused him most trouble because they were too large. He wore two pairs of socks and foot rags, artfully folded. Later he bought his own boots.

The regiment consisted mostly of young volunteers all filled with

Colonel von Stockhausen, regimental commander, says goodbye to the soldiers on Pferdemarkt in 1914

the same determination and spirit. The camaraderie was sincere in pursuit of one aim: the salvation of Germany. At the end of the month they moved off in long trains. The soldiers travelled in goods wagons, the lucky ones on straw, officers in passenger carriages and equipment was transported in open carriages. They came to camp in Lockstedt, north of Hamburg. Georg shudders at the memory of the terrible night march from the station to the village where they were to take up quarters: deepest darkness, incessant rain, swampy paths and such heavy luggage. He was lucky to find a good room with a real bed in the house of kind people.

Over the next days there were even longer marches and exercises with other divisions, followed by preparations for war. They exchanged their old blue uniforms for grey, which were more modern and a better fit, and they were kitted out with mess-tins, tent, blanket, bandages and the iron ration, which was not iron but a bag of hard rusks on which to feed when no other food was available. Each soldier had an identity disk, a little piece of tin worn round the neck showing name and troop. By 1916 all identification such as the disc and the number on the cap were abolished because if taken prisoner, it would help the enemy. They were given regimental postcards to send home, such as this one from 1911.

Last preparations done, on 12 October they marched out towards Belgium and Flanders. The first stop was to take up rations at Kirch-Weyhe near Bremen. They had been able to

Oldenburgisches Infanterie-Regiment Nr. 91.
Oldenburg.

A regimental postcard, 1911

write home to relate where they were going so family had the opportunity to see sons and brothers once more. Georg's mother had come with other women from Oldenburg, loaded with butter, eggs, sausage, chocolate and tobacco but... they were too late. All they saw were the rear lights of the train as Georg and his comrades left the station. Many a mother missed the chance to see her son for the last time, because so many soldiers never returned. Georg was told later that another battalion then arrived at the station and was delighted to receive these unexpected gifts.

They travelled via Osnabrück, Münster and over the Hohenzollern bridge in Cologne over the Rhine. Thousands of young voices roared in unison:

O Deutschland hoch in Ehren,
Du ewiges Land der Treu

Oh Germany, highly honoured,
eternal land of loyalty

They sang through the night and the songs boomed with defiance:

Es braust ein Ruf wie Donnerhall
Wie Schwertgeklirr und Wogenprall :
Zum Rhein, zum Rhein, zum deutschen Rhein,
Wer will des Stromes Hüter sein?
Lieb Vaterland, magst ruhig sein,
Lieb Vaterland, magst ruhig sein,
Fest steht und treu die Wacht am Rhein!
Fest steht und treu die Wacht am Rhein!

A call roars like thunder
Like clashing swords and crashing waves:
To the Rhine, to the Rhine, to the German Rhine,
Who will be the guardian of this river?

Dear Fatherland, put your mind at rest,
Dear Fatherland, put your mind at rest,
Firm and faithful stands the watch on the Rhine!
Firm and faithful stands the watch on the Rhine!

They sang old and beautiful songs about Germany while others were humorous or melancholic, such as this lament for lost loves to which the soldiers added grim humour at the end:

Die Vöglein in Walde, die sangen so wunder-wunderschön
In der Heimat, in der Heimat, da gibts ein Wieder-Wiedersehn
Drum Mädchen weine nicht, sei nicht so Traurig
Wisch Dir die Tränen ab mit Sandpapier;
Denn dieser Feldzug, das its kein Schnellzug
Wisch Dir die Tränen ab mit Sandpapier

The little birds in the forests, sang so beauti-beautiful
In the homeland, in the homeland, there will be our reunion
Therefore, do not cry, my girl, and do not be so sad
Dry your tears with sandpaper,
For this campaign is no fast train,
Therefore dry your tears with sandpaper

They travelled on via Aachen and through half-destroyed Liege, via Brussels towards the west. Their mission was to strengthen the right wing of the German army which had progressed through France. Many regiments joined in the effort to win the Belgian coast and to rob England of its harbours and bases on the mainland. They disembarked in Haltert, west of Brussels, during the night. 'Break step, load and secure!' This was the first command Georg received on hostile soil.

They continued marching west. They would arrive, dead tired, in the evening at quarters in abandoned, half-destroyed houses or in barns of farmhouses that had been burned to the ground. Then they had to collect firewood and peel potatoes. The food was bad because they did not have proper field kitchens in which to prepare it. Around midnight they went to bed on a bare floor or on a little straw. It was painful but they remained steadfast to the cause. Georg's adaptability was tested – from an accomplished student living a life of fun and comfort to a soldier roughing it and expected to kill for his country.

In his account, written nearly twenty-five years later, Georg relies on his memory to follow the advance, having no maps and not being able to refer to his letters home which had been kept by the family. He recalls that they went via Thielt and Roulers towards their first combat with the Belgians, the French and the English. The battle proper started in early evening of 22 October when the men of six regiments, including Georg's, crossed the swampy ground riven by trenches and entered the little town of Bikschote. The German troops sang their patriotic songs, some even blowing bugles and banging drums. With throaty shouts of 'Hooray' and *'Deutschland, Deutschland, uber alles'*, they ran at the enemy. Many of these reservists were barely trained and knew little about the art of war, such as showing the enemy as small an angle as possible. It was considered cowardice to seek cover. They were pounded by British artillery and it was chaos in the darkness. Burning houses and explosions cast an eerie light. Officers tried desperately to regroup their men but the splintered German units retreated in the face of the British counterattack and managed to turn their advantage into defeat. Losses were huge. Georg says:

'Many a comrade of mine lost his life that day and many a mother cried, at home, for the son who would not return.'

Georg and his regiment arrived at a little smallholding outside Bikschote. The enemy lay hidden behind a hedge opposite, about 100 metres away.

Georg knelt down, took aim and shot, as he had been instructed. Suddenly there was a terrible blow, the rifle butt hit his face and he was knocked over. With shock he saw that both his hands were bleeding: a bullet had grazed his left hand underneath his rifle, gone through two fingers of his right hand and continued through his shoulder flap where it had torn the number of his regiment 216 to shreds.

A comrade bandaged him up using Georg's own first aid pack and, with great effort, Georg retreated over a water-filled ditch. His squad also retreated to this ditch to avoid being surrounded but their line was weak and in disarray. Georg retreated further to the first aid tent. He passed a house behind which a squad of his company stood in readiness. Georg informed the sergeant that the line of riflemen at the ditch urgently needed reinforcements. The sergeant refused because he had no orders. Georg urged haste but the sergeant was unmoved. Being wounded, Georg felt he had the right to give the order and called out: 'This squad will listen to my command! Directly to the trees, at the edge of the water, spread out!' Those who realised faster than the sergeant what was going on obeyed and rushed forward. The sergeant rushed after them. Many years later, a fellow soldier asked Georg if he was the same Hahlo who had shamed the veteran sergeant. Georg's qualities had shone, despite his physical frailty.

Georg could not find the first aid tent in the darkness and therefore crept into a stable in which already lay a number of wounded men, giving off a constant, keening moan. His wounds were torturing him under the improvised bandage. A goat lived in the stable and resented these intruders. It trampled over the wounded men, many of whom were unable to move out of its way. Their howls pierced the air as the goat wreaked vengeance on its unwelcome guests. Georg and his comrades endured a terrible night.[3]

[3] Did the Germans achieve their objectives? The Battle of Langemarck, 21-24 October 1914. See p254

4

RAWARUSKA, UKRAINE, 1914–15

*'So I lit my pipe and dreamed a bit
in the mild evening's air'*

The next morning, Georg and some wounded colleagues walked to the field hospital. They passed others still involved in the fighting who were keen for Georg to pass messages to their loved ones at home. Towards midday he reached his goal where he was at last bandaged expertly and he received the best offer he could imagine – a warm meal. A nurse had to feed him because with his dressed hands, he was helpless. Everything had to be done for him. He couldn't even wipe his own bottom, the greatest indignity.

From there he travelled on the top deck of a requisitioned Berlin bus. There was nearly an accident, and the bus had to swerve sharply. Georg was not able to hold on and the man next to him had to grab him to prevent him from falling. The bus took them to Thielt, the end station of the repaired one-track railway. A long train was soon filled with about 1500 wounded men and started to move east at a snail's pace. They sang songs of longing for home:

In die Heimat möcht ich wieder,
In die Heimat möcht ich fort,
Wo man singt so traute Lieder,

Wo man spricht manch trautes Wort!
Teure Heimat, sei gegrüsset,
Aus der Ferne sei gegrüsst,
Sei gegrüsst aus weiter Ferne,
Aus weiter Ferne sei gegrüsst!

I want to go home again,
I want to go home,
Where one sings such sweet songs,
Where one speaks many a sweet word!
Dear homeland, we greet you,
We greet you from afar,
We greet you from great distance,
From afar we greet you!

Georg was taken to a large military hospital in Remscheid. He had a bath, was fed and given a clean bed. In the next days they amputated one joint of his third finger. On 31 October he received a surprise: 'Visitors from Oldenburg!' and in the next moment he was in his parents' arms. Their embraces were hugely comforting. Georg's father had taken over management of the Department for Charitable Gifts in Oldenburg and had an authorisation for Georg to be moved to a Red Cross hospital in the town. The next day, Georg's 19th birthday, they set off home by train. Georg was allowed to travel first class free of charge and at the larger stops well-wishers showered him with gifts.

Back in Oldenburg, Leopold collected them in his car, something special in those days, and took Georg to the hospital at the converted agricultural college. Food and treatment were excellent but on account of his injuries he was not allowed out and Georg lamented that he did not make it home for Christmas. Healing was slow due to ingrained dirt and his fingers festered. They never did heal fully; two fingers remained distorted and had restricted movement, on another the nail never grew properly. I remember being fascinated by these war wounds as a young child.

It was February 1915 before he was discharged. Georg was detailed to join a reserve battalion of No. 216 stationed in barracks in Bundesstrasse, Hamburg. The place was overcrowded and he managed to lodge in Osterstrasse with his Aunt Bertha, his father's sister. He had 'a very agreeable time in that hospitable household', helped by being excused from military work on account of his fingers remaining agonising, especially when it was cold. Gradually he got used to handling his rifle again and performing drills such that by the end of April he was again ready for active service and, well provisioned by Bertha, he boarded another long train of troops. By now the rules had changed and when writing home they were no longer allowed to say in which direction they were travelling. Georg decided to use code. He agreed with his parents that if they were going east, he would write 'The sun is rising', and if west 'The sun is setting'. He was soon writing '*Die Sonne geht auf*' (the sun is rising) as they headed towards Berlin and the Eastern Front, to the Galician border.

Galicia had long been a disputed region that nowadays straddles southern Poland and western Ukraine. Before the war it had been the largest, most populous and northernmost province of the Austrian Empire. It had already seen heavy fighting and Russian forces had overrun most of the region after defeating the Austro-Hungarian army in a chaotic battle. The area was now to be contested again by a combined German and Austro-Hungarian offensive, in which Georg intended to play his part. German General Mackensen made the breakthrough at Gorlice-Tarnów (east of Krakow) in early May. German troops, buoyed by victory, marched on eastwards.[4]

[4] What were they fighting for? The Gorlice–Tarnów Offensive, May–July 1915. See p255

Georg and his battalion travelled by train over the border into Galicia near Oderberg where they were unloaded because the railway had not been repaired. They had to proceed on foot through terrain that was flat and sandy with sparse woods. It was not fertile ground and therefore was thinly populated. They needed to catch up with the German fighting units as quickly as possible, themselves steadily moving forwards which meant marching faster than usual, despite heavy loads on their backs. Every hour was fifty minutes of marching and ten minutes of rest, hour after hour. They had to drink their water in little sips, despite the scorching heat, because it was believed that frequent drinking tires and increases perspiration. They were told not to moisten temples or lips and to allow sweat to linger, even when their eyes were burning, because it had a cooling effect. Georg stuck to the rules and had to conquer extreme physical strain in order not to slacken.

After twelve gruelling days, they eventually caught up the fighting units. Together with friends from Oldenburg Georg applied to join the company using machine guns, an important new addition to German warfare, and they were detailed to Reserve Infantry Regiment No. 267. They were most likely to have used Bergmann MG 15 light machine guns developed for greater accuracy because they could be mounted on a surface. Serving in the machine gun company was at first a little easier than being in the infantry because Georg's knapsack and his gun were loaded onto wagons so he didn't need to carry so much himself. But Georg quickly found that using the weapon in battle was a lot harder because he had to carry the heavy gun and the ammunition boxes.

The advance went east via Tarnów, Rzeszow to Jaroslau, north of Przemyśl that had already been conquered. They could see the smoking ruins in the distance. Only a few Russians resisted and few could hold out against the German advance. Thousands were taken prisoner. Georg describes them as 'mostly dull, stupid figures', who were overjoyed that for them the war was finished. As they moved over the Polish border, the only people they met were peasants whose poor dwellings had been burned down by the Russians and who had lost everything. The nationality of who now ruled their country didn't appear to matter to them.

The soldiers marched on. They were constantly damp due to perspiration but at least it was not the nerve-racking war in muddy trenches. There were a few rest days and these brought the wonderful treasure of letters from home. Greetings from parents, brothers, sisters and relatives, often accompanied by *Liebesgaben*, meaning gifts of love, that made the soldiers' hearts sing. German field mail was a model of organisation because the army knew that letter writing was critical to the mood of the troops and their families, so letters from home sometimes arrived within a few days. The men loved the socks, newspapers, tobacco and foodstuffs that provided a welcome supplement to rations. Later in the war, when food shortages became chronic in Germany, the scarcity of parcels made soldiers aware of the depth of civilian suffering and contributed to a deterioration of morale in the German and Austrian armies.

Georg's next destination was Rawaruska, north of Lemberg (now Lviv), which they failed to take, condemning them to have to keep moving from village to village. On 29 July his regiment regrouped and Georg had to transfer to the infantry. Towards evening Georg duly reported at the clerks' office in an old farmhouse where they did administration and sorted the mail, organised the field kitchen and compiled the lists of wounded and dead. The sergeant was glad when he saw Georg's papers because he had been on the lookout for former high school pupils to join the officers' training course. Until now the sergeant had not found someone of sufficient calibre and his joy now was immense, telling Georg he was a 'gift from heaven'. If the sergeant had not been able to find a suitable candidate, he and his fellow officers would have felt humiliated.

Georg too felt joy. He had been a basic soldier for almost a year and disliked the suffering of lowly rank. He longed for promotion, through both personal ambition and confidence in his abilities to make a good officer. It promised an easier and more interesting service. After hearing such enjoyable news, Georg sat down opposite the clerks' office under a shady tree and prepared his evening meal. Georg says that he remembers the evening with total clarity. He had received a package from home and his table was richly laid. As an entrée he ate sardines on army bread toasted over the open fire. This was followed by warm meat from a tin, with more bread. For dessert he treated himself to a rusk from his reserves and pears, which he had collected unripe and now cooked. He calmed his conscience about having eaten from his iron rations, because his duties at the front would soon be finished: he would be off to a training centre for officers, far from the fighting. Sweet and happy thoughts coursed through his mind. He ended his lavish meal by lighting a cigar from his gifts of love. What a delight this would be.

He never got to smoke that cigar.

There was an ear-splitting noise and hissing. A tremendous blow. He lost consciousness. When he came to, he saw that the clerks' office was burning fiercely. He tried to get up and found that his left leg was badly wounded and blood was running from his trousers. Despite the pain, he staggered away from the burning house and immediate danger. The Russians had fired into the village with incendiary shells.

He hobbled for about 100 metres to a square which had been transformed into an emergency first aid station. They removed his trousers and saw that a shrapnel bullet had entered above his left knee and come out on the opposite side. Shrapnel bullets are marble-sized and made of lead. Russian shells were packed with dozens of shrapnel bullets that sprayed over a wide area when the shells burst, designed to kill and injure targets in open spaces. Amid the suffering and carnage around him, Georg describes it as 'No serious wound; the kneecap, bones and important tendons were not hurt.' He had been lucky.

Beyond the pain, there was disappointment. His dream of being promoted was on hold. But maybe his wound was severe enough to justify a transport home? That would mean seeing his parents again and living in comfort. When he had been wounded in Flanders, he had left his personal belongings behind. This time he desperately wanted to avoid this as he had recently received gifts of underwear, socks, food, tobacco. His haversack and water bottle would be vital on transport out. He described where he had sat to a comrade and asked him to fetch his things. The fellow returned without them. Everything had been burned, or they had been collected by someone else.

So he would have to make his way back in the clothes he was wearing. The only comforts he had were his pipe and tobacco pouch which accompanied him throughout his war. And so he lay back, lit his pipe and watched the smoke swirl in the warm evening's air as he dreamed sweet thoughts of home and awaited his fate.

5

KISIELIN, UKRAINE, 1915–16

'When I heard bullets whistling, I threw myself down.
When it was quiet, I ran on.
My nerves were like bowstrings'

The next morning the injured were loaded onto carts pulled by tough little farm horses and driven off. It was still boiling hot and they had inadequate supplies of water and food. Wounds had been treated rudimentarily but there was little that could be done to alleviate the pain. Georg lay on straw wedged between other wounded soldiers, unable to move. They went from village to village for four long days. One day Georg lay next to a soldier who had been shot in the stomach. The poor man's torment was made worse because the carts had no springs and the roads were rutted. With no medical assistance, his despair and his screams were terrifying. Georg doubted that the man survived.

Eventually they arrived at a military hospital in Lemberg. Compared to the ravages of others, Georg's wounds were slight and he feared he would not get home. Yet a few days later a first-aid train went back to Germany and he was on it. It was a mobile hospital, clean, with good food and treatment. Better still, there were young and pretty nurses. Georg was in a top bunk and able to look at the scenery as he daydreamed that every mile took him closer to home.

Nobody knew where they were, so they passed time trying to follow the route on maps.

Georg alighted in Hannover on 11 August 1915 and was admitted to the military hospital in the grounds of the technical university. It was an ideal place to recover, set in a magnificent garden. In later years, he would visit this garden with his children. He wrote a postcard home and within a few days his parents came to visit. Everyone was overcome with joy and Georg was able to limp over for an embrace. Before long he was out and about with a walking stick to enjoy the city and its glorious parks and lawns. His only disappointment was that his uniform was not adorned with the black and white ribbon of the Iron Cross. As a foot soldier with relatively few days of action, he was not yet deemed worthy.

Georg's reserve battalion remained in Bromberg, near the German-Polish border. He applied from hospital to rejoin Regiment No. 91 in Oldenburg but he had heard nothing by the time he was healed a month later, so he set off for Bromberg and arrived at old, dank and overcrowded barracks. He was miserable, feeling like a stranger. Three days later the authorisation to return to his old regiment came through and so he was back on a train across Germany with his bread ration for two days, which had to be officially weighed before he could take it.

In Oldenburg, he moved into his old quarters at Pferdemarkt. Because his leg had still not healed completely, he was employed to drill the young recruits, which was enjoyable compared to fighting. On 18 October Georg became a lance-corporal and helped with training and the running of the garrison and had responsibility for the cleanliness of the barracks. He had his foot on the first rung of the ladder to becoming an officer and it meant a lot to him. He wore a button on each side of his tunic collar to denote his status. When he went home, his mother, beaming with joy, took him in her arms and bade him to walk up and down Lange Strasse to show off.

In mid-November there was to be an officers' training course, causing excited debate about who would be sent. The captain promised Georg that he would be going so it was a shock when his companions received new uniforms and only Lance-Corporal Hahlo did not. A clerk told him that the captain was on leave for a few days and in his absence Sergeant Riesebieter had adjusted the order, saying: 'Little Hahlo will never be an officer, why should we send him?' There was nothing Georg could do, except watch as the others left without him. But when the captain returned, Georg appealed personally to him and was soon despatched to join the other officer candidates. They were all filled with ambition to lead platoons and eventually regiments. Every day they marched out to do battle drills; they exercised, staged battles and repeatedly stormed and defended the little village of Wietzendorf. In the afternoons they received instruction in battle theory, topography, map design, the duties of an officer and about the technical features of armaments. There were lessons on administration, military catering in garrison and field, the handling of personal papers, and much else.

At times they were 'pretty rowdy', baiting the man in charge, Sergeant Senf, whose name happens to be the German word for mustard. It was hard to give him full respect because he was not a commissioned officer and they expected to be his seniors by the end of the course. One week, they asked for leave to go to Bremen on the Sunday and knew that leave permits had been prepared. On the Saturday evening they made merry in a pub and returned to barracks worse for wear by which time Sergeant Senf was asleep. They started to yell for mustard, using the colloquial word *Mostrich*. Sergeant Senf was predictably enraged and next morning he declared leave to be cancelled. They asked again on Monday but Sergeant Mustard continued to thwart their plans. They stood in line for inspection but suddenly buttons were not polished sufficiently or boots were not shined well enough, or the tassel on the sabre had not been tied properly. All this had to be put right before leave permits could be issued, one by one.

By this time, they had ten minutes before the departure of the train. Even when running, the station was fifteen minutes away. Sergeant Mustard knew that. They raced to the station but the train had left! The stationmaster knew how much their leave meant to them and telephoned the next station to change the signal and ordered the train back so they could get on. Now they were boisterous again, shouting that they had won the Battle of Mustard. In the evening they rewarded the stationmaster with a box of cigars.

One day it was announced that the group had lice. Whether true or not, Georg did not know. Lice are tiny creatures that fasten to the private parts, especially of soldiers. Delousing was done in true military style. Uniforms were put into huge vats of chemicals and cleaned, coming back in a pitiful state. The soldiers had to stand in large tubs and be covered in soap. Then barbers shaved them all over, with alarming thoroughness. It was borne by the soldiers with humour. When the hair began to regrow, it itched terribly, which is when the oaths started. It was worse than anything caused by lice.

The months of November, December and January went by. Following practical and theoretical exams, on 17 January 1916 Georg became Staff Sergeant Hahlo and was nominated as a potential officer. He had stripes sewn into his collars and cuffs; he exchanged the plain cockade for the silver one. He tied the sword knot to his bayonet, the sign of a military leader. Some received stronger commendations; he put this down to the disparaging words of Sergeant Riesebieter. The end of the course was celebrated on 31 January with several rounds of drinks.

He reported to the captain: 'Staff Sergeant Hahlo back from the course.' He was entitled to a new sword. They were no longer worn in the field, so that the enemy could not recognise a leader from afar, but in the garrison they were still worn. The problem was that the new sword was too long for him and he had to find someone to shorten it. Once done, he proudly led his detachment through the streets of his home town, saluting the young women and his old teachers at the school with his sword, his head held high.

In February they set off to meet with Regiment No. 91 in France, south of Laon. The enemy frontlines were opposite in trenches on the River Aisne. Georg was in charge of a platoon (forty to fifty men) that he had to lead, during the night, to their own trenches, where they undertook earthmoving work. The trench network was like a small town, a maze of main streets and side streets with dugouts as houses. Each street and dugout had a name and number, carefully noted on maps. Georg was stationed in a fine house in the village of Bouconville. Even so, it was overrun with rats that scampered to and fro in his room. Bread and food had to be put into bags and suspended from ceilings, in the dugouts as well. Enemy artillery frequently shot towards the village and the smell of bombs and ammunition thickened the air. His house was hit twice but he did not move. There were too many advantages, mainly a proper bed. They had a good time in this village, despite knowing they were training to join the battle for Verdun. Georg says: 'Soldiers never think of tomorrow, today is today.' Overcoming the huge French fortress at Verdun had become a key German objective. Many soldiers had already perished without getting much closer.

Then everything changed. One afternoon all their luggage was packed and loaded, ready to go to an unknown destination. In haste they marched to the station and the train set off eastwards. Russian General Brusilov had launched a strong offensive between Kowel and Lutsk, had defeated the Austrians and taken hundreds of thousands prisoner. Northern Austria was now under threat and Germany had to divert troops as reinforcements. We can detect a disparaging view of Austro-Hungarian army capabilities when Georg says 'As many times before, the Germans had to help them out.' In fact, Brusilov's operation achieved its goal of forcing Germany to reduce the intensity of its attack on Verdun and transfer considerable forces to the east. It most likely saved Georg's life. The Battle of Verdun lasted for 303 days, the longest and one of the most costly conflicts in human history. Each month 70,000 men, almost equally French and German, were killed and in total 700,000 died. The Germans never did capture the citadel at Verdun. This is one reason why Georg had a lucky war.

The war on the Western Front was essentially a stalemate with all sides locked in concentrated, entrenched positions and unable to make significant progress despite mass casualties. The war on the Eastern Front was different, a conflict of rapid movement and bouts of aggression resulting in large-scale breakthroughs and advances (and retreats) of hundreds of miles. As Winston Churchill observed: 'In the west, the armies were too big for the land; in the east, the land was too big for the armies.'

Georg and his regiment proceeded in hurried marches to the front, to the region in which Georg had last seen action. One evening they had to rush on to a castle in which the division's staff was housed, to dig trenches and to protect them. The Austrians had departed without waiting for relief, leaving the divisional staff unprotected. 'Lace-ups' the Germans contemptuously called their Austrian comrades, in reference to their fancy footwear. The staff had not been aware of their vulnerability but luckily neither had the Russians and they had not attacked.

Soon there was heavy fighting. The Russians tried to advance but the German troops halted their progress. For several days Georg and his colleagues lay by the River Stochod, a swampy area with an unhealthy climate; hot and oppressive during the day, cold and misty at night. Drinking water was bad, and the health of the troops deteriorated. Dysentery and typhoid were the most feared enemies. On 1–2 July they started to attack the village of Kisielin, 500 metres away on the River Stochod, and the Russians defended doggedly. The countryside was treeless and hilly with loose, sandy soil. It was impossible to dig trenches so the soldiers operated at night and had to dig holes for themselves to hide in, to be invisible by the time morning dawned. Georg had just started excavating his hidey-hole when an order was relayed from mouth to mouth: 'Staff Sergeant Hahlo to go on patrol and find out if there is barbed wire or other obstacles between us and the Russians.'

Georg crept off, armed only with a revolver and accompanied by his orderly, a soldier assigned to him as a personal servant. They edged forwards right up to the Russian lines and discovered that all obstacles had been removed during the fighting of the past few days. Georg inched back to relay this information to the company commander. Now he had to dig his hole, sharpish. The other soldiers had disappeared into theirs. Dawn came swiftly. He could soon see the outlines of the church steeple, of houses and of the Russian positions in the village. He and his orderly dug as quickly as they could but not quickly enough. Suddenly Georg was knocked flying by a blow to his face. He had been shot. Wounded again. As he says himself: 'I wasn't surprised. After all, I was used to it by now.'

Blood dripped from his face and ran down his left arm. His orderly whispered that a bullet had penetrated Georg's chin, gone through his lower lip, back out of the other side of his chin and had grazed his left upper arm on its way. This peculiar line of shot was explained by Georg's crouched position: he had not been deep enough in his hole, making him a target.

There was no chance of being bandaged because the smallest movement would expose him to greater danger. What were his options? To remain on the frontline when they were expecting heavy fighting? That would mean having to lie quietly and chancing it as the battle raged around him. If the German attack were unsuccessful, he would become a prisoner of war, at best. Or to retreat? This was equally dangerous. He would have to get over a treeless hill which could be easily seen by the Russians in the village, making him a first-rate target.

He opted for retreat, trusting his luck. As soon as he set off running up the hill behind the German line, the Russians started to shoot. At each volley of shots he flung himself to the ground. He would make a few metres at a time before bullets came whistling and he had to throw himself down. Behind he heard shouting: 'Who the hell is running back there?' 'It's Staff Sergeant Hahlo, wounded.' The second German line lay on the other side of the hill. Eventually he made it, blood streaming from his wounds and in unspeakable pain. He was exhausted: 'My nerves were like bowstrings.' Georg sat down and lit his trusty pipe, his only solace in this hell. He does not report if the smoke came out of both sides of his chin.

It turned out to be an horrific and disastrous day. His regiment suffered huge losses and did not take the village. The revered commander of his battalion and a schoolfriend were among those who died. Georg had made the right call; had he stayed on the field, he almost certainly would have been killed.

6

DAUGAVPILS, LATVIA, 1916–17

'What sigh of relief came from my heart!
A tunic with epaulets lay in readiness
and I quickly exchanged it for the old tunic'

Georg was soon bandaged and found that by some miracle, his teeth and jaw were not damaged, nor the bone in his arm. Calmly he walked through the valley, protected from the sight of the enemy, to give his report. He was not sure that his injuries merited further treatment but his luggage was loaded onto carts and he went by train to military hospitals, first in Warsaw, then Bromberg. After five weeks of medical attention and good food his wounds were healed. On 13 August 1916, he was sent back to Regiment No. 91 in Oldenburg. Meeting his parents and sisters was 'an indescribable joy'. Each time when returning from the front, being sheltered in his own home fully restored him. His mother spoiled him as much as was possible given the growing scarcity of food. She traded the goods they had, such as material, in return for extra rations. The dockets for the necessities of daily life, such as bread, meat, butter, sugar, coal and clothing were as important to them as a passport is to a traveller.

Thanks to his scouting report he received the Oldenburg Friedrich August Cross 2nd Class and the Iron Cross 2nd Class. The latter came with a ribbon that was threaded through the second buttonhole for everyday wear. He was proud.[5]

Georg served a few weeks again at the garrison in Oldenburg. Machine guns had gained importance and he applied to join a machine gun reserve detachment of the X Army Corps, stationed in Eilvese, near Hannover. In October, after training, Georg left for the front for the fourth time. They travelled to the end of the railway at Svencionys (in Lithuania) to join Reserve Infantry

Portrait with ribbon of Iron Cross, 1917

Regiment No. 425 near Daugavpils (in Latvia). The position was on a lake and the surrounding area was a swamp. The Russians were on the opposite shore, protected by huge mounds of earth. Digging trenches was out of the question so all they had were makeshift huts. Georg was in command of a machine gun section, responsible for testing the condition of the guns and training the men. There was a large number of machine guns, which meant a lot of work. It was preferable to open warfare, but the winter of 1916/17 was hard, even for this region. Ice and deep snow dominated outside. Georg's fingers, which had been hurt in 1914, caused him a lot of pain and he had to wear a muff that his mother, in her great care, had made

[5] The Iron Cross. See p257

for him. To keep warm they burned wood and drank strong spirits. To pass the time they played a card game called Skat.

Here Georg spent his first Christmas in the field. Every shelter had a small fir tree which they decorated with items received from home or bought from the canteen (including even stronger spirits). Somebody played carols on a mouth organ to try to get everyone into the Christmas mood. Georg's brother Fritz married on 30 January 1917 in Kassel and Georg sent him a telegram that arrived in time, showing that things were well organised behind the lines.

There was a small hill as part of the German frontline. It acted like a fortress and was of strategic importance, with machine guns built in to the defensive position. Three officers and their units alternated the guard, each doing a shift of twenty-four hours followed by forty-eight hours' rest. But there was little fighting and few losses and it became almost monotonous. By this stage, even on the front, they could sense the internal disintegration of Russia and a seepage of the will to fight from its troops. The Russian revolution was on its way.

Georg's firm ambition was to become a full officer. After a few months in his new regiment, he asked the leader of the company to recommend him for promotion and was pleased to get a positive reaction. On 1 April 1917 he heard that the recommendation had been ratified and he was elated. In his baggage a tunic with epaulets had lain ready for weeks. He quickly put it on. He called on the Regimental Commander, the Commander of the Battalion and the Commander of the Company: 'Lieutenant Hahlo of the Reserve, with respect, reporting for duty!' There was a great deal of cap touching and bowing as he accepted congratulations with what he imagined was an appropriate sense of hauteur. After that he made his way to the Officers' Mess, reciprocating salutes as he went, all the time checking his shoulders to see that the epaulets were still there. He celebrated well in the Officers' Mess, pleased to be a social equal with the other officers. At age 21, he was the youngest officer in the regiment and had already fitted in an enormous amount of experience. He sent a card home with the joyous news, adding that it was not an April Fool. This promotion, and his career, were important to him. It is likely that as a small man he felt the need to prove himself.

He received extra money as an officer and he requested three days' leave, in order to go to Vilnius to get items for his uniform. In a merry mood he bought new epaulets, thigh-length boots, an officers' suitcase and other articles. He had never taken full leave, having only been able to escape the frontline due to injury, and now he had a strong desire to go home. When his turn came at the beginning of July he sent a telegram and set off on a rail journey that was long and tedious but he didn't mind because he felt so happy. Back in Oldenburg, along with his parents and sisters, was Fritz, also on leave by chance, and he had become an officer as well. The family was overjoyed. 'Fat' Sergeant Riesebieter who had not wanted to send Georg to the training course was still at the town barracks. Georg made a point of tapping him on the shoulder: 'I have become an officer after all!' The sergeant was forced to salute and congratulate, preventing Georg from saying what he thought of the man – which was probably just as well. He enjoyed his time with family and friends and his leave passed too quickly but not before he had used family connections to have an elegant uniform made by the best tailor in town.

On 10 July he returned to the front where he found that they were expecting an attack, reconnaissance planes having ascertained that the Russians had amassed forces around Dünaburg. On 18 July a heavy bombardment began to hit their positions. German artillery fired back but their defensive system was primitive. Everything was poorly constructed and far from bomb-proof. They sat in shelters squashed like sardines, quaking at every hit. Many a hut was blasted and the occupants blown to smithereens. Twisted bodies of dead and wounded soldiers lay everywhere. The stench of warfare curdled the air. There was little to do except count the hours and days.

Georg and his comrades passed four days and nights in frightened waiting for the ultimate attack. It was imminent, but where? The Russians were most likely to aim for the railway embankment and for Georg's field guard position, the hill which protruded from the line. At dawn of the fifth day, the guns fell silent and a guard with a telescope-cum-periscope overlooking enemy lines shouted 'The Russians are coming!' They rushed out of their shelters and could see the Russians in a tight line only thirty metres away, fortunately being hampered by barbed wire.

In the lower valley, the Russians had already penetrated German positions and their riflemen were swarming in. Georg was in command of the right section of the field guard and he and his section rushed to defend their position. He had placed machine guns in the trench at the side to defend against Russians moving in from the right with their rifles and hand grenades. Georg and his men reached their guns and unleashed their devastating power on the enemy. Georg shuddered as his gun cut swathes through the marauders. The field guard had to be defended under all circumstances, and it was. Their survival had depended on it.

By evening the area was clear. The Russians suffered substantial losses and their assault was halted. The relief detachment arrived at dusk and Georg's unit could breathe again. In the next days there were no more attacks, following which the Germans undertook counterattacks and removed the enemy from the positions it had gained. With that, the war on the total length of the Eastern Front was virtually at an end. Russian involvement dwindled to nothing as the Russian revolution took its course, fuelled by the losses incurred in the war and the subsequent widespread deprivation that had followed.

Georg and his contingent marched back to barracks sheltered by a small wood. On his way he saw the huge destruction caused by the Russian attacks to their reserve positions, their shelters, the paths and large tracts of forest. The air had fallen silent. There were no birds or animals, not even rats. It was an eerie wasteland of stumps where trees had been felled like matchsticks. The soldiers were dog-tired, hungry and thirsty. The battle had kept their nerves at breaking point. Now there was complete exhaustion. Georg dropped on to a bed and slept for one night and one day. On waking he took his first wash for days and, at last, paid lengthy attention to his stomach.

7

HALLE, GERMANY, 1917–18

'With the plane on its nose, the propeller broke into thousands of pieces and I was flung out in a high curve'

Georg's regiment had been resolute and brave in defending the field guard position and he had hoped to be recognised with the award of the Iron Cross 1st Class but the leaders of the detachments received nothing. Georg was disappointed as he resumed the monotonous life of the garrison, so he acted to change his situation and applied to join the air force. This branch of the military had recently come into existence and its importance was growing fast. The construction of aeroplanes and training of pilots and observers were being pursued with energy. He felt life would be more interesting than the daily routine of the infantry and that, when in action, the air force demanded greater skills and initiative from its men. He says that pilots had become 'the most respected troops'. He craved some of their glamour.

On 25 September 1917 the order arrived for him to report to the air force base in Halle for training to be a pilot. The aerodrome was outside the town, a huge open square with one side occupied by hangars, workshops, barracks and offices. Georg took a furnished room in town, using his bicycle to get to the aerodrome. His first task was to obtain his new clothing: a heavy woollen tracksuit to be worn over his uniform, a short fur jacket, a crash helmet, fur gloves, a scarf, goggles and many smaller items.

Training started with being strapped into a swing, to simulate what it is like to have no terra firma underfoot. At the next level, five men had to squeeze into the observer's seat of a plane and a trained pilot flew them over the town and performed a couple of loops to test their mettle, and to show off. They declared this to be a day worthy of celebration in the officers' mess, which was in

Georg in 1917 as Air Service fighter ace (briefly)

the Hotel Hohenzollernhof, near the station. Over the next few months, Georg often sat there with his comrades for what they called a *Liebesmahl*, a love feast, a decidedly sociable evening of food and drink. Officers always ate together in the evening and delighted in making newcomers buy a round of spirits for all as the fine for saying they had 'driven' a plane instead of 'flown' it.

Georg was to be a pilot, nicknamed an 'Emil'. The observer was known as a 'Franz'. Emil and Franz had to become inseparable companions, the one depending on the other when they were in the air. If a plane lost its way, this was called 'Franzing', because it was Franz who had not paid attention. This jargon remains in the German air force to this day. There was training in the workshops, about the engines, the parts of a plane, aeronautic rules and much besides. Observers were trained in scanning the country from the air,

in designing maps, taking photographs and using a machine gun
while flying. Soon they had their first trial flights, accompanied by
an instructor, when weather allowed given it was autumn. These
were Georg's best days.

AEG planes were the most common in use, which were biplanes
with a single-propeller engine at the front and two wings, one above
the other, held by struts and attached to the fuselage. The pilot was
seated in the forward cockpit behind a simplistic windscreen and the
observer manned the rear cockpit, facing aft, with a machine gun to
engage trailing enemy fighters. These planes had a top speed of 98
miles per hour but were extremely primitive as the air force, and
aviation, were still in their infancy. The only instruments were a
throttle to control engine speed and a joystick to gain height and to
control the tail of the plane. There was also side steering which had
to be done with the feet. There were gauges for height, petrol and oil
and that was it. Safety mechanisms were inadequate and piloting an
aeroplane was difficult and dangerous. On training flights, the
trainer took the observer's seat which had been adapted so he could
also control the plane. Speaking was impossible due to the fierce
airstream over open seats and the noise of the engine. The apprentice
simply had to feel what he might have done wrong through his
teacher's counterbalancing movements with the joystick and
steering. Everything was discussed when the flight was over.

The two main challenges were obvious. After takeoff, if the plane
lost speed because it had climbed too steeply (there was no
speedometer; the pilot had to estimate), there was danger of
pancaking, in other words crashing backwards. For landing, the pilot
had to reduce speed, push the joystick to lower the nose of the plane
and approach the ground. It was crucial to estimate the distance to
the ground, as well as the speed of the plane, in order to set down the
tail at the right moment. If going too fast, the plane's landing gear
would be overwhelmed; if too slow, there was a danger of the plane

landing on its nose. And if the plane was not even, it landed on its side and the wings were destroyed.

Georg completed training and embarked on a few solo flights in a single-seater plane. It was a peculiar feeling, to be alone, reliant on his own skill, flying through the air and looking down to see people as tiny as toys and to see the house where he was living. It was unavoidable to wonder if he would get home that night or be in a hospital or a grave. But all went well – until it didn't.

He had moved on to the larger two-seater plane that would in time accommodate him and an observer. On his first flight he was solo and the flight itself went well. But in landing the plane came down on its nose, the propeller broke into pieces and the engine burrowed into the ground. Georg was flung out of the cockpit in a high curve, landing ahead of the plane in a crumpled heap. He had no serious injuries but his body and his pride were much bruised.

These planes were built for taller people. He had tried putting cushions on his seat so that he had good all-round vision but then his feet could not reach the side steering controls. On his approach to the airfield, he could not lean out far enough to estimate the distance to the ground. There was some bad luck because it had rained and the ground was muddy, which made landing more difficult because the wheels did not roll easily. An investigation showed that his small stature was the primary cause of the accident and he had to give up his fledgling career as a pilot. It was the first time that his lack of inches had caused him serious setback. To rub salt in his wounds, some joker drew a cartoon of the incident and pinned it to the mess noticeboard. It showed Georg and a great number of cushions flying through the air. The ineptitude with mechanical contraptions that afflicts many of the Hahlo family perhaps started here.

What would become of him now? Another role in the air force or back to the infantry? For the time being he helped with drilling the teams and was allocated the unpleasant task of arranging the estates of dead airmen, of which there were quite a few. He even had to attend funerals as the air force representative and to give the bereaved the relevant details and the dead man's personal belongings.

So he was glad to receive an order in May 1918 to move to the Air Cannon Section in Döberitz, near Berlin. It meant that he remained with the air force, suggesting he had not blotted his copybook entirely. Here new tests were underway of small, quick firing guns that were being built into the planes to target tanks. They tried out these guns from the ground and from the air. They experimented with star shells in which the bullets were phosphoresced, meaning they lit up as they went through the air so that the military could follow their course and see if they hit their target. It was interesting work.

8

JÜTERBOG, GERMANY, 1918

'I wrote a heart-rending letter home;
I wished I had not lived to witness this shame,
an edifice reduced to rubble'

On 11 July 1918 an order came for Georg to go to Jüterbog, just south of Berlin. Nobody knew why. When he reported his first question was: 'What am I doing here?' He received a surprising reply: 'You are our new law officer.' Georg almost keeled over with shock. 'You are a lawyer, aren't you?' In 1915 he had enrolled at the Law Faculty at Kiel University, hoping that it would help him later but this he did not anticipate.

It turned out that the Observation School of the air force needed a law officer and when senior command had leafed through the papers of their officers, they discovered Georg was a 'lawyer'. Having heard the adjutant's assertion, Georg rallied and answered: 'Of course I am a lawyer.' The adjutant responded: 'Good, please start your duties straightaway' and led him to his office. The truth was that his studies had been curtailed by the war, and that he knew little of jurisprudence. But he thought to himself that he had managed difficult situations before, so he strode in and took his seat on the senior chair, trying to make it look effortless so that nobody would guess he was a total novice.

Georg's assistant was a junior barrister who had already passed his first law exams. When Georg did not know a particular detail, he asked the man how he had handled it to date, and then said: 'Yes, I have always done it a similar way myself.' Georg stumbled through the difficulties that came his way with chutzpah and resourcefulness, gaining the confidence of his captain, who later certified that he had fulfilled his role well. Georg was allowed to attend law lectures at the University of Berlin, about forty miles away. Lectures were in the evening, so he rented a room in Schöneberg, at Bahnstrasse 1, and would spend the night there before returning to Jüterbog on the first train the next morning. So began his law studies.

He found the work interesting. Discipline was slack in the air force and offences among the ranks and NCOs had increased to startling levels with widespread theft of materials stored at aerodromes and in workshops. Georg had to interview witnesses and conduct criminal proceedings himself or participate in cases that were taken to court. He was in control of visitors to the aerodrome, especially suppliers, and people working on counterespionage based in Jüterbog reported to him. He had independence and the bonus of an official car at his disposal.

A key part of the role turned out to be as a type of air policeman. Pilots were forbidden to land outside the aerodrome. If they had to make an emergency landing, they had to telephone air command immediately. But pilots were a law unto themselves, with a tendency to land near a village where their girlfriend or other friends lived in order to pay a little visit, and to acquire hoards of butter and other coveted articles that were otherwise in short supply. These became known as 'butter landings' in air force slang. Suspicions were raised when an airman reported that he had been forced to land but had been able to repair the engine trouble himself. If a pilot did this a second time or there was a reason to suspect a butter landing, Georg flew to the village in question and caught many a wrongdoer red-handed. Nasty but necessary work, he says.

Georg worked for four months like this, whilst beyond the horizon events started to spiral beyond Germany's control. Up to the spring of 1918 Germany had fought battles on the Western Front in style but had achieved merely local successes. Attempts to break through French lines had failed. The enemy had more troops and superior armaments, on top of which the recent involvement of America was having a significant impact and curtailing hopes of a German advance. Conditions at home were also sapping the confidence of the troops. The British blockade combined with poor harvests and a lack of manpower to get the crops in had reduced swathes of Germany to near-starvation. The notorious 'turnip winter' of 1916/17 had had a detrimental effect on morale, when turnips had become the only food available in bulk. They were cooked, canned and eaten in all ways: turnip stew, turnip meatballs, even turnip jam. The hardships were keenly felt and soldiers worried about their families on top of constant anxiety over their own daily rations. By August 1918, when fresh troops from France, Britain and America attacked German positions, they did not encounter the previous energetic resistance. The Germans were worn out and hungry.

Oldenburg Infantry Regiment No. 91 had lost about 50 per cent of its men: fallen, wounded or taken prisoner. In letters home soldiers described the harrowing reality of war. It became clear to people that German invincibility was a myth and this hit them like a thunderbolt. The sombre frame of mind of the population and of the army was further undermined by socialistic and communist propaganda that fell on fertile soil. The time was ripe for revolution and, on 9 November 1918, it arrived.

Georg does not comment at length on Germany's defeat and collapse. He says, rightly, that the superiority of the enemy, being abandoned by its allies and the overwhelming food shortages were factors that combined to undermine determination to fight and led to internal and external disintegration. He and his fellow officers knew that the enthusiasm of 1914 had disappeared and that the war could not be won. He believed that they still had responsibility, during those difficult days, to set an example to the ranks, to the whole nation. It was not easy to find the balance between maintaining discipline and adjusting to the changing mood as the officers continued to do their duty for the fatherland. Georg showed a loyalty to his country that was manifestly not reciprocated by Germany a mere decade and a half later.

Georg's experience of the end of the war started with being sent by his commander on 8 November to the railway station in Jüterbog to ascertain how the situation was developing. In uniform, he took his official car to the station, not realising the grave risk. The stationmaster told him that the soldiers had formed their own councils with leaders who had the audacity to give orders. Georg saw one train after another rolling away to Berlin filled with noisy, undisciplined ranks who had departed without permission. He saw that the revolution was coming and returned to base. Opposite the aerodrome were infantry barracks known to house radical elements. Georg and his men feared an attack and had to form a plan to defend the aerodrome. Machine guns were placed on every hangar, to be manned by officers. When they heard the phrase 'The Commander requests the officers for a discussion', they were to take up their positions. Fortunately, nothing happened. Soon, the order came from Berlin not to use force against the revolution. News rushed news. The Emperor abdicated. The Social Democratic leader announced in the Reichstag the formation of the German Republic, saying that the nation had been victorious. For Georg it was the beginning of defeat, the unbelievable economic and moral defeat of a once mighty nation.

That afternoon he walked across the exercise square and was approached by a sergeant with a cigarette hanging from his mouth.

Once, Georg had ordered a search of this man's home because it was suspected that he had stolen clothing. The search had been unsuccessful. Now the sergeant wanted revenge. In a tense exchange, the sergeant claimed to have been disgraced by Georg's actions and demanded damages, insisting that Georg arrange his divorce, as he could not face his wife after what had happened. He barked on, insulting Georg in imaginative ways, while the ranks grinned from the windows of the barracks, hoping for fisticuffs. Georg showed remarkable restraint and walked away, filthy abuse ringing in his ears. He told the commander and together they approached representatives of the soldiers' council and it was agreed that it would be better if the officers left the camp: they had made too many enemies. Georg understood that the situation could not be salvaged and was relieved to get away. He dressed in his civilian clothes, packed a few effects into a suitcase that he left with a friend and travelled in the evening to Berlin, posing as an ordinary soldier. His war was over.

On his way he saw the depressing consequences of the turmoil and hardship of his once proud country. Officers in uniform were insulted, taunted and openly assaulted by the rabble, their epaulets and decorations torn off. There was shooting in the streets. Who against who? Nobody knew. There was no armed resistance to the revolution, it was simply the rule of the mob. Somebody opened the prisons and the underworld poured out, adding to an unruly, lawless throng. Georg sat in his room in Bahnstrasse and wrote a heart-rending letter home, lamenting that if only he'd been killed in Flanders in 1914, he would not have had to witness this shame. For him, the edifice of Germany and all he believed in, the mighty fatherland, had been reduced to rubble. He had believed in the German Empire with all the idealism of youth. Now it had gone.[6]

---

[6] Who against who in the German revolution of November 1918? See p257

Georg had been disheartened by the Emperor's flight. Nobody knows how history would have gone if the Emperor had attempted to quell the revolution by force but Georg could not understand why he had not at least tried. He felt betrayed. Doubtless, there would have been a bloody civil war but perhaps the Emperor could have altered fate. To Georg, it was cowardice. A true emperor, a true Hohenzollern, should have found a more dignified departure from world history than to board a train to Holland and to surrender his sword to a customs official. This was the same emperor who had expected devotion until death from his soldiers, who had reiterated at every opportunity that he expected loyalty to Germany and to himself. He had no right to desert in the country's hour of need. Georg expected the captain to perish with his ship.

The next few days were turbulent. Power battles raged between radical communists and moderate Social Democrats. Strikes paralysed the economy. There was insecurity in all spheres of public and private life. There was a flood of returning soldiers and no preparation for their arrival. Plus no one knew what the enemy would do with a prostrate Germany. The German population was convinced that the German army remained undefeated, that in terms of military prestige, they were the victors. It was the treacherous politicians who had stabbed them in the back together with a lack of food caused by the cowardly Allied blockade that had forced Germany to surrender. An estimated 800,000 people had died of starvation in Germany during the war. The brave soldiers at the fronts had never given way. There was little sense of guilt or remorse, just regret at their own bad luck.[7]

---

[7] Why did Germany lose the war? See p258

9

BERLIN, GERMANY, 1918–19

*'My desire was very great to find soon a basis for my life
and to be able to marry my dear fiancee'*

A week later the University of Berlin reopened and at last Georg
could start his real law studies. Students poured into the University
from the forces and from the schools. It became overcrowded
because the age groups from the four war years were now clamouring
for their courses. In some lectures there were fights over seats.

Georg was determined to succeed in life and placed a high value
on education. This was shown in later years by his support when I
went to university in 1973, sending a small monthly stipend to help
me through my studies. Richard received money too and Georg sent
Michael a good shirt when he started work. These were generous
gestures because he hardly lived a life of splendour by the time he
was a grandfather. We wrote to express our thanks but I might have
divulged too much about social life at university because in a letter
to my father in December 1973 Georg admonishes:

'I can imagine how much Gerald is enjoying his new footloose life
but I hope he will soon realise that success comes only from hard
work. Tell him that I was already 23 years old when I came home
from the war in 1918 and started studying. For those of us who had

been in the war, special courses were introduced so we had virtually no holidays and I was able to sit my final exams in January 1921. It didn't leave a lot of time for sports, going to the pictures or dancing.'

He was right of course. Georg's mindset was: War is over! It's time to get on! He worked tremendously hard to overcome the obstacles that life and war had thrust in his way. His attitude was to look forward, to find solutions, to do well. It is remarkable that his journal has such a breezy tone and that he appears to display no mental suffering. I would not expect details of how grisly war is, remembering that his account was written for his teenage children, but it might have referred to mental anguish, the strain of readjustment to civilian life, the ingratitude of the country for whom he so nearly died, three times. Not a bit of it.

Across Europe, everyone had to get on with life again and this phlegmatic attitude was also demonstrated by my maternal grandparents. I recall that my mother's father, Wilfrid Foley, never mentioned the war and jovially dismissed childish enquires about what it was like to wield a sword or to engage in combat. And then there was her mother's brother, Arthur Kings, who did clerical work following his wartime experiences and, we were told, suffered from shellshock. It is now recognised as post-traumatic stress disorder and an understandable reaction among those who have seen comrades blown to pieces and had to live for days on end with the threat of annihilation. But at the time, his sister, Doris Foley, would have none of it. She told me: 'He should have gone out and got himself a proper job.' This was her brother. Generally, trauma was not spoken about. People were expected to get on with life and to deal with the mental fallout themselves, quietly. Talking about it was liable to be seen as self-indulgent at a time when everyone had suffered.

At university, Georg wanted to join a students' club, by which he meant one whose members, when insulted, demand satisfaction with a rapier. To him, with his officer background and an Iron Cross, it was the natural thing to do. It was difficult to get into a club because of the huge crowd of students but he had connections and joined a new club, the Suebia Fraternity in Potsdam, which seems to exist still. Their colours were red-yellow-black with black caps and he wore the two-coloured ribbon of the freshman. Georg spent many happy hours with his 'brothers' in their favoured bar in Potsdam and on the duelling ground, where they trained for friendly duels against members of other clubs. In his first duel he received a cut to the artery on his temple and was forced to retire. When he duelled a second time, he received a few cuts to the head but unfortunately not the cut to the cheek that was the most desired marking. But this duel he fought to the end and so became a Senior Man. With pride he now wore the tricolour ribbon of the fellowship.[8]

Georg's studies were soon interrupted. People faced a miserable future and unrest simmered across the country. Many had lost faith in their leadership, dreaded communism and, with the Allied blockade still in place, continued to go hungry. Market places had been converted into public kitchens where thousands of people were fed but with food of so little nourishment that their ability to work became seriously compromised. Germany in 1919 was a bleak and desperate place. Civil war loomed.

The provisional government planned elections for 19 January 1919 but the communists threatened to prevent them by force. The success of the Russian proletariat and peasantry in overthrowing their ruling classes had raised both hopes and fears that a revolution could take place in Germany as well. On 4 January protesters erected barricades in the streets of Berlin and seized several newspaper offices. Communist factions called a general strike in support and over half a million protesters surged into Berlin. One

[8] Why would Georg want to become scarred? See p261

of their demands was the redistribution of land, particularly of the nobles' estates.

Returning soldiers felt that they had been forgotten, returning to little thanks or recognition and paltry charitable handouts. They felt disconnected from civilian life because the world in which they had grown up no longer existed. They were angry at their inexplicable defeat and they had been brutalised and traumatised by their experiences such that aggression had become second nature to them. They joined Freikorps (volunteer paramilitary groups) in their droves and made themselves available to the government to counter any possibility of a communist uprising. They had been allowed to retain their rifles. It was the perfect recipe for a bloodbath.

The University closed to make it easier for students to join the volunteers. Georg put on his uniform and joined the Freikorps Lützow, a paramilitary brigade in Dahlem, a suburb of Berlin. It evoked the memory of a supposedly heroic volunteer regiment that had sprung up to help defeat Napoleon. It was a varied crew, determined to prevent a disastrous civil war. Georg was in charge of the machine gun. On 18 January they moved into Berlin and were greeted as liberators as they strode through Potsdamerstrasse to the Reichstag and spent the night in tents. The next day, the day of the election, they went to Gesundbrunnen, a notorious communistic quarter in the north of the city. Their task was to secure a school which was due to be a polling station and which was occupied by communists. They set up position opposite the school with Georg's machine gun and two cannons. They demanded that the communists leave the school at once. The occupiers saw that they would be overwhelmed and marched off without attempting to fight. In other parts of Berlin, it did not go so smoothly and more than a hundred were killed in brutal clashes on the streets.

The veterans emerged triumphant, recapturing the city centre, and a shaky equilibrium was established. The elections went ahead, and the National Assembly gathered in Weimar to give the German nation a new constitution. In Georg's view it had been essential to save the country from communism and to preserve the unity of the realm. In the evening they relinquished their weapons and went home. Georg took off his uniform for the last time. On the next day the University reopened its doors and he returned to his studies. Being a soldier was finished for ever.[9]

Georg studied hard in order to achieve his goal as fast as possible. The University supported ex-servicemen by wedging in an extra term so that they could finish the course in two years, with no time off. This demanded intense work but Georg's overriding desire was to lay the foundations for the rest of his life. He now had an extra motivation: to be able to marry his new fiancee.

---

[9] Why was Georg involved? The Spartacist uprising of January 1919. See p261

10

HALLE, GERMANY, 1919–22

'Sincere regards, Doktor Hahlo'

Georg had the habit of taking a stroll in the grounds of the
University of Berlin during his lunchtime break from his law studies.
There he spied an attractive young woman who would sit on a bench
in the gardens to eat her lunch before returning to her work in the
bank. One day, he tried his luck and introduced himself, using a
characteristic, formal German greeting, something like: 'Good day,
I am honoured, gracious young lady.' His charm brought a smile and
they fell into easy conversation. The girl's name was Ella Luise
Pauline Drewin, known as Elli. She had been born and raised in
Berlin and worked at Dresdner Bank. The regular lunchtime
meetings turned into courtship as they shared their love of arts, the
classics and theatre. He admired her poise and gentle manner. She
admired his earnest knowledge and listened patiently as he recited
endless facts he had to learn for his law exams.

Georg was mainly studying in Jüterbog but they wrote and they met
in a cafe or went to the theatre when he could get to Berlin. When
finally he moved to Berlin they could meet frequently, and soon they
'fell in love'. On 11 March 1919, after five months, they exchanged
engagement rings. Georg was eager to get on with a new phase of life
and to put his war experiences behind him. They had many happy

times at dances in Georg's club, or at restaurants in Potsdam, or in the houses of Georg's friends. He writes that one afternoon they rowed on Wannsee Lake in Berlin, Georg sporting the black duelling bandage on his forehead. Elli was terribly worried that he would feel ill. He could not let on that he did indeed feel faint.

He made her laugh with his witty remarks and ability to find the humour in everyday situations. Georg made increasingly strenuous efforts to impress his new girlfriend, such as when he was seeing her off at the station to visit her parents for the weekend. She seldom travelled alone and was nervous at the prospect. Georg found her a suitable compartment and installed her in a window seat so that he could issue last-minute reassurances. He stood by the open window, stressing where she had to change trains. As the train gathered to leave amid great gusts of steam, he took out his handkerchief and dutifully waved it. The train started to move and he jogged after it, and he was still waving as the train pulled away and he disappeared from her sight. Unbeknown to her, he opened a door and jumped into a moving carriage. At the next station he got out and ran up the platform, pretending to be seriously out of breath, and gasped 'And one more thing I want to tell you...'

In summer 1919 Elli's father, Friedrich Wilhelm Drewin, bought a small house with a little land in his birth village of Grabow, midway between Berlin and Hamburg in the north of Germany. The photo shows her parents happy and proud in front of what appears to be their thatched cottage. On 19 November 1919 Elli's mother Pauline Drewin was suddenly taken ill with a stroke and expected to die. Georg received a telegram in Jena, where he was now studying, over 200 miles to the south. He had to get to Grabow for the funeral.

The railway was in a state of chronic unreliability. It had received huge wear and tear during the war and in this period of economic and political unrest, repairs had not been started. Georg managed to catch the one fast train that ran each day to Berlin, where he spent

At the cottage in Grabow, c 1919

the night. The next day he met Elli and one of her brothers at Lehrter Bahnhof, the main station for the north. It was mayhem. An enormous crowd jostled for tickets because there had not been a train for a week in the direction of Hamburg due to strikes among railway workers. It seemed impossible to get a ticket but Georg found a railway official and could show that they were going to a funeral and in this way they obtained tickets and even seats.

It had snowed heavily in the preceding days and this was the first train. The rails were covered by snow and the points had iced over. Instead of one hour, the train took more than four hours to cover the first fifty miles and then they had to change. After a delay, they set off on a branch line which took several hours to reach Blumenthal, still fifty miles from Grabow. They travelled this last part on a horse-drawn sleigh. It was slow, cold and deeply uncomfortable on the uneven roads. Fortunately they arrived in time to see Elli's mother before she breathed her last. The next day they carried her to her rest in the village church. Shortly after, Elli moved to Grabow to keep house for her father.

Georg continued to study in Jena. He was interested in journalism and wrote political and law articles for newspapers leading his professor to suggest he should write his doctoral thesis on the Press Laws. He moved back to Berlin in spring 1920 and lodged in the hospitable home of his cousin Tilly Bing in Grunewald, Niersteinerstrasse 4. He worked in the Seminary for Journalism because he had decided on a journalistic career, judging that this was a less crowded field than pure law and a faster route to a well-paid position, as well as being an interesting occupation. He spent time either with his fraternity friends or travelling to Grabow to visit Elli. He joined the Deutsche Volkspartei, a party to the right that represented the interests of the industrialists, stressing family values, secular education and lower taxes. It generally opposed welfare spending and subsidies and was hostile to socialism and to communists. It grudgingly accepted the Social Democratic government of the new Weimar Republic.

During the summer of 1920 he wrote his dissertation in the State Library on Berlin's main thoroughfare, Unter den Linden. The title was: 'The History of the Prussian-German Press Law from 1815 until Today'. The theme was highly relevant as the new republic had for the first time granted the unlimited freedom of the press. He could not have guessed how drastically and how soon this would all change. On the first page of his thesis he wrote: 'Dedicated to my dear fiancee.' In November he handed it in and requested to be admitted for the oral exam in March. He applied for the position of editor of the Merseburger Tageblatt (Merseburg Daily) and was offered the job. After passing his exam, he would start on 1 April 1921. Meanwhile he continued to cram his studies, using the extra term. It was strenuous.

His oral exam was unexpectedly brought forward to January, which made Georg nervous. He did not feel well enough prepared and requested deferment but this was not possible because they had to examine four students together. And so he arrived back in Jena in an agitated state, not helped by a difficult journey in the January snow. It was the custom to visit the professors of the examination committee beforehand. Georg put on his top hat, a family heirloom, and set off for the home of the first professor. It had started to pour with rain and he and his ancient top hat soon looked bedraggled, but he was received kindly and assured that he was well prepared. The next morning, after fitful sleep, he visited the remaining examiners ahead of the exam at 5pm. The candidates entered the room in single file. Georg was at the front, dressed in a tailcoat, another heirloom. A new one would have been far too expensive given that materials were scarce and inflation had started to bite. His war medals were displayed on his chest, which encouraged sympathetic smiles – the other candidates could not boast such markers of past bravery.

The exam went better than he had feared, despite his thumping heart. Three hours later it was over. A few worried minutes were spent pacing in an anteroom with the other students before they were called back in and met by cheerful words from the chairman: 'Gentlemen, I can give you the positive news that all of you have passed the exam. My congratulations, doctors.' Handshakes all round! What relief and liberation! Studies were finished and his life lay before him. Georg went straight to the Post Office and sent telegrams to his fiancee and to his parents, none of whom knew that he had travelled to Jena for the exam. The telegram read 'Sincere regards, Doktor Hahlo.' Germans like addressing people by their titles and so Georg became Herr Doktor. He went with a friend to a well-known wine bar, Göhre, in the historic market square, where they celebrated long and hard. The days leading up to the exam had been stressful and Georg admits that the excess of food and wine that night proved unwise.

The next day he went back to Berlin, packed his belongings, signed off at the University and travelled home for two months off before starting his new job. As the first Dr Hahlo he was received with elation. He was able to introduce his fiancee to his parents when she arrived a few days later in Oldenburg. At the end of March he travelled via Grabow to Merseburg, a small industrial town south of Halle, to begin work. It was hard to learn the ropes. He knew nothing about the technical aspects of the production of a newspaper. Usually editors worked their way up but Georg immediately received complete responsibility, giving his signature to each edition. He worked and learned as fast as he could to master his new trade, the model of a purposeful, professional young man.

Soon he felt secure and he wrote to his fiancee: 'Let's get married!' He could not wait any longer to settle down. The war years had fixed his desire to live calmly in his own home. A fragment of a letter exists which suggests that Georg's parents had a serviette ring or similar 'prettily engraved' for the couple to commemorate their engagement. It was not simple to find somewhere to live because no new homes had been built since the start of the war and demand was high owing to the marriages of returning soldiers. He rented furnished rooms in Halle, Yorkstrasse 2.

The wedding day was fixed for 2 September 1921. Georg travelled to Grabow the day before, as did his mother, his sister Else and Elli's brothers. In the morning they drove by car to the registry office for the district in Königsberg, fifty miles away. It was a hot day and Georg claims he had last minute nerves on the way and that his mother had to hold on to his coat-tails. At 3pm, decorated with his war medals and the red-yellow-black senior's ribbon across his chest, he led his fiancee to the altar of the village church. It was a typical Christian wedding reflecting the Drewin Protestant faith. His colleagues in the Suebia Fraternity sent a glass boot, bearing the crest of the Suebia.

In the evening good food and drink helped them to celebrate a memorable day. A honeymoon was unthinkable because, after only five months of work, Georg was not yet entitled to much holiday and they lacked the money, due to the effects of rampant inflation. When his salary was paid at the end of the month, its buying power was less than at the start of the month and its value sank further in the following months. Yet they moved to Halle full of hope and the first weeks of marriage were 'happiness and delight'. In the mornings at 7am he set off for Merseburg with his breakfast and a thermos of coffee. His suit was pressed and his shoes shined. Around 5pm he returned home and they ate a meal together. They took advantage of free seats to first nights in local theatres so they had many enjoyable evenings. Georg even began to write the reviews for the paper but confesses that Elli helped him with these as she had a strong interest in theatre and music.

The marriage was fully approved by Elli's family. She had attracted the son of a wealthy business owner, an educated and qualified man. Georg's parents were not so thrilled, according to my father. Elli was two years older than Georg, born 10 January 1893. They felt Georg should have found someone from their own level and with financial backing. Elli's father was merely a packer in a porcelain factory, although this was an expert job because porcelain was sent all over the world and packing it properly was an art. Dieter recalled a number of oddities about his mother's family, such as the family having to chew each mouthful of food thirty-two times, which was a health fad of the day, being one chew for each tooth.

Georg was pitched into work at a time of great stress to the German economy. As a condition of the peace treaty, Germany had given up enormous quantities of goods, materials and gold reserves to its former enemies. On top of this, the expenses of the state were increasing at a greater rate than the productivity of the economy, which was struggling due to strikes, the introduction of the eight-hour workday and for other reasons. The state simply printed money to cover its expenses. Consequently there was more money than there were goods for people to buy for their daily needs, so prices increased. Therefore the state had to increase wages and so printed more money. Prices increased further until it was a race between the value of the money and the price of goods. Georg remembers when his salary of 10,000 Marks per month enabled him to buy what he formerly could for 100 Marks; the next month he could buy even less. The salary was enough for daily life, but it was unthinkable to acquire anything other than the basics.

The Merseburg Daily soon faced difficulties. Businesses could sell their goods without needing to advertise in the paper. When subscribers' money came in at the end of the month, it was already devalued. Georg had differences of opinion with the owner of the paper about his salary, which was progressively worth less. Georg saw that there was no prospect of advancement because all newspapers were struggling. He decided to find a role which made better use of his qualification in law and applied for various positions.

In September 1922 Elli met him at the station in Halle with a telegram that invited him to present himself for interview for the role of legal adviser at the Employers' Federation in Bad Kreuznach. His wife was questioning whether to show him the telegram because Bad Kreuznach lay in the occupied zone and there were stories of violence perpetrated by the occupying French troops. Luckily, she gave him the telegram and Georg took a day off to travel to Bad Kreuznach. Once there, he soon agreed his conditions of employment and was asked to start immediately. Georg returned overnight and surprised his wife at morning coffee with the words: 'Let's pack our bags, we're off to Bad Kreuznach!'

11

BAD KREUZNACH, GERMANY, 1922–23

*'I had a dangerous post; there was many a search
of my house and office and Elli worried if I would
return from my travels'*

The decision to start a new life in a new town was so quick that it
was decided Georg would go ahead and set up while his young wife
returned to Grabow. Georg started his new employment on 23
September 1922, renting two rooms at Salinenstrasse 48. The
bedroom was so small that he had to open a window to put his jacket
on or take it off. The Employers' Federation was an organisation of
factory owners, wholesalers and retailers in the Nahe District,
between Bingen and Oberstein and its main activity was wage
negotiations between workers and employers. There was only a
week's crossover with his predecessor to acquaint him with his new
tasks and he knew nothing about industrial law, most of which was
newly drafted. After a difficult beginning, he was soon familiar with
the demands of the job. Elli arrived a little later and they took a small
flat in the home of Georg's colleague, at Winzerheimerstrasse 18. It
was on the edge of the town on a small hill with views but was not
well protected from the bitter winters. They made a small circle of
friends through associations which had formed to link university
graduates, with whom they would enjoy meals and drinks, especially

at Felsenkeller (the Rock Cellar) in the town, as well as 'marvellous excursions' into the countryside.

Bad Kreuznach in 1922 was a small town of around 30,000 inhabitants on the River Nahe, which flows into the Rhine ten miles away. Today, it still has quaint old houses and a stone arch bridge dating from around 1300 that originally spanned the Nahe and neighbouring canal, though only the section over the canal is intact. With four houses on its piers, it is one of the few remaining bridges in the world with buildings on it. The town is surrounded by vineyards on three sides. The peaceful landscape of vineyards, orchards and meadows is interspersed with striking cliffs and gorges, the result of ancient volcanic activity. The mild climate and mix of steep rock formations and deep clefts of soft soils foster diverse microclimates ideal for wine cultivation. The area is famous for its white wines, dominated by Riesling grape varieties. Georg loved the local wines and in his memoir he yearns to taste them once more: 'If only I could drink again a Kreuznacher Kauzenberg, a Castle Böckelheimer Felseneck, a Niederhausen Rosenberg or a Münster Schlossberg Beerenauslese.'

The town is the starting point for excursions along the river and its tributaries to the upper valley of the Nahe, to the Hunsrück mountains, to the Palatinate Forest and to the majestic Rhine itself. The town has a spa, with lovely gardens and a splendid spa house. The sanatorium was used by those with tuberculosis, comparatively rife at the time, inhaling the natural salts and minerals. The bath waters contain the noble gas radon, with supposedly curative properties.

French, British and Americans occupied the Rhineland after the war as security that the terms of the peace treaty would be properly executed. The English occupied the first zone centred on Cologne, the Americans had the second zone around Koblenz and the French occupied the third zone with its centre in Mainz. According to the

Georg and Elli, c *1923*

treaty, the first zone would be freed in 1925, the second in 1930 and the third zone in 1935, ending occupation. The French had also taken over administration of the Saar district to the south and on the border with France. A referendum was planned for 1935 to decide if the Saar should remain French or return to Germany.

Bad Kreuznach had a strong French military presence. Occupying troops would march up and down wherever they pleased. The French commandeered the best buildings for their barracks and confiscated the most beautiful houses for officers and their families. Most Germans had no experience of non-white people and were unsettled by the fact that many of the troops were from French colonial divisions, seeing the deployment of Algerian and Moroccan soldiers as a conscious attempt to heap yet further humiliation on Germany. There were rumours of women being molested in the streets and most Germans were nervous and would not go out at night alone. Georg describes French officers swaggering around and behaving arrogantly in bars and restaurants. Every German would keep away from them and avoid having to show the required respect to the French flag.

Regulations affected the details of civilian life and were deeply resented. They were beset with petty rules, such as needing permissions to travel or to make long distance telephone calls or to publish newspapers. The local population was restricted to drinking nothing stronger than beer or wine, while the occupying forces guzzled whatever they could. The troops' canteens were in the best hotels with notices outside declaring 'No Germans allowed'. German children would gather at the windows to watch these people gobble up steaks paid for by German taxes while their own stomachs twisted with hunger. It was a vulgar time.

By January 1923 Germany was no longer able to meet the reparations demanded by the peace treaty. France and Belgium were intent on extracting the coal that had been promised, and which Germany was failing to deliver, and sent 60,000 troops into the Ruhr, a region just to the north of Cologne. This was Germany's industrial heartland, its centre of production for coal, iron and steel, and was vital to the economy. The English and Americans left the French to it. It seemed that the French were preparing to get what they had wanted at the end of the war, which was to separate the Rhineland from Germany: the long strip of territory that included the Ruhr and the mighty Rhine itself, a major transport artery. Germany would be powerless to resist because it had been disarmed, and the French were armed to the teeth.

Soon there was a desperate shortage of coal, because most of it had been appropriated by the French. Industry and transport were crippled and people could no longer heat their homes. Despite the political and social struggles, the nation was united against the French and determined to preserve the Rhine, the most German of all rivers. There was widespread passive resistance and various acts of sabotage, such as wire cutting. Greater confrontation started with railway workers downing tools, disrupting passenger and goods transportation. The French reacted by taking the railway under their own administration. The trains emptied. No respectable German would travel on that railway; those who did were considered traitors. The French introduced a customs border between the occupied zone and the rest of Germany. No German firm would pay French customs duties, so no goods travelled over this artificial frontier. Hence the economy, already weak, was shattered.

The economic paralysis gave Georg new problems. Factories and other businesses were out of action but the Government ordered that they keep the workers employed even though there was nothing for them to do, because widespread unemployment would demoralise the workforce. It was forbidden for the Government to pay wages and thus support the passive resistance, so Employers' Federations were tasked with doing so by the Government because the French could not interfere in the activity of private firms and organisations. Companies sent their payrolls to the Federation and Georg had to examine them, verify that they were concerned with unproductive work and request the amounts required from the Government.

He was in a dangerous position because being caught by the French authorities risked eviction or prison for being active in the resistance. There were searches of his home and office by French officials looking for evidence of 'illegal' payments. In order to obstruct the French from looking into his work, Georg set up a second office in the unoccupied zone in Frankfurt. He often stayed over, alternating fortnights between Frankfurt and Bad Kreuznach. Documents were worked on in Frankfurt in order to evade confiscation by the French and communications between the two offices were through messengers or the employers' companies. Georg and his secretary developed a code to use during their telephone conversations for the names of firms and amounts of money. There was danger that the French would occupy Frankfurt and his office was linked to the secret telephone service of the police station, so that he would receive a warning if needed. On days when the threat of occupation appeared real, he packed his documents and took them to a hotel or to a private room which he rented for this purpose. Georg was 27 and had been a working man for less than two years. With a wife to support, this was an extremely demanding situation.

Getting between Bad Kreuznach and Frankfurt was difficult. Travel by road was perilous because cars were often stopped and searched for forbidden documents and smuggled goods. There was only one station on the border between the British zone and unoccupied Germany that was not under French control. To travel through there, Georg needed a passport for the British zone, only available to those who lived in Cologne or its surroundings. His Federation belonged to a branch based in the British zone in Cologne so this office arranged a false certificate saying that he lived in Cologne which enabled him to get the passport.

Because Georg had to go via Cologne in order to travel from Bad Kreuznach to Frankfurt, a journey that should have taken eighty minutes by train took more than twenty-four hours. For the return journey, he would leave Frankfurt at 5pm and arrive in the morning in Cologne. From there he took a Rhine steamer that arrived in Bingen (between Bad Kreuznach and Mainz) in the evening from where he took a bus to home. Elli frequently worried if he would return from his travels but the system worked and he even obtained a fake passport for his wife so that they could spend a few days in Oldenburg. He had to take good care of her – she was now pregnant.

The continuation of aid payments and of passive resistance became more difficult with the ongoing devaluation of the currency. The Rhineland needed huge sums for payment of wages and other expenses, while the economy was producing little. The Government continued to print more money in order to pay their dues but the Mark dropped into a bottomless pit. Sums fixed one day for payment of wages would the next day be insufficient. A 1 million

Mark note would buy goods that used to cost one Mark. In August there had been 12 million Marks to the British pound, by November it was 2.8 billion and by the end of the year a dizzying 18 billion. The Government and the Federation were swamped. It was clear that something would have to give. In October 1923 things came to a head.

The French capitalised on growing unrest among dissident Germans by funding a separatist movement calling for a Rhenish Republic, fronted by unpatriotic German rogues. It was obvious that France was manoeuvring to enhance its power base by separating the Rhineland from Germany and Georg and most others stiffened their resolve to protect the unity of the fatherland as best they could. One morning on his way to the office in Bad Kreuznach Georg saw the new red-yellow-green separatists' flag fluttering from the town hall. The separatists had occupied it and other public buildings during the night, under French protection. At a street corner Georg met a man with whom he was slightly acquainted and they discussed the situation. Georg said he thought it could not last because the workers remained patriotic and anti-France. If they went on strike, or were dismissed, the chaos would be impossible to manage without the support of the majority of the population.

Half an hour later three German separatists wearing red-yellow-green armbands appeared in his office. They announced: 'In the name of the Rhenish Republic we arrest you!' Georg kept his cool and asked for their warrant, which they did not have. They said he must accompany them to the district administrator's offices. He knew that he had incriminating papers, so he told the men that he had to give his staff instructions before leaving. This allowed him time to hide the papers and tell his two secretaries to inform the chairman of the Federation. On no account were they to tell his wife. The women sat at their desks and wept. He went with the men to the district offices. A few more men he vaguely knew were there –

people with a bad reputation, opportunists hoping to gain influence in a new Rhenish state under French leadership. A conversation ensued:

'Herr Doktor, on your way to your office this morning, you were overheard to have said that you and industry would fight us with all available means.'

'No, I did not say that at all.'

'Oh yes you did, when you were standing at the corner of Mannheimerstrasse and Poststrasse.'

'No, I did not say that at all.'

'Well, it could be an error. But you are an expert and know exactly the political and economic circumstances. What do you think we should do now?'

'Gentlemen, if you are to undertake a campaign, you yourselves will already be clear about the most urgent tasks. It is essential to know how far you want to expand your region politically.'

'From the ocean to Switzerland!'

'Then the most urgent thing would be to eliminate the passive resistance and stabilise the currency.'

'Yes, the first point would not cause difficulties, because we have good relations with the French authorities. But for economic issues, we need experts like you and your colleagues. If you, or the gentlemen working with you, would like to make themselves available for this kind of work, we would welcome it very much.'

'At the moment, I cannot give you any assurances. I would have to talk to my board. But, as I am arrested, this is not possible.'

'Ah, of course, you are free. Please speak to your board and kindly inform us afterwards.'

This uncomfortable but incompetent conversation on the part of the separatists amused Georg to such an extent that he reproduced the exchange in his journal. He had found out what they aspired to, he had avoided giving specific advice and had extricated himself such that he was able to give a full report to his board. The decision was to keep silent and give no answer at all. And it was a good reminder that informers were on the streets.

The separatist movement did not last long because the population ignored it. Negotiations took place between Germany and France over reparations aimed at breaking the passive resistance and returning the Ruhr to Germany. France saw that they could not achieve an independent Rhenish State due to the hostility of the population so it withdrew its protection from the separatists and they got what they deserved: the leaders fled to France while hangers-on were beaten and chased out or simply treated with disdain.

There was progress economically with a new currency unit, the Rentenmark, introduced in November 1923. Despite some difficulties, it succeeded in bringing inflation under control and stabilising the economy which seemed like a miracle. Chancellor Stresemann encouraged an end to passive resistance and acceptance of a new plan that would see Germany regain control of the Ruhr while reparations would be paid on a sliding scale. The short-term fixes stimulated the modest resumption of loans and investment from overseas. The recovery gathered pace with such speed that by the mid-1930s Germany was once again one of the world's great industrial powers. But times remained turbulent.

The Beer Hall Putsch in November was a ham-fisted attempt at a coup d'état by the National Socialist German Workers' Party, led by Adolf Hitler. Around 2000 supporters marched on the centre of Munich, where they clashed with police, resulting in several deaths. Hitler was arrested, charged with treason and sentenced to five years. Georg was bewildered. He was used to surprising political events, yet this was no time to attempt an uprising when they had just fought off the threat from France and the unity of the people was paramount. Hitler was released having served nine months, by which time he had clarified his tactics and started to develop the Nazi doctrine. He was on the prowl again.

12

BAD KREUZNACH, GERMANY, 1923–33

*'Mum was frightened that our car could be
hit by a stone and lifted up the baby,
requesting by this gesture to spare us'*

During the country's turmoil, Georg and Elli had the excitement of
the birth of their first child. They had prayed for this and here she
was. Georg placed a birth announcement in the local newspaper:

> 'My dear brave sweet wife
> presented me today with a healthy little daughter.
> Her name will be Ursula.
> Counsel Dr Hahlo.'

The date was 2 October 1923, auspiciously the birthday of Field
Marshal Hindenburg who had commanded the German army during
the war and was President of the Weimar Republic. Ten days later
Georg fetched Elli and Ursula Pauline Susan from hospital. As the
young family drove through town, they found themselves caught up
in separatist unrest. Elli was frightened that the car could be hit by a
stone and lifted up the baby, hoping to ensure safe passage. Georg
and Elli adored their daughter, called Ulla for short, and looked to
the future with new confidence.

They prayed for another child and on 11 April 1926 Dieter was born, named Dieter Friedrich Wilhelm, the middle names tributes to his two grandfathers. A postcard with this photo was sent to family to announce the birth. These early family years were carefree. The first home was Brückes 25, where both children were born, after which the family home was Rheingrafenstrasse 5, in the spa quarter and near the river. It is an imposing block of brick architecture, typical of this area of

Dieter birth announcement, 1926

town. There was a level crossing on the road and opposite was a farm – the street was on the edge of town then. Dieter only had to turn right out of the house and walk five minutes in order to reach the River Nahe and its landscaped walks, although at his young age it seemed to take forever. Horse-drawn taxis plied the town and there was a taxi rank at the junction with the main road where he enjoyed patting the huge but calm horses as they waited for their next customers. The baker's boy would cycle down the road each day ringing his bell, which was the signal to rush out and buy *broichen* (bread rolls) still warm from the oven. We had been told this story by our father when we were small boys and when my brother Richard first visited Bad Kreuznach, he heard the sound of a bell and dashed outside, excited to see the baker's boy. But there was no boy, no bike and everyone was laughing at his crestfallen face. It had been the peal of the church bells.

The family lived on the ground floor in a large apartment with a beautiful garden. Friedrich Drewin had sold his home and had become 'our dear house guest'. The household had affluent trappings: a maid, a salon with deep armchairs and a wireless for entertainment. There was a separate dining room with a bell to summon the maid, who would come to serve the next course. Ursula and Dieter could be relied on to squabble over whose turn it was to ring the bell. Their best friends lived next door but one, Ingrid and Gisela Knaul. The four played together and were in and out of each other's houses. Ulla loved playing horses; she had reins which she attached to her arms and Dieter would have to drive her round the garden. Dieter, about five in the photo, was a typical German boy: clean, well-behaved and, like his father, packing a lot of energy into his tiny, wiry frame.

Rheingrafenstrasse 5 in 2017

Dieter, 1931

Dieter was proud when his father had to fly by plane for his work. Bad Kreuznach didn't have an airfield so the plane landed in the field opposite to collect him and bring him back again. This was sufficiently newsworthy for a picture to appear in the local paper of Georg emerging from

A Hanomag

his plane. The Knauls had neither a maid nor a salon which made the Knaul girls envious of the Hahlos. But Dieter envied the Knaul girls because they had a car, as their father was a mechanic. It was a Hanomag and looked like an upright matchbox on wheels. Dieter was not put off that its rounded front and rear had gained it the nickname *Kommissbrot* due to its resemblance to a loaf of army bread. It had seating for two people with a tiny boot at the front and the bonnet at the back housing the engine. To start the car Herr Knaul had to pump hard on a lever inside, where a handbrake would be today. They developed a routine whereby Dieter held the door open so it didn't squash Herr Knaul's leg while the man leant in to start the engine. This made Dieter feel terribly important and he was impressed by the car, despite the strenuous performance required to start it.

Elli was a homemaker, providing a happy and loving environment for her children. Bedtimes were special and even if Elli had been out for the evening, she would be sure to lean over the cot to kiss her children goodnight. Dieter recollects her perfumed scent and the bliss of waking enough to be comforted by her presence. They called her Mutti, meaning Mummy. Dieter was astonished to learn later that she had a real name. Dieter went at age 6 to primary school, a short walk from home. On the first day children were given a funnel filled with pencils, rubbers, notebooks and sweets and chocolates. Dieter's cone had to be held with two hands and reached up past his shoulder. It was an exciting day.

It was unheard of for married women to go out to work in their circles. Even so, Elli had a housemaid to help manage household chores and a washerwoman who came twice a week. Germans were house proud and things had to be just so. Elli enjoyed being in the kitchen where she cooked marvellous meals and treats. Dieter was allowed to scrape the spoon around the cake bowl and lick it clean, making sure he got every speck. He liked pressing out shapes for home-baked biscuits. Eating well was an obsession with Germans. Whenever Elli took Dieter to a doctor, the doctor would ask 'Does he eat enough?' and Elli would say 'Well he could eat more. He sometimes refuses his food.' The doctor would say 'I'll give him something to make him eat more' and would turn to Dieter and say: 'You need to eat more or I might have to operate on your stomach to make it bigger.' This made Dieter scared of going to the doctor.

The maid's name was Flörchen. She had her own room in the attic. Her boyfriend would come to keep her company when Dieter's parents were out for the evening and the two children liked playing tricks on him. There was a rickety old chair in the kitchen which was due to be thrown out but Dieter and Ulla managed to cobble it back together. They persuaded Flörchen to offer it to her man. They listened with bated breath at the bedroom door and yelped with glee when they heard a big crash as he fell to the floor.

Everyone had to be punctual for mealtimes. When they heard the instruction *'Kommt Kinder zum Essen hier'*, the children dutifully took their places at table. No one could start until Georg started to eat. Meals could be elaborate and took time. Chickens were purchased whole and had to be prepared from scratch. A favourite on Sundays was *Eisbein* (cured pork knuckle) with sauerkraut and mashed potatoes. Other popular foods were pumpernickel bread, sausages, including Dieter's beloved liverwurst, lentil soup, roasted and braised meats with potatoes or dumplings, sauerkraut, red cabbage, apple pies and various baked desserts. *Pflaumenkuchen* (plum cake) was a seasonal treat, cashing in on the abundant plum harvest in the region. If Dieter was lucky, he was able to devour it when it was still warm. He loved *Rote Grütze* (stewed red berries), rich and sweet and juicy and the juices would trickle down his chin. Their afternoon rambles would, when possible, involve picking luscious bilberries and grapes for scoffing there and then, or to have later with cream or to be stewed and used in more elegant desserts.

Like most families, the Hahlos didn't buy ready-made clothes. Material had to be chosen and the clothes made. A lady came to measure up, as often as once a week because there was always something that needed to be done. Dieter enjoyed her coming and it was interesting to see what would be created. The family shop in Oldenburg had provided this sort of service.

Dieter's parents were affectionate and caring, especially his mother who wrapped her children with cuddles and kisses. She thought it was good for children to have a rest in the afternoon and Dieter hated being made to go for a lie-down. Georg's main contribution was to instil a love of stories and rhymes, none more so than 'Hoppe Hoppe Reiter'. Dieter sat on his father's knees, facing him. Georg moved his knees up and down, imitating riding a horse, and holding his son's hands as if holding reins. At the end line, Georg would open his knees so that Dieter slipped towards the floor, shrieking with joy.

Hoppe, hoppe, Reiter
Wenn er fällt, dann schreit er
Fällt er in den Graben

Fressen ihn die Raben
Fällt er in den Sumpf
Macht der Reiter... plumps!

Hop, hop, rider
If he falls he will cry
If he falls into the ditch
He will be eaten by the ravens
If he falls into the mud
The rider falls with a... splash!

This rhyme has stood the test of time, proving popular with me and my brothers and becoming a highlight of my father's visits to his young grandchildren, at least as far as they were concerned.

Elli was nervy, often for little reason. Dieter remembers being on the light suspension bridge over the River Nahe in the town. When you walked, it wobbled. His mother fretted: 'Oh, do be careful Dieter, do be careful, it's dangerous.' It wasn't but she couldn't bear the thought of anything happening to her precious children. She could be so petrified in case her children should fall that it spoiled their outings.

Germans revered the idea of fresh air and exercise and a daily walk was regarded as obligatory. If Grandpa Drewin or their mother could not take them, they would go with the maid. They would cross the road to avoid the big house at the corner where the occupying French soldiers lived – the North Africans who were so unfamiliar. Dieter found the music they played peculiar and, to him, they appeared half-wild. He felt intimidated even though they were behind a high fence, not helped by his mother who would not even look at the soldiers, rushing the children past and refusing to talk about them. Dieter loved going out with Grandpa Drewin, a calm, reassuring man who dressed in a three-piece suit every day. His trimmed white whiskers and beard gave him a kindly, almost stately, air. Dieter and Grandpa Drewin would walk down to the swimming pool and the *salinental* (saline valley), the site of huge brushwood fences down which water from mountain springs dribbled. The wood trapped the salts and the breeze became saline. Fat Germans sat and sucked the salty air into their lungs. Salt residue was collected and sold as a cure for aches and pains, to be added to baths or diluted for drinking. Elli would insist that they breathe deeply in order to benefit from the saline air but Dieter never did. Dieter would need to sit on a bench and rest his tired legs before the walk back home. He let his feet dangle and could not understand how adults could feel better when they kept their feet in contact with the ground, the very cause of his fatigue.

Dieter and Ulla were taught to swim by their mother in a cordoned area of the river. Elli also taught her children to skate when the river iced up in winter. Most children had skates that clipped on to their boots. People flooded their tennis courts and charged admission for people to skate.

Sundays were important and there was often a family walk that brought them back to town along the other side of the river. Dieter

Rotenfels and spa in 2017

loved ascending to the top of the valley from where their home town looked tiny. Bad Munster, on the other side of the river, was dominated by the *Rotenfels* (red rock), a steep, wide cliff above the river over 200 metres high. The town was reached by a ferry that could take about twelve people and looked like a rowing boat. But there were no oars, the boat was guided by a pilot using a rope strung at head height. He wore special thick gloves that Dieter yearned to touch but never dared ask. This trip took twenty minutes and was exciting but the children were more focused on getting peppermint sweets from the automatic dispenser on the other side. Nothing tasted as good as those peppermints, except perhaps the lemonade that they gulped down. The adults scoffed coffee and cakes, whether it was a morning or afternoon outing. Long-established cafes with steep roofs and wooden beams could be relied on to ply them with bread, cakes, pastries and chocolates. They loved *Pflaumenkuchen* when plums were in season and the cafe did a good *Apfelstrudel*. The cakes were sometimes so smothered in cream that the flavour chosen was immaterial.

The tram route home started at Bad Munster, by the boat jetty. In the summer, the trams had *anhängers*, open carriages with just a roof, which were towed by the leading tram with its driver. His father had already organised that Dieter was allowed to stand next to Otto the driver and survey the route ahead. Drivers had to stand all the way and were exposed to the weather. Otto would press a bell with his foot to signal that the tram was about to set off and people should board. One day Dieter begged to be allowed to ring the bell and Georg asked Otto 'Do you mind if my little boy rings the bell?' Otto agreed and so Dieter stood next to him and rang the bell to announce departure. He loved that. But he hadn't grasped that this was a one-off privilege. The next time they went to Bad Munster, Dieter went straight to the bell and rang it. Everybody appeared out of houses, hotels, cafes and boats, thinking the tram was leaving.

The driver wasn't Otto and he was furious: 'Who rang that bell?' Poor Dieter was terrified that he would be sent to prison but Georg was amused.

Georg made time to spend with Dieter. At weekends they might go rowing, down by the town bridge where there were boats for hire. Excursions further afield, to the upper Nahe valley, the Hunsrück mountains and to the Rhine were usually by rail and sometimes by car. Herr Michel was a friend and colleague of Georg who had a Mercedes, no starter handle for him. The Michels had a lovely, old house on the high street which Dieter loved going to because it had an entrance with triangular mirrors, which allowed him to look up the street and down the street at the same time, as well as to see himself.

Sometimes the family used the ferries on the Rhine. Elli was always nervous stepping on to the small launches which carried up to forty people and were open to the elements. They had metal railings all way round so no one could fall in and a gate made of metal bars that was pulled back to let people on and off. When everyone had boarded, the man shut the gate, prompting Georg one time to say 'That will keep the draught out.' Everybody laughed at the joke and Dieter was proud of his father.

Many Easter traditions originated in Germany, such as egg hunts in the garden (or in the house if wet outside). There was great excitement as the children tried to find them all. Often there were large, highly decorated eggs made of cardboard that split in half and had chocolate treats and little presents inside. Elli would take the children to church for Easter services. Easter was traditionally a time for father and son to go wandering and Georg took Dieter away for two or three days' walking as he got older. Germans took walking seriously, using sticks to which they attached metal shields to flaunt where they had been. From the sticks they could tell immediately who were the old-timers and who were the novices. Georg had the proper walking attire: sturdy shoes, knee-length woollen socks and shorts that met them at the knee, held by leather braces and with practical deep pockets for a penknife and other walking kit. He never failed to pack his pipe which would be clamped in his teeth as they tramped through the countryside. Dieter had his own walking outfit, his baggy shorts held up by braces, which, like his father's, had a chest strap to keep the assembly in place and comfortable. Georg and Dieter stayed

Georg ready for walking, with pipe, c 1932

at modest hostels which had sprung up to cater to these new enthusiasts for the great outdoors. They were models of orderliness, cleanliness and simplicity, qualities that encapsulated the rising generation of Germans.

They walked and talked, mostly about Georg's young days, his schooling and his life as a soldier. It was an opportunity for Georg to stress the value of education and he would follow this up with close scrutiny of school reports and exam results. He impressed Dieter with his broad knowledge, such as of Homer, Schiller, Goethe and Shakespeare. Georg would recount Schiller's gothic tales of revenge in dramatic tones and Dieter would be awed by his ability to tell stories with such impact. It seems these expeditions were only for the men of the house – there is no mention of excursions with Ulla.

Georg and Elli enjoyed an active social life, thanks to Georg's club at the Stadthaus, nearby on the river. They could eat at its restaurant and drink and gossip, or they would play Skat, the most popular card game of the time. Germans tended to play with vehemence, slapping their cards down in order to intimidate their opponents. The club was an important part of Georg's life giving him and his wife a large circle of friends who would often visit each other's homes.

Elli had a taste for the arts. She loved going to the theatre and her critical eye would enhance, if not shape entirely, Georg's reviews when he wrote for the local paper. They continued to go the theatre in Bad Kreuznach, liking the social aspect and being seen in local society. Elli sang and played the piano, trying to teach both her children. She also enjoyed the cinema. It was a thrilling era for German film, spearheaded by the glamour of Marlene Dietrich. Dieter recollects that the first film he saw starred Charlie Chaplin, but in no time he became a fan of Dick und Doof, the German names for Laurel and Hardy, and was a cinema enthusiast. Before long, he was a theatre lover too, with his mother's encouragement. Germans had become great theatregoers and towns had their own theatre companies. The ingenuity of scene-shifting was mesmerising as whole sets dropped out of sight while new scenes, with actors, rose on elevators or descended from above. Dieter remembers the theatre in Bad Kreuznach, with its scenery waving in the gusts of air as it moved back and forth.

The family enjoyed visits to Oldenburg and holidays on the beautiful North Sea and Baltic Sea coasts, in Grömitz and the Frisian Islands. One summer, when he was aged 7 or 8, Dieter went on holiday to Denmark, to Apenrade (the German name for Aabenraa) with his grandparents, aunts and cousins. It was Dieter's first holiday away from his parents and he cried on the first night.

When going to the Frisians they travelled by train to Wangerooge or Juist. This was exciting because the rails went along a causeway and at high tide the train looked as though it was steaming on water. Whenever Georg had to catch a train, he always said 'That

Photos from
Juist, 1931

On holiday at Apenrade, 1933 or 34. Back: Else Hochfeld, Lotte Giessel
Middle: Dieter, Sofie, Wilhelm, Wilfried Hochfeld, Heinrich Giessel
Front: Wilhelm Giessel, Ruth Hochfeld

train will not leave until I'm on it.' Dieter was impressed because he was right every time. It seemed that his father, the man who could do everything, even had authority over the railways.

Georg and Elli saw to it that the Hahlo Christmas celebrations were special. My father would reminisce dreamily of the Christmases of his youth, before his world was torn apart and joy was extinguished. Festivities started on 1 December, when a fir wreath was hung in the lounge with four candles. One was lit every week and, as the excitement of the children built to fever pitch, by the time they lit the fourth it was Christmas Day. The children were not allowed to see their tree in advance and never saw it being decorated. It was a big secret and they would start to fret that a proper Christmas wasn't coming. Georg and Elli kept this pretence, making the moment when it was revealed stand out. The big day was 24 December with ceremonies getting underway in the evening, when it was dark. First, Ursula and Dieter sang carols at the piano with Elli playing. They sang *'Stille Nacht'* (Silent Night), *'O Tannenbaum'* (Oh Christmas Tree) and *'Leise rieselt der Schnee'* (Quietly Falls the Snow), which was Dieter's favourite, a haunting tune.

The doors between the lounge and the main living room were kept shut and only a sliver of light showed beneath. The children had to wait outside until they heard the tinkle of bells to signal that Saint Nicholas had left. The doors were folded back to reveal a room in darkness except for the Christmas tree, shimmering from the flames of real candles. Georg would burn a twig of fir to give the pungent but pleasant smell of... Christmas! The delight of this smell never left Dieter. The tree was decorated with baubles and chocolates and biscuits, with presents for the children at the foot of the tree wrapped in shining colours: red, green, gold and blue. On a table was a witch's house made of gingerbread and covered in sweets, with figures of Hansel and Gretel and the witch. The little coloured windows glowed from a bulb inside powered by a battery. This and the tree were the only light, creating a special aura. Dieter believed firmly in Father Christmas and in the Christ Child, who was the one who brought the presents. One Christmas he was allowed to place a call to Father Christmas himself from the family telephone, which he was not normally permitted to use. The surge of emotion through his tiny frame almost overwhelmed him as he asked the operator to put him through.

Presents could be lavish. Dieter was proud of his *tretroller*, an early 'kick scooter' which had a board sticking out at an angle of forty-five degrees. He stood on the platform with one leg and put his weight on the lever with the other leg to propel the scooter forward. He could scoot along fast without having to use his other leg. It was a rare and advanced little machine which he was proud to have until somebody stole it. Georg informed the police and a burly policeman turned up and took particulars from Dieter. Some weeks later the policeman brought it round saying they had found it in someone's loft. Dieter was delighted to have it back. One Christmas, when Dieter was five or six, when the bell rang inviting them into the room it sounded different to the usual ting-a-ling. It was the sound of Dieter's first electric train set. Georg had set the train going and when it went over a level crossing it rang a little bell. The engine had a tiny light at the front, so Dieter could see it whizzing round: he was overcome with joy. His father became preoccupied playing with the train set and later admitted this to a friend at the local paper. They published a cartoon showing Georg playing with the train set and Dieter crying because he couldn't have a go.

Goose was the centrepiece of the Christmas feast, accompanied by delicacies such as apple and sausage stuffing, red cabbage and potato dumplings. Dessert typically included a Christmas stollen cake and *lebkuchen*, soft biscuits in the shapes of stars and hearts. The spicy taste, laced with cinnamon, is rare in England and my father would seek them out for our own celebrations many years later, creating a link to his Christmases past.

Georg's professional position went from strength to strength, as did his income. He was entrusted with the management of more trade federations, such as for the wine growers of the Nahe valley, and he was in charge of the Tourist Information Centre, which was vital to the spa. He had become a teacher and examiner of industrial law and of political economics for the district of Bad Kreuznach. He had a prominent position in public life in a wonderful part of the country. He had a wife he loved and two happy and healthy children. This bliss would soon be crushed by economic and political events.[10]

Before long the family was forced to move and all their precious belongings, including Dieter's much-loved toys, went into storage. Dieter never saw his toys again. His gushing recall of these days betrays exaggeration. Dieter would not have been aware of the depth of his joy until it was snatched away. His feelings of happiness and security would not return until he had a family of his own and he came to regret that he had no mementoes of his happy childhood to pass on, other than a few photographs, many of which are in this book.

---

[10] Why was inflation rampant and what happened to the Weimar Republic? See p263

13

BAD KREUZNACH, GERMANY, 1930–33

'Dismissed without notice. Jewish descent
prevents me from representing the Federation,
I am no longer politically reliable'

In June 1930 a remarkable event took place. The French departed
the final occupied zone five years early and Germany felt free again.
In the evening there was a procession by torchlight and a military
band played in the spa gardens, for the first time since the
occupation. Everyone belted out the national anthem. Georg at long
last was able to help set up an association of former German officers,
which had been forbidden by the French, and so enlarge his circle of
friends. Together they organised events and appeals to support the
widows and children of soldiers. Georg was elected as honorary
manager of the local group. He also became one of the board
members of the Deutsche Volkspartei in Bad Kreuznach, the right-
leaning liberal party representing the interests of industrialists.
Georg's loyalty to the German nation ran deep and he remained
sceptical of the Weimar Republic. The circles he moved in virtually
ignored noises from Adolf Hitler, believing his fire would soon burn
out. They dismissed him and his supporters as Bavarian separatists
with little influence outside Bavaria.

Two elections were held in 1932 and the National Socialist German

Workers' Party attracted surprisingly significant support, although not the numbers needed to form a government. President Hindenburg tried to build a coalition that did not include Hitler but it became clear that nothing stable could be created without including the National Socialists (Nazis). After protracted negotiations, in January 1933 Hindenburg reluctantly nominated Hitler as Chancellor. The old warrior believed that he and his allies could control Hitler. A subsequent election in March 1933 produced an overwhelming win for Hitler. No one foresaw that he would use his parliamentary majority to eradicate the foundations of the state and of democracy. Hitler demanded use of a clause in the constitution that allowed the Chancellor to govern without parliament in a time of crisis. Almost overnight, Germany became a dictatorship based on the Nazi party and the army. Many people's futures collapsed within the year but Georg felt the effects as soon as April.[11]

Anti-Jewish rhetoric had begun to appear straight after the end of the war, with the inaction of Jews cited as one of the reasons for German defeat. Although Jews had been emancipated in 1871, antisemitism remained rife. Jews could not become officers in the German army and it was difficult for Jews to become university professors or to hold other state positions. The post-war government had not been regarded by many as a government of the people, but a government of Jews. Posters proclaimed that there had been almost no Jews at the front, yet they held the majority of government posts. The clamour for the people to be ruled by those of their own race had grown steadily in the intervening years.

On 1 April 1933 Joseph Goebbels, the Minister of Propaganda, appeared on the wireless calling for a boycott of Jewish businesses. Mobs formed in small pockets on the street in front of Jewish premises and heckled customers who attempted to enter. Thousands

---

[11] How did Hitler rise to such power, and so quickly? See p267

of shops were daubed with yellow Stars of David and the popular slogan became *Die Juden sind unser Unglück*: the Jews are our misfortune. In his diary, Goebbels praised the 'excitement in the air' and the unity of this 'moral victory' for Germany. The following day newspapers acclaimed the patriotism of those who participated in the boycotts. Not one article criticised the campaign or reflected that Jews were only 1 per cent of the population and could pose no realistic threat. Jews were in jeopardy, but yet to know they were on their way to the brink of an abyss.

Government policy with regard to Jews was enacted with great swiftness and an iron determination. On 7 April 1933 a law was passed that banned Jews from working for the Government and previously loyal workers were summarily dismissed. This included bureaucrats and office workers, teachers, judges and professors. An exception was made, for now, for war veterans. Two weeks later, another law restricted the numbers of Jewish students who could attend schools and universities, to 'solve the overcrowding'. Later in the year Jews were barred from working as journalists. Around this time, the owner of the old family store in Oldenburg changed the name of his business to his own, August Melching. He no longer wanted an association with the name Hahlo (although he didn't buy new awnings).

A colleague from the Federation's head office in Berlin attended a meeting of managers in Frankfurt that included Georg. In the evening they sat and talked over beers in the *Ratskeller*, the bar beneath the town hall. It was quiet and dark with its old wood panelling. The man from Berlin related that an official from the National Socialists had appeared unannounced and said that they should expel all Jews from the boards of the federations. It became increasingly clear that it wasn't only practising Jews who were in the Government's sights: antagonism extended to those who were of Jewish descent. Georg went home depressed and told Elli that he might not be able to keep his position.

He was right. The next day as he entered his office, the deputy chairman of the Federation asked to see him. It wasn't the chairman himself – that was Herr Michel, the family friend, and he, a Jew, had stepped back from his position a few days before. It was a deputy, Herr Kufrian, who started by saying that Georg should take a holiday. Georg replied that he had always acted with the greatest loyalty, which Herr Kufrian agreed was true and added that not all Jews were alike. But the party principle was that people were still Jews even if they had been baptised. He hoped there could be exceptions but it would be better for now if Georg would take that holiday, until the situation was clearer. He pressed a bell and another man entered the office to be introduced to Georg as his successor. Everything had been arranged. Hitler had in effect made him Jewish.[12]

Georg's replacement later said that he did not intend to usurp his position but Georg felt the man was not being honest and as a consequence he became anxious. The following weeks were nerve-racking. The rule that gave protection to ex-servicemen, including Jews, in government roles gave Georg hope and he attempted to put his case, saying his role was important to the reorganisation of the economy, even though he was not a state official. He had friends in high places and the German Officers' Union and his old regiment supported him. Georg went to Berlin to get the President's Office interested in his case. They promised to help but had little influence. Local officials were enjoying their power and making their own rules.

New men joined the board of Georg's organisation with Herr Kufrian's patronage. A board meeting at the end of May was attended by a *Kreisleiter*, a National Socialist official appointed to oversee local government. That same evening Georg received a letter

---

[12] Why was Georg Hahlo, a God-respecting Protestant, classed as a Jew? See p269

saying he was dismissed without further notice. The letter stated that this was due to his Jewish descent and that he was no longer politically reliable. The letter referred to irregularities that had been discovered by his successor, trumped-up charges relating to contributions to Georg's sick fund, to his private telephone, which was essential for his work, and asserting that he had altered his contract with the collusion of the (Jewish) chairman to ensure a favourable tax rate. It overlooked that payments to the sick-fund and the home phone were audited and authorised every year and that his tax arrangements were perfectly legal. The next day Georg asked former colleagues why he had been deemed politically unreliable: 'The *Kreisleiter* said so.' Courage was in short supply as everyone toed the line for their own safety. They all knew that his conduct had been impeccable and that the objections to his management were preposterous. He had simply become *untragbar*: intolerable. This was the new word to account for decisions for which there was no explanation.

His professional activities had meant everything to Georg. His contract was valid for another one and a half years but this was not a legal battle; it was a political one. He agreed to leave his position and his employers agreed to rescind the dismissal notice. Georg wondered if his job would even exist in the future and he foresaw correctly: within a few months all employers' federations and unions were dissolved.

14

DARMSTADT, GERMANY, 1933–34

*'It was rumoured in town that an Aryan
did tax consulting with a Jew and this endangered
the reputation of my partner'*

Word went swiftly around and the next day a business connection in
the town, Dr Warthorst, a tax consultant, told him that a tax
business in Darmstadt was available for acquisition because the
Jewish owner had emigrated to Palestine. They would pay half each
for the firm with confidence that the income would support their
two families. Georg was pleased to have found new work so quickly
and to show the people of Bad Kreuznach that he did not depend on
them. The small town had become uncomfortable.

On 15 June 1933 they took over the consultancy with Dr
Warthorst fronting representations to clients, as Georg was not a
qualified tax adviser. At first, Georg lived with his new business
partner at Bismarckstrasse 57 above the offices. On 1 October the
family joined him in an apartment at Victoriastrasse 28. Everything
looked promising. The apartment was above a tiling business, which
used the back garden to mix clay and where they had a furnace to
bake the tiles. The flat was quite large and had huge coal ovens. In
the living room there was a seat built into the stove where Dieter sat
to warm himself when it was freezing outside. The kitchen stove had

a cubbyhole for keeping dishes warm once they had been prepared before serving in the dining room. The apartment was opposite Ulla's school and Dieter would look out of the window to glimpse Ulla during her playtimes or to see her crossing the road to come home. Dieter was still at primary school, which had shorter hours.

Darmstadt is where Dieter found out that he was not a 'good German boy' but a Jew. The Nazis had said so. He was in bed and his mother suddenly said she needed to talk: 'It's time I should tell you that your father is Jewish.' Dieter was astonished. He was 8 years old and didn't know much about Jews, didn't even know what being Jewish meant. He only knew that Jews were talked about and were not well thought of. There was no further discussion with his mother. It was not something to raise around the dinner table.

The atmosphere in Germany became increasingly oppressive. Newspapers were censored and extolled the glory of the Nazi state and carried little news of the outside world. Swastikas swamped the streets and it was unwise not to display them. It was also unwise not to step aside for uniformed Nazis or to refuse a donation when they came into cafes or cinemas rattling collection tins. Criticism of the regime would have been suicidal. Most people sang its praises, despite continuing food shortages and widespread poverty. To them, Hitler was the *Übermensch*, a visionary, an inspired leader who, at a time when so many other nations languished, was putting his people back to work, building imposing new infrastructure and, best of all, restoring his country's pride. The discomfiture of a small number of Jews was a small price to pay for the restoration of the nation and resistance of a slide towards communism.

In November Dr Warthorst received a letter saying that work between an Aryan and a Jew was not permitted and that if he did not dissolve the partnership immediately, he would lose his licence. On 10 November Georg appealed to the district tax office. Outside the window, university students made a torchlight procession to honour students who had been killed in the war. Georg mentioned to the official that he had fought in the war and been recognised for his bravery but the official shrugged his shoulders. The decree from the Ministry of Finance was clear and it was signed by the Head of the Ministry, who was Professor Hederich, Georg's old colleague from Cologne. He had to help! Georg contacted Professor Hederich and told him what had happened, and the man was speechless. He wanted to help and after consideration, Professor Hederich decided that his decree related only to tax matters. Those could be dealt with by Georg's partner and Georg could work on other areas, such as management of assets and property and liquidations of Jewish possessions. Georg was grateful, although he knew it was an artificial distinction.

The two partners separated their work and income was split accordingly, which meant Georg's income was considerably lower than before. The separation did not work in practice because each asset or property transaction had a taxation element. Rumours began to circulate that an Aryan did tax consulting with a Jew, endangering the reputation of the firm and causing some clients to stay away. Dr Warthorst feared that the district office would denounce him. Georg sensed that this fight against Jews would make his position untenable before long. Although ex-servicemen should have been exceptions, it was clear the intention was to push all Jews out of positions of trust. Georg tried splitting the partnership, hoping to get back some of his investment by enabling Dr Warthorst to continue his work. In the end, they had to dissolve the enterprise and Georg lost all of his investment. He had been cheated by the system and there was nothing he could do, as Jews were not allowed to start legal proceedings. His livelihood having been stripped from him for a second time, Georg would have to look for something new.

The sinister atmosphere, the constant obstacles and the fact that Georg no longer earned enough money created stress at home. Elli took it badly. Dieter believes that Georg's father sent an allowance to alleviate the financial strain. The parents shielded their children from the realities, shielded them from their own suffering in the face of overt provocation. Dieter remembers being made to sit and listen at school to one of Hitler's first major speeches. He didn't understand the ranting but the power of his oratory was clear, as was the applause thundering from the wireless.

The state controlled industry, banking, infrastructure, education, the youth movement and elections. Reforms benefitted industrial and agricultural workers at the expense of professionals whose way of life was eroded. They were taxed more highly, family life was disrupted, parental influence diminished. Religion and education were interfered with to such an extent that they focused almost entirely on Nazi doctrine. No one could stand up to authority without risk of exile or martyrdom, for themselves and for their dependants. It was an ugly, fearful time and, for Georg, looking on the bright side became increasingly impossible.

Persecution of Jews intensified. Stormtroopers took up positions in front of Jewish shops, blocking their entrances. They held placards saying *Deutschland erwache: die Juden sind unser Unglück*: Germany awake: the Jews are our misfortune. Windows bore bright yellow posters. Newspapers, radio and the streets filled with anti-Jewish propaganda. Georg's sister Lotte lived in Eichwalde, a smart suburb of Berlin. She was a doctor and had married a doctor, Julius Giessel, who practised at home and was a Jew. In May 1934 the Government outlawed the reimbursement of Jewish doctors through the public health insurance funds, dramatically reducing their fees, and doctors were banned from treating non-Jewish patients. A stormtrooper was stationed outside the Giessel house to intimidate patients. Leaflets were stuck to every tree along the road: 'Anyone who goes to this Jewish doctor is *'ein strolch'* (a rogue or ruffian). Dieter started to notice Der Stürmer (The Attacker), a newssheet displayed at bus and tram stops, posted on walls and on notice boards that had been erected to display propaganda. It appeared each week in every town and village. It contained nothing but outrageous claims against the Jews and perpetuated nasty caricatures to stir up hatred. This edition's lead article is titled 'Jewish Murder Plan Against Non-Jewish Humanity Discovered'. At the bottom of the title page there was always the same motto: *Die Juden sind unser Unglück!*[13]

Der Stürmer, front page from May 1934

[13] Who produced Der Stürmer? See p272

15

HANNOVER, GERMANY, 1934–36

'Do you belong to Hitler Youth?'
'Not yet because we've just moved, but I shall be joining'

It took an anxious year for Georg to find something he could do and hence the time the family spent in Darmstadt could not be remembered with any positivity. They hardly knew anybody and Dieter recalls a dour town. Georg's new role was with a firm in Hannover that dealt with the collection of claims and the financing of savings contracts. Georg had little experience but he needed a job and it was the only opportunity available. Georg and Elli moved the family to Hannover in July 1934 so that he could start work straightaway. They found a small flat at Am Listholze 8. Grandpa Drewin came with them. By now he paid less attention to his appearance and his beard had grown shaggy. Dieter had to share a bedroom with him, which gave Dieter some comfort, even though he would be asleep by the time Grandpa Drewin turned in. Ulla slept on a divan in the study-cum-dining room, leaving one room for everyday use.

The business venture was a failure. The people running it turned out to be conmen who had hidden how weak the firm was. In no time the business had gone to pieces and Georg lost a further investment. Despite running a modest household, the family's savings had disappeared. Georg had to cash in his life insurance policy for the family to survive; they could no longer afford the premiums anyway. On 2 August 1934 Hindenburg died. He had endeavoured to protect Jews against the new measures. After his death, there was nothing to stop Hitler combining the offices of Chancellor and President, making his dictatorship unassailable. The assault on Jewish activities carried on without restraint and now Jews working in Aryan companies were subject to persecution. The increasing violence wore down Georg and Elli. All their joy in life had gone but they hid their despair as best they could from their children.

They were fortunate to be living in an enormous block of flats with several mod cons such as double glazing and heating and hot water supplied by a central boiler. This was marvellous but for the children there was one drawback. The heating pipes ran from one block to the next under the paths used by residents. When it snowed, the snow melted on these paths and this interrupted the otherwise-excellent toboggan run, much to Dieter's disappointment. It snowed a lot in Hannover and Dieter knew when it had snowed overnight because he could hear the scraping of shovels as people cleared the pavements. The

Grandpa Drewin, Elli, Dieter, Ursula in Hannover c 1938

sound excited him and made him eager to get his sled moving on the crunchy whiteness.

Behind the block was a communal garden with sandpits and apparatus for gymnastics. Dieter played football there with other boys who lived nearby, with Dieter liking to leap about as goalkeeper, irrespective of whether he caught the ball or not. If he was hungry he would whistle up to his mother who would prepare a sandwich and throw it down to him from their second-floor balcony. When his budgerigar died he carefully placed the bird in a little box and put a cloth around to make it comfortable before conducting a solemn ceremony and burying it behind a hedge in the gardens. He marked the grave with a little cross and some decorative stones. Two days later he decided that he wanted the box, so he dug it up and laid the bird to rest a second time, in the same hole but without the box.

The apartment was close to the Eilenriede, a forest in the centre of Hannover with a sumptuous tree canopy where they went walking. One day they saw an elderly man hiding Easter eggs for his grandchildren. The old man hadn't seen that his dog had twigged what was going on faster than the children and was snaffling the eggs before the children could find them. Further on was the lake, the Maschsee, which had been built as part of a government drive to use the labour of young men in order to reduce unemployment. The family would take out rowing boats or swim at the open-air pool and beach. The lake was stocked with carp which were reared for eating over the new year festivities. Nearby was a smaller lake where the ice in winter would be thick enough to support lots of people and Dieter loved skating in the magical evenings, when the rink was floodlit and stands sold snacks and hot drinks.

Outside town were the Deister hills, popular with hikers, to which Georg and Dieter managed a walking trip. The family also went to Steinhude a village on the shore of the huge lake Steinhuder Meer, about twenty miles from the city. It was originally a fishing village but had become a small resort offering swimming, water sports and fishing. The local delicacy was eels, which were trapped in large numbers and smoked over beech wood. Great racks of drying eels stood outside the numerous smokehouses and they used to sit and sample the fishy treats at the end of their days out.

A chance meeting with a regional official working in employment law led to an offer of help for Georg. Jewish companies, the few still existing in 1935, were excluded from German judicial process and advice. Through this official, Georg gained permission from the Ministry of Economic Affairs and Employment to advise and represent Jewish firms in questions of economic and industrial law, for which Georg was well qualified. He sent a circular to local Jewish firms and they clamoured for help. At first he was kept busy but one by one, these Jewish firms disappeared or fell into the hands of 'pure' Germans and his sources of work diminished. Local labour organisations obstructed him and the Ministry did not have the courage to defend the permission he had received. One day Georg was summoned by the *Geheime Staatspolizei*, known as the Gestapo, and forced to sign a declaration that he would give up his work for good.

Nazi policy was designed to bring Jews to the brink of despair. Oppression and persecution became part of everyday life. It is feasible that Georg and Elli did not suffer as much as some; perhaps they eluded the attentions of local officials through moving around. Georg does not mention, for example, daily pressures such as being forced to wait in food queues until all non-Jews had been served. Possibly they avoided these privations due to not being formally identified as Jews and not attending synagogue. Rules were interpreted differently by the various local authorities and often depended on personal connections. There is no talk of the family having to wear a yellow star. These became nationally mandatory in 1941 but it was demanded in many areas that Jews wear them long before this date.

Dieter and Ulla were largely unaware of the severity of their situation. It was not the custom to speak about grave or delicate matters in front of the children. Dieter spent four years in Hannover, transitioning from primary school to attend the Leibniz School in the centre of the city, a walk or short tram ride away. This was the *gymnasium*, for which he had to pass an entrance exam. He was proud to wear his school cap, a different colour to denote each year. Dieter declared he wanted to be a doctor, and Grandpa Hahlo set aside money for him to receive the extensive and costly training. The interest had started simply because when young he believed that his father was a doctor, not realising that a lawyer would also be addressed as Herr Doktor.

It was at this school that Dieter first showed interest in the theatre, no doubt encouraged by his mother. The school had a house in the country, on a mountainside about an hour outside Hannover. Every class would go there for a week at some point in the year. They would play games and Dieter enjoyed the trips. Parents came at the end of the week to collect their children, who put on a performance. Dieter somehow seemed to be the one in charge for his class, performing and helping to direct his first show at the age of 10 or 11. One skit demonstrated what it was like to be a naval officer in a German U-boat. Somebody lay on the floor covered by a mackintosh holding up one arm as the periscope. The dialogue covered the approach of an enemy warship which was in the U-boat's sights. At the crucial point there was the sound of an alarm as the warship attacked. Someone shrieked 'It's a hit! Water's coming in!' and poured a glass of water down the arm to soak the poor chap below. According to Dieter, the audience found that amusing. The children also acted out a poem, with Dieter hoisting a sword over his shoulder and marching about. His mother was so worried about him poking somebody in the eye that she stood up and said 'Dieter, do be careful what you do with that.' Dieter was mortified.

The applause at the end was followed by the audience standing, arms outstretched, and shouting three times *'Sieg Heil!'* Elli merely flicked a glove each time. Dieter was thankful that her actions went unnoticed. Dieter never let on that his father was considered a Jew; that he himself might be part-Jewish. He longed to blend in, to join the Hitler Youth as all his contemporaries were doing. He saw them practising their parades in the open ground by the side of the flats, looking smart in their neat uniforms and their slicked hair. He admired their controlled marching and their sense of purpose. He envied their huge drums which they played with such vigour. He wanted to be part of it, to belong. At his age, he could not comprehend what it all meant.

Hitler Youth was primarily for those aged 14–18; there was a separate branch for 10–14-year-olds. From 1933 it became the sole youth organisation in Germany and others were forced to disband. It indoctrinated its members in Nazi ideology and expected total obedience. Activities focused on sports, physical fitness and military training, such as shooting. Camping trips promoted a love of the land, which was a central strand of the Nazi movement, and another stick with which to beat the Jews who, as mainly city dwellers, were derided for their 'asphalt culture'. It was said that Jews were afraid of real work, preferring to build businesses that profited from the toil of others. This ignored the fact that many Jews had become traders and shopkeepers because for centuries they had been banned from owning land. By the end of 1933 membership of Hitler Youth reached 2.3 million and by 1936 it was over 5 million. Parents who refused to allow their children to join were subject to investigation and students who did not sign up were assigned essays with titles such as 'Why am I not in the Hitler Youth?' and were taunted by fellow students and teachers.

The pressure on Dieter was immense but he knew that he could not belong. He fobbed off classmates with the excuse that having recently arrived in the city he was not yet able to join, though he would do so soon. Every morning at roll call, the form master asked name, address, father's name and 'Do you belong to Hitler Youth?' Dieter's answer was 'Not yet because we've just moved, but I shall be joining.' He said, falsely, that they were members of *Der Stahlhelm* (the steel helmets), an ex-servicemen's organisation with right wing affiliations. He was terrified of being exposed but was never rumbled. It was made slightly easier by never having been a practising Jew.

The school had its own squad of *Schutzstaffel* (meaning protection squadron, the SS), which included an impressive band. They had endless drills with marching, torchlit processions and other displays. A delight to the kids was that one pupil attained a higher rank than a young master, who therefore was obliged to stand to attention in the pupil's presence.

It was all part of the groundwork for war. Propaganda highlighted the aggression of other nations. There was an exhibition in Hannover to which every schoolchild went. They were shown a model of a town with an aeroplane on wires which would drop its bombs causing the houses to collapse, with thrilling sound effects. It showed that Germany was prepared to defend itself if attacked by other nations that were willing to put civilians at risk – the dastardly rogues.

The Nazis reformed education, aiming to indoctrinate and to deter pupils from asking questions or thinking for themselves. They believed this would instil obedience and belief in the Nazi worldview, creating their ideal future generation. They changed what students learned, switching the emphasis to sports, history and racial science. In 1936 sport took up a minimum of two hours of every school day and by 1938 this had been increased to five hours every day as part of the grand plan to boost the fitness of the nation's youth in preparation for war. Subjects such as religion were removed from the curriculum altogether.

A Young Girls League had been created that promoted activities including camping, sports and instruction in ideology. Girls were instructed in domestic chores such as making beds, in line with Nazi views on women's place in society where they were expected to conform to the ideal of *Kinder, Küche, Kirche* (children, kitchen, church). Their role was to bear children for the Fatherland and to support their husbands, so they were discouraged from working and from seeking higher education. They had to sacrifice the freedoms they had enjoyed under the Weimar government and it was frowned on to wear makeup or to smoke in public. Lipstick was discarded, but sales of blonde hair dye boomed as everyone tried to make themselves appear as Aryan as possible.

The Nazis promoted simple and traditional aspects of Germany, removing new ideas and rejecting an intellectual approach. The Reich Chamber of Culture was established to cover the press, art, theatre, radio, music, films and literature – to exert a vice-like grip on all areas of life. Music composed or played by Jews was banned: no Mahler, Mendelssohn or Debussy, who had married a Jew. They acclaimed Aryan composers such as Wagner and Beethoven and suppressed 'degenerate' music such as jazz and swing. They blacklisted authors who were Jewish or deemed to be communists, socialists or adverse influences. This blacklisting led to a series of book burnings fronted by university students who led parades and threw blacklisted books onto huge bonfires in towns throughout Germany. Art in the modernist style was despised, believed to be the work of communists. In 1936, the Nazis carried out a review of everything on display in Germany's museums and galleries and removed 13,000 paintings that they considered 'degenerate'. They staged the Degenerate Art Exhibition to show how modern art was corroding traditional German culture. It was to contrast with the nearby Great German Art Exhibition which epitomised good

German art. Gallingly for the Nazis, the Degenerate Art Exhibition attracted twice as many visitors.

If there was one thing the Nazis excelled at, it was propaganda, and the country's hosting of the 1936 Olympic Games gave them the ideal opportunity. The Winter Olympics were held in a Bavarian resort. Although not as politically charged as the summer Games in Berlin, the event was manipulated with suppression of unfavourable press coverage and staged, lavish celebrations to mark the opening of new facilities. For the summer Olympics, the Nazis went to town. The organisation was impeccable, the atmosphere was festive and the population was swept along on an orchestrated wave of patriotism and pride. To outdo the previous Games, held in Los Angeles in 1932, Hitler had a new 100,000 capacity stadium built, as well as many smaller arenas. The Nazis invented the concept of the torch relay from ancient Olympia to the host city. They promoted the event with colourful posters and magazine spreads. Imagery drew a link between Nazi Germany and ancient Greece, symbolising the belief that German civilisation was the rightful heir of classical culture. Publicity promoted the myth of Aryan superiority and idealised athletes' muscles and strength, reflecting the importance placed on physical prowess – a prerequisite for military service.

FACKELSTAFFELLAUF OLYMPIA-BERLIN

Poster for the Berlin Olympics, 1936

The Games were the first to have live television coverage, not that many people had sets to receive the

125

pictures – certainly not Dieter. He was caught up in the enthusiasm via the chatter of classmates and newspapers which regaled the nation with tales of Aryan heroes. He followed the exploits of German athletes as they amassed a hoard of medals. Visitors came away from the Games dazzled by the impression of Germany as a thriving, efficient and friendly nation, albeit one obsessed with uniforms.[14]

In March 1936, three weeks after the closing ceremony of the Winter Olympics, German troops reoccupied the Rhineland, which had been a demilitarised zone. This was in flagrant breach of the Treaty of Versailles. Hitler gambled that the French would not react aggressively, and it paid off. Nobody tried to stop him and the majority of the population celebrated. Hitler's standing and political support were stronger than ever.

[14] How did the Nazis manage the Olympic Games? See p273

16

HANNOVER, GERMANY, 1936–38

'I cannot understand what they are saying.
I think of you all the time. Daddy, Mummy,
I shall never learn English'

By now Dieter was well aware of the consequences of being regarded as Jewish. When friends called round, they would raise their arms and say *'Heil Hitler!'* as the standard greeting. One day Georg said to a boy 'When you come here, you don't have to do that.' Dieter was stricken with embarrassment, spiced with fear. Luckily, the boy accepted it. The saying of *Heil Hitler* had become a reflex – people did it in the street, in shops, at events, everywhere they could. Even visitors to the country were expected to join in.

Another tricky moment was when the SS turned up at the house and asked Georg for a donation to the *Winterhilfswerk* (winter relief). This was an annual drive to help finance charitable work, with the slogan 'None shall starve or freeze'. It was to provide food, clothing, coal and other items to less fortunate Germans during the winter. Each Nazi association had its own badges to give in exchange for a pfennig or two. The can-rattlers, as they became known, made sure every good German gave their share. Neighbours and even family were encouraged to whisper the names of shirkers to local leaders and the names would be printed in the paper to highlight their neglect. Some workers risked losing their jobs if they did not give enough. Georg declined to give, saying that he already had. There was a tense exchange as the SS men demanded to know where he had donated. In the end, no trouble ensued. The idea of being a good German was uppermost in everybody's minds. Once, Dieter and his sister helped a blind man at a tram stop and a witness asked for their names and wrote to the family to say what fine German children they were.

There was a Jewish family living in the same block whose children never came out to play. Dieter was with a group of boys when one of them said 'My father said if a Jew is cheeky towards me, I should pick up a stone and smash it in his face.' Others agreed and another boy said 'Let's get those Jews!' So they stood outside and chanted *Juden raus!'* (Get out Jews!). Dieter likes to believe he didn't shout abuse but he was there; it was part of his survival strategy. The Jewish mother saw him and later admonished him: 'What a pity to see you amongst the others.' My father still felt guilty decades later. He thinks that the lady must have spoken to his mother and knew the family secret.

Georg turned his hand to something different: an agency to help with the sale of firms, which again was quite successful but he could see that this was only temporary and no basis for safe living. It already seemed likely, in 1936, that there would be war in mainland Europe with Germany at its heart. It was becoming clear the family could not stay in Germany much longer and emigration had to be discussed. Ideally Georg would emigrate first, on his own, in order to establish their new life. But how could he work abroad? His knowledge of German law would not get him far. How could they survive with no money? Dieter started to sense the strain as the atmosphere at home soured further. Elli became increasingly agitated and her loving attention to her children seeped away. On one occasion when his mother was upset Dieter took it upon himself to relieve the tension. He went down to the cellar and retrieved a bottle of wine, fetched some glasses and poured his parents a glass of wine each. They were suitably touched and had a drink which calmed the air.

The priority became to find somewhere safe for their precious children, somewhere where they could receive a good education. The decision to tear the family apart was so heart-rending that they delayed as long as they could, even though, in fact, they acted much more swiftly than most. In August 1936 Georg and Elli spotted a communication from a voluntary relief organisation (most likely the Inter-Aid Committee for Children, possibly the Hampstead Garden Suburb Care Committee) announcing that English families were willing to take girls of non-Aryan descent. Georg wrote immediately but it was not until 27 October that they received a reply. It stated that the Northcott family in north London had agreed to take Ulla into their family. But it came with a momentous proviso: she should depart as soon as possible. Georg and Elli decided to accept the offer.

The plans had to be kept under wraps until they were certain. One day Ulla came home from school and her parents told her: 'From now on, you will not go to school anymore.' Ulla started to cry, thinking she must have been naughty. Then they said: 'Because next week you will travel to England.' She laughed, the enormity of what this meant could not sink in. A charming letter from Mr Northcott direct to Ulla arrived. He prepared her, in a fatherly way, for all the new things she would have to face. Georg and Elli were comforted that their daughter would be well looked after. Dieter only remembers a 'blank acceptance'. He got on well with his sister and would miss her. It is hard to know how much he had to suppress the pain that he felt, for self-protection, and how much he was unable to grasp the magnitude of what was happening at his tender age. His parents tried to make life as ordinary as possible leading up to Ulla's departure in an attempt to lessen the trauma, or simply to ward off the terrible reality.

The date of arrival in England was set for 9 November 1936, less than two weeks after receipt of the first letter. There was a passport to prepare and get stamped and other bureaucracies to complete. By this time Ulla could hardly wait for what had been billed as a great adventure for someone who was a big girl now. Besides, she would be met by her Aunt Else, who had emigrated to England earlier that year with her husband Richard Hochfeld, who had been able to obtain a visa because his fruit import/export business was partly based in England. At 2.45 in the morning, Georg settled Ulla into the night train to Vlissingen, with instructions to find for herself the boat, the SS Mecklenburg, to take her to Harwich.

Ulla travelled through the night to begin her new life – she had just turned 13. Soon after departure the reality of life away from her mother and father started to hit. She was miserable and uncomprehending: why had she been sent away when her little brother had not? What had she done wrong? Why did she deserve this? Was she unwanted at home? She knew nothing about a war. She knew of the hardships they had endured but the strength of the family had insulated her and kept her secure. The crossing took almost eight hours and Ulla recounted waves as high as houses and the boat pitching violently. And it was there, alone in her bunk, that she had her first period. She did not know what was happening and thought she might be dying. Worse, she had no one to ask. Her mother, in the stress of the times, had not prepared her for this. Some unknown women tried to help but they spoke no German and Ulla didn't speak a word of English. The isolation gripped her. It is arguable that she never recovered from the trauma.

Georg cannot describe his and Elli's feelings when Ulla left home. They wanted nothing more than the best future for their children. Unfortunately in those days, frank conversations between adult and child were restrained and subjects such as menstruation, persecution and civilian atrocities were not talked about. As loving parents, their feelings and intentions were pure; their implementation and communication were perhaps lacking. Georg could only hope that when she was grown up and had children of her own, Ulla would understand how difficult it was to see their child depart for a strange country, under such difficult circumstances. Their only consolation was their conviction that it was for the best.

Ulla was met in Harwich by Aunt Else and for a week stayed with Else and Richard in London but her visa was linked to her staying with her sponsoring family, so she could not stay longer. She later reported that she had a cool reception from her aunt and uncle, presumably due to the stress of the times and the various arrangements that Else and Richard were being required to make. She then moved to the Northcott home at 1 Avenue Road, Highgate, a substantial property ostentatiously called Budleigh Towers. A first letter arrived at the Hahlo home in Hannover, opened with great ceremony in front of Dieter. In no time Elli burst into tears and was inconsolable:

'Mummy, I'm so homesick. I cannot understand what they are saying. All I ever think about is you, and when they stop talking, I jump with a start and notice again where I am. Daddy, Mummy, I shall never learn English!'

It is possible she was intimidated by the home itself, a gothic mansion built in 1876. It became known locally as The House of Dracula and was reputedly haunted before mysteriously burning down in 1969. The derelict building was eventually replaced by sheltered housing but a fragment of the original house still stands at the front of the new block.

Her next letter sounded happier and more confident. In the summer of 1937 Ulla came home for a holiday, and to renew her visa – she had become English. The Northcotts had given her a good home and Georg was grateful, chiding Ulla in his memoir: 'It is your duty always to think of them in gratitude. Perhaps one day there will be an opportunity to give back a little to them or their children for all the good they have done to you.' This does not seem to have come to pass. In later life she made no mention of Mr Northcott and his family. They treated her well, as far as we know, but had three children of their own and she never felt the warmth and closeness of her own family. These years of her life seem to have been obliterated from her memory.

Mr Northcott had originally offered to take Ulla for one year but prolonged his support to spring 1938, meaning she lived at Budleigh Towers for sixteen months. In this time she went to St Aidan's High School in Stroud Green. Then Uncle Richard added his financial support and this influenced the relief committee to allow her to attend a boarding school, St Monica's at Clacton-on-Sea, which she went to from spring 1938 until the end of summer term 1940, when she was 16. Georg came to London in May 1938 to discuss with Richard the possibilities for his own emigration and made time to visit Ulla in Clacton as well. By now Georg could not work in Germany, a decree having declared that agencies such as his were forbidden for Jews. It was the fourth time that Georg had lost the foundations of his existence. Emigration had become his only option. His sister Lotte and her husband Julius had emigrated to Texas in 1936 and were willing to be guarantors for his American visa, but the rush for emigration to the US meant that the country had now closed its borders to stem the influx of refugees.

And before he could depart Georg had to get his son, Dieter, to safety. England was preferable because they hoped to get an English visa for Elli, so that his wife and children could be in the same country. As yet, there was no simple way to get Dieter to England. Sweden was another option. Dieter had been to Sweden on an exchange trip in the summer of 1937, staying with a clergyman and his family at the vicarage on a lake in Bromölla for several weeks, enjoying it immensely and getting on well with the children. They kept chickens that were named after the Nazi leadership, so everyone took extra pleasure from eating them. Georg got back in touch to see if they could provide Dieter with a home.

The family wrote back to say that they were willing to foster Dieter and in September 1938 his suitcase was packed and he was ready to go, looking forward to an extended holiday. A few days before he was due to leave, they received a telegram saying there was an outbreak of polio in the area and he was advised not to come. This was a blow, both to Dieter and to his parents.

Strangely, there is no mention of this in Georg's memoirs, or of Dieter having had a holiday in Sweden. My father never mentioned it to me until I interviewed him. The village of Bromölla is by a lake with its church close to the shore, just as he said. And there were spikes in reported cases of polio in Sweden in 1937 and 1938, which lend credence to the story.

17

OLDENBURG, GERMANY, 1938

'The Gestapo are searching house by house'

The Nazis had thwarted all avenues that Georg might pursue in order to make a living in Germany. He could no longer afford the apartment in Hannover and so he moved with his family into his parents' house at Taubenstrasse 22 in Oldenburg on 28 September 1938. They shared a cosy room, furnished with a selection of their belongings, a few favourite toys (but not the train set), a couple of ornaments and some books. Everything else went into storage, to be reclaimed when the troubles had blown over. Dieter's Grandpa Drewin, with whom they had lived for the last fifteen years, went into a rest home in Hannover, aged 85.

Dieter had a key role in removals, sticking labels onto furniture to indicate which went to storage and which came with them. He was allowed to sit at the front of the removal lorry, looking out at the journey from Hannover to Oldenburg, which delighted him. He was positive about the move, realising it had become inevitable. He liked his grandparents, especially his grandmother, who was a lovely, kind lady. His grandfather was the domineering head of the family and could, at times, be rather terrifying but they got on well enough and it was comforting to live with them. Dieter attended the same school as his father had done but had little chance of enjoying it.

Apart from the tedium of lessons, the new devotion to physical education meant endless rounds of exercise in which the better athletes constantly showed off their physical prowess and mocked those who were unable to match them, such as Dieter. Even worse was the excessive number of visits to the baths where the ability to dive seemed to matter – a lot. Dieter never mastered the art of diving and endured the blistering condemnation of his fellow pupils, all of whom repeatedly propelled themselves into the water with gusto.

Within a few weeks, an event took place which shaped the future of the Hahlos and that of all Jews in Germany. On 9 November in Paris, a German diplomat was assassinated in protest by a Jewish teenager. The Nazis saw this as martyrdom to their cause and lost no time in stirring up even more hatred of the Jews. Sporadic violence was already breaking out when, that same evening, the Nazi leadership gathered in Munich and declared that protests should continue, so that, according to Hitler, 'the Jews should feel the rage of the people'. Police and fire services were instructed to stand aside unless Aryan people or property were affected.

Taubenstrasse was ten minutes' walk from the centre of Oldenburg in a residential district. The family was unaware of events escalating in the town during the night. In the morning of 10 November, Dieter set off for school as usual. His route took him close to the centre where he saw much activity and smoke and damage to buildings. People roamed the streets and the atmosphere was menacing. He did not know why. No one was in school, even the teachers were not to be seen. He returned home, highly agitated, pressing the doorbell with such force that it startled everyone inside.

On hearing the news, Georg set off towards Peterstrasse. Getting closer, he saw that the synagogue had burned to the ground and the adjacent Jewish school was also smouldering. The central domes of the synagogue had collapsed and only the blackened front wall was recognisable. Shards of glass from the windows had been blown onto the pavement. The buildings had been set on fire with gasoline and acrid smoke churned in the morning air. Fire engines were in attendance but standing idle, the crews chatting. City dignitaries had assembled in front of the stricken buildings, among them the mayor and a councillor, with his young daughter holding his hand. Georg hastened to Leopold's apartment. The mood of the town had changed – there was palpable tension everywhere and it was hard to know who was friend or foe. He was shocked to see widespread destruction. Stormtroopers and their cronies had rampaged through the town, smashing the windows of Jewish homes and businesses. Two Jewish stores on Kurwickstrasse had been destroyed. When Georg reached Leopold's apartment at Staugraben 4, he was stunned to learn that Leopold had been arrested and taken away to an unknown destination.

Georg hurried home. It seemed that the whole population had turned against Jews. Ordinary Germans were joining in to terrorise their neighbours, even their friends. The family drew the curtains and cowered indoors in the dim light, even though all seemed quiet in their neighbourhood. No one knew what might happen next. Elli sat upright, twisting her hands in her lap as anxiety filled the room. Dieter kept a low profile, too unsettled to read or do schoolwork but sensible enough to keep quiet and not ask questions. It seemed that they had been spared the worst, as the mob in the town had focused their attention on more openly Jewish families. Georg thought that Nazi persecution had reached its pinnacle, unable to grasp that it would soon outstrip his worst imaginings.

The telephone rang, a rare and ominous sound. Wilhelm picked up the heavy Bakelite handpiece from the solid wooden desk. It was an ex-neighbour from Hannover. He asked to speak to Georg.

'Herr Doktor, it's good to hear your voice. We have been worried about you. They have been looking for you.'

'Are you sure it is me they are looking for?'

'Yes, yes. The Gestapo were searching block by block, house by house. They broke down the door to your apartment. They demanded to know where you had gone. I told them I didn't know. Georg, it will only be a matter of time before they discover where you are.'

'You are right. I am most grateful to you for warning us.'

'These are desperate times Georg, take care. Look after yourself and your family. Goodbye and good luck.'

Georg knew he must act. After hurried farewells, he rushed to the station, sticking to lesser-used streets. He caught the first train he could find, which was to Hamburg. On board were a few men like him who had decided it was safer to be on the move than to hide in their own homes. In Hamburg there was a swelling band of restless men hoping to evade the attention of the mob in the towns. No one had a plan, it was a case of keeping going, hoping things would settle, that the SS would lose interest. Georg caught another train, and then another. He stayed on trains for four harrowing days and nights, sleeping when and where he could. Returning to Hamburg, the news from the community of people on the move was bad. There seemed no hope that the police or the people would lose interest in hounding Jews.

Georg reasoned that he could not continue life on the run. It had to end somewhere, somehow. He needed to get himself and his family out of the country but an idea that at first seemed impossible started to have a glimmer of potential. Mr Northcott had been extremely helpful in providing for Ulla. Georg's sister Else and her husband Richard were already in London and could facilitate arrangements. It had to be worth a try so he returned to Oldenburg and placed a call to Else and Richard. They agreed to ask Mr

Northcott if he would be prepared to provide a guarantee for Georg to travel to England. It could only be for a temporary visa because work permits for male professions were not available. Meanwhile Richard investigated what visas might be available in England for permanent emigration.

This was his only chance. All the fevered discussions had reached the same conclusion: he had to get to England in order to arrange his onward emigration. His survival depended on it but there was one hurdle, perhaps an insurmountable one. Georg needed a permit to travel abroad. Permits were only available from the state police, the organisation that just a few days before had facilitated the rounding up of the Jews of Oldenburg. If the plan misfired he would be sacrificing himself to no avail. It was a huge gamble and Georg knew too well that the future of his family depended on it, on him.

Georg put on his best suit and made his way to the police administration building, the Polizeiamt in Pferdemarkt. This building had once been his barracks and had held good memories; now its red stone vastness was forbidding. It was five stories high and had twelve sets of large windows across each storey. Why did the police need so many rooms? What did they do in there?

He steeled himself and walked in with as much sense of confidence as he could muster and asked to speak to the officer responsible for issuing permits to travel. He was shown into a room where he was received by an officer who wore his uniform with obvious care and pride, a pressed earthy-grey jacket with high lapels over shirt and tie. Around the parade of bright buttons were insignia and collar patches to denote rank, with cuffs and diamond patches on the sleeves to indicate membership of the SS. On the left sleeve was an armband with a swastika. His cap was firmly in place and above the peak was the national cockade surmounted with the eagle crest, its widened wings symbolising the power of the state.

Georg cleared his throat and announced in what he hoped was a measured tone:

'My name is Doktor Georg Hahlo. I am of Jewish descent and in the current circumstances I am obliged to search for possibilities to move abroad. I am here to request that you allow me a permit to travel.'

The officer acknowledged the request with a nod, took Georg's passport and walked to his filing cabinets, jackboots ringing on the hard floor. He started riffling through folders. After a little time he looked up and said:

'That is strange. Why can't I find your files? Are you registered here in Oldenburg? You know it's the law?'

'Yes, I registered my arrival at the end of September.'

'Hmm, well, in that case I would have expected you to have been picked up in the... in the action the other night.'

'Oh, I didn't know you had to volunteer for that' quipped Georg, belying his anxiety.

'Ha ha, you're quite right!' The officer smiled at Georg's little joke.

The mood in the room eased. The officer turned to look through a stack of pending folders.

'Ah, here it is. We haven't added you to the town lists yet, which is not very efficient of us, is it? Let me see... yes, everything seems to be in order. Going abroad might be the best thing for you now. Here is your stamp. I wish you good fortune.'

Georg went on his way, with a look to the heavens. The plan had worked and he had been saved by a miracle.

18

OLDENBURG, GERMANY, 1938

'He had been in a camp.
He couldn't join the group, he couldn't say anything,
he just stood there with his head bowed'

Leopold was less fortunate. On 10 November 1938 he was rounded up with forty-two other men who were Jewish or believed to be of Jewish descent. The objective was to detain leading members of known Jewish families and businesses. Leopold had been a prominent citizen, serving as chairman of the committee of wholesale merchants. Officials wanted to display their power over those who had been notable in the town. The men were marshalled in the square in front of the police building on Pferdemarkt. From there they were paraded through the town as an event for the populace to enjoy. Passers-by taunted them, including boys who had been excused school and were on hand to make fun of the men. Some spat at them. The captives were marched along Peterstrasse so that they could see the destruction of the synagogue, which had been reduced in most part to smoking rubble. A small crowd of police and people gloated.

The parade turned left at Café Klinge, a town institution that had been serving coffee and cake to the well-heeled of Oldenburg since 1884, into Haarenstrasse, lined with traders who stood in their shop doorways to watch. It reached the junction with Lange Strasse, turned

SA and SS men drive their Jewish captives past the destroyed synagogue to the prison. Leopold could be in the photo

The destroyed synagogue in Peterstrasse, 10 November 1938

right and in a few steps reached the junction with Gaststrasse, at which stood the old family shop. The procession continued to the *Rathaus* (town hall) in the market square at the centre of town. The route was calculated to maximise the attention and the satisfaction of the locals. The faces of the captives in the photos are tight and their expressions grim. Some look down, unable to face the photographers, others look imploringly for help, for decency. A terrible sense of foreboding must have flooded their minds as they walked. They continued past the glorious castle to the town jail on Richtstrasse, where they were detained overnight. The euphemism in the police department records is that they were placed in 'protective custody'.

Leopold had celebrated turning 70 just a couple of months earlier. On 11 November he and others aged 70 and over were released, as were two disabled ex-servicemen – eleven men in total. Leopold may have been helped by the fact that he, his wife (who had died in 1933) and his children were not outwardly Jewish. It is assumed that Leopold swiftly agreed to arrange emigration and managed to secure not only his safety but also that of his brother Wilhelm and Wilhelm's wife Sofie. The Hahlos were fortunate in that they had assets to entice the Nazis to treat them cooperatively, and they had contacts in Britain who could provide the guarantees required for emigration.

The remaining thirty-two prisoners were marched again though the town centre to the station, where they were herded onto a train. It accommodated prisoners from several districts, the fruits of a highly satisfactory night's work for the Nazis. The journey took all

Jewish men being marched through the streets of Oldenburg as bystanders look on. Two women pose, clearly enjoying the spectacle. This is an official photograph of Nazi measures to control Jews

day and no one knew where they were being taken. It turned out to be Sachsenhausen, a model concentration camp on the outskirts of Berlin. The prisoners disembarked in Oranienburg and were walked through the town to the camp's main entrance tower. Its central arch featured forbidding metal gates with ironwork spelling out *Arbeit macht frei* (work sets you free), a slogan used at various camps. The camp had a radial layout in a semicircle with watchtowers that ensured there were no spaces in which prisoners could loiter unobserved. The security system consisted of a death strip, an electric fence and a high wall.

The Jews of Oldenburg were housed in one of fifteen barracks hastily erected in a sub-camp. Jews, as a detested group, had to be kept apart from the main body of prisoners. First, they were stripped of clothes and valuables, which were confiscated. Their heads were crudely shaved and a thin uniform issued. They received a number and a coloured triangle to attach to their uniform: a yellow triangle representing the Star of David. Jews were on the lowest rung of the prisoner hierarchy.

Prisoners had to assemble for roll call three times a day. They were shoved together with blows and made to stand outside for hours. The prisoners' uniforms were no match for the bitter cold or the rain and the men suffered horribly. Anyone who collapsed was not to be helped. If a prisoner was ill, or had died overnight, they still had to appear for roll call, so fellow prisoners were compelled to drag the ill or dead body to its place on the parade ground.

The purpose of the action over the night of 9–10 November was extortion of Jewish assets and forced emigration. Pressure was put on detainees to write letters to their remaining family asking them to sign over assets to the Nazis and to arrange emigration forthwith, and when agreement was secured, the prisoner might be released. By the end of 1938, Sachsenhausen held 1345 Jews out of its original 6000, so most were detained for only a few weeks. One of Leopold's thirty-two comrades who was removed to Sachsenhausen did not return to his family in Oldenburg, having died in the camp.[15]

Dieter remembered he and his mother talking to a woman in the street, whom his mother knew well. The woman said 'This is my husband, he has just been released from a detention camp.' The man held back, he couldn't join the group, he couldn't even speak. He stood with his head bowed, skin raw under a newly-cropped stubble of hair, and took no part in the conversation. The Nazi strategy of breaking the will of the Jews had been extremely effective.

The events of 9–10 November 1938 became known later as Kristallnacht, meaning the night of broken glass, because of the devastation left in its wake. Thousands of men, women and children were brutalised and had their places of worship desecrated and destroyed and their homes plundered, right across the country. Life would never be the same again. Over 30,000 men were deported to detention camps where they were further ill-treated before being allowed to return home. Some did not survive.[16]

A barrage of anti-Jewish legislation followed Kristallnacht, intensifying persecution, and there were even fines on the Jewish community to pay for the damage caused. This intimidation and forced emigration were the first instalment of the Nazi's solution to 'the Jewish problem'. A hefty levy was imposed for transferring assets abroad that meant emigrating Jews often lost up to 95 per cent of their savings.

Meanwhile in Berlin, the Nazis prepared to move the enormous Victory Column and to add a fourth segment, to signal another victory in an upcoming war. The prize held out to Germans was the prospect of a vast empire in which they, the chosen people, would have the most glittering of futures. Euphoria was in the air.

[15] How did Sachsenhausen fit with Nazi ideology? See p275
[16] Background and aftermath: Kristallnacht 9–10 November 1938. See p280

19

OLDENBURG, GERMANY, 1938–39

*'You had tears in your eyes. When I said that you had
been so brave, you answered: "Yes, but you have to go so
far away!" That was the last thing you said to me'*

Immediately after the horror of Kristallnacht, American and British
relief agencies swung into action, discussing how to get food aid and
relief to the Jewish population. Many Jews had stuck it out in
Germany believing, like Georg, that their record as war veterans or
as model citizens would protect them, that it would all blow over in
a matter of weeks. Kristallnacht shattered that illusion. By the time
realisation was upon them, for many it was too late to act. The relief
effort was led by Quakers and a delegation went to Berlin to meet
with senior officers of the Gestapo. They reminded them of the role
of Quakers in preventing famine in the years after the Great War and
reassured the Gestapo that they did not represent any government,
political party or other organisation, nor were they interested in
propaganda. The Quakers were authorised to initiate a relief
programme and as they set to work, the delegation discovered that
food was not the main priority for Jews. The priority was to find a
way to emigrate.

A group of Jewish activists in London began working with
Quakers in Germany and England and, with the help of the British

passport control officer in Berlin, identified families in most urgent need, such as Jewish children whose parents had been incarcerated, those who had lost one or both parents or who were impoverished. Out of this despair the Kindertransport was born (although the name was not popularised until the 1980s). Dieter met none of these criteria and might not have made it if Georg and Elli had wavered. Many families did not act in time, because they did not believe that the worst could happen, until it was too late.

Georg realised that Germany had become too dangerous and that the further separation of the family was only a question of time. Dieter says he accepted that they had to move abroad and that it was his only route to survival and a future. He was comforted by the intention of his mother and father to follow him to England. They struck lucky in getting a place for Dieter on the scheme to transport children to England, not directly to a family, as for Ulla, but still the opportunity they prayed for. Georg does not say how this was arranged but it all happened quickly.

People had to be in the know in order to apply and be accepted for a place. It was a time of chaos amid a swirl of unreliable information. German newspapers published nothing that might be helpful, or even that could be considered news, and foreign papers were unobtainable. Georg was rewarded for being alert and having good connections such that Dieter seems to have gained a place on only the second Kindertransport train departure from Germany, about two weeks after the first. This was before the escape route became well known, the clamour for places escalated and it became an increasingly demanding process of forms to be filled, documents to be stamped, permits queued for and financial guarantees provided. The brutal truth was that a family had more chance of escape if they consented to be separated. Georg was sharp in mind and sharp in practice. He and his wife were willing to risk everything for the safety of their children and their clear-sightedness in realising there would be no escaping their roots thus avoided the most terrible of fates.

Dieter stopped going to school in Oldenburg and waited for his adventure. His suitcase was packed as they had been told to be ready even though the exact date of departure was not known. As a child he was free to roam the town on his own which he did for almost two weeks. He liked standing on the pedestrian bridge over the railway line near the station, as traffic waited at the level crossing, to admire the sleek, pounding locomotives – he liked being enveloped by the steam and smoke, the sounds and the commotion of the station. The Nazis had made sure that the trains ran on time. Schoolboys had a theory that these thundering steam engines would be brought to a halt if you spat directly into the funnel. With time to practise, he became much better at this than he was at diving, although despite strenuous effort it never had the desired impact. There was also the Cäcilienbrücke to occupy him, which had been the largest lift bridge in Europe when built in 1927. It had towers on each bank and a steel carriageway with two lanes for traffic and a lane for pedestrians. A mechanical lift pulled the entire roadway up to allow ships to pass through. Dieter would climb the stairs inside the towers and stand on the walkway, where he could gaze down at the huge cargo boats going in and out of the town port. He would travel on the large trolleybuses that trundled up and down Lange Strasse, past the old Hahlo shop.

The shop today. Georg was born above it in 1895

He also went to the vast, sprawling fair which was in town in the build-up to Christmas. There were roundabouts, ghost trains and bumper cars. There were great glasses of beer, sausages and mountains of filled rolls, lots of sweets too. The fair had sideshows and a booth for short theatrical performances that became another trigger to Dieter's theatrical ambitions. He recalls vividly the 'electric woman' who stood looking pale and unwell. A man attached various cables to her and put light bulbs at the ends of her fingers. A switch was flicked and, as she appeared to suffer the agonies of conducting electricity, the light bulbs would glow. Dieter was astonished. He didn't realise the deception or that the woman was wearing makeup and he went time and again to see her. There were also amazing displays of ventriloquism by the *bauchredner*, literally a belly speaker. At home Dieter tried fruitlessly to master the art until his abdominal muscles ached. He was entranced by miniature cabarets, for which Germany was famous, each show lasting about twenty minutes. Two men played a range of sketches and Dieter thought they were hilarious. He saw as many as his pocket money allowed, learned the sketches off by heart and tried to perform them whenever he could persuade a friend to be his fall guy.

Eventually the call came that the transport was arranged and would depart in two days' time. On a cold wintry morning in early December, Georg and Dieter travelled together to Berlin from where the train to England would depart. Georg boarded the same train and stayed on until Hannover. From then, Dieter, aged 12, was on his own with a crowd of unknown children. This was the little boy who only a few years earlier had been frightened by the thunder that boomed in the hills around Bad Kreuznach.

Elli was traumatised by the agony of losing her children and her home but she prioritised the safety of her son, despite her emotions and with no idea how he would deal with the future that awaited. It was an extraordinary leap of faith that this was the best chance of giving her son the gift of life. The Holocaust was not yet underway and the fate of those left behind was at the time not clear. Parents could not be confident that in sending their children to a foreign country, into the care of strangers, they were doing what was best. The anguish and uncertainty were immense and made worse because the plan to get Elli to England was not sure to be successful. Dieter feels that his mother had the hardest time of all. She was not under the same threat because she had no Jewish ancestry but to her credit, she stuck by Georg and his plans. If she had divorced him, she might have avoided potential difficulties but she refused to do this. She loved him.

Back in Oldenburg, Georg busied himself with closing down the family home and seeing to their tax affairs. He prepared his own parents for emigration to England – they and Leopold had been sponsored by Wilhelm's sister Helene and her relative Charles Ruttenau who lived in Manchester. The family was forced to leave their assets in the hands of the Nazis and would arrive in London with almost nothing for their new life, save the support of those already there. The house at Taubenstrasse 22, once an emblem of achievement and contentment, was sold cheaply. Everywhere, property and riches were being requisitioned by the Nazis. Party officials moved in as soon as they could, relishing the splendour of their new surroundings and all the trappings of prosperous life, the furniture, ornaments, china and glassware, even clothes, with no thought for the lives of the owners.

Mr Northcott again helped by agreeing to be the guarantor for Georg to obtain a visa for a stay of three months from late December. He travelled to England at the end of the year, leaving Elli behind in Oldenburg. Georg was not eligible to remain and work in the UK and, besides, what did he have to offer? What work could he do? He had neither capital assets nor relevant experience. He was a proud man, used to providing for himself and his family, and it would have been unbearable to be dependent on the charity of relatives. Georg stayed with his sister Else and her husband Richard in London and took great joy from being able to see his dear son at his temporary accommodation for refugee children. Georg was determined to find his son a family to be part of and, being in the same country, was able to be assured by the refugee committee that the chosen family would give Dieter a second home.

Emigration was Georg's only option, but to where? The US had closed its borders to the tide of refugees and Georg was deeply upset at being unable to reach there. Overwhelmed by the perpetual obstacles, it was the only time that Dieter saw his father cry. Most countries had taken measures to prevent being swamped with refugees. Richard Hochfeld had found a travel agency in London that could procure visas for Honduras and Bolivia, for substantial amounts of money. It was on the black market but Georg had to grasp this opportunity. Helene and Charles Ruttenau gave him a vital £100 (equivalent to around £7000 today). He knew little about either country but concluded that Bolivia had a healthier climate and better economic prospects. He secured an agricultural worker's visa and a ticket to travel.

Georg left London on Monday, 20 February 1939. Ulla came to London beforehand and Georg spent time on the Sunday with Dieter. He accompanied Dieter to the underground for his journey back to his new home in south-east London and there were tears. Georg said that all day long Dieter had been so brave. Dieter answered: 'But you have to go so far away!', the last words he said to his father for more than ten years.

Georg does not record an emotional farewell from his daughter Ulla, no last words, no tears. Perhaps she had already closed down emotionally, to shield herself from the pain of separation. By now she had been apart from her parents for over two years and was a teenager aged 15. It might be thought wonderful to be reunited with family after a painful separation but relationships cannot always be picked up where they had been left earlier. Life and people do not stay still and Ulla was deeply changed by experiences that proved too harrowing to talk about and she blamed the breakup of her family on her father. I imagine that, having left early in the era of persecution, she had little understanding of how desperate life was for those of Jewish descent who had remained behind. She never accepted that her father saved the family and she never forgave him.

Georg returned to Germany to say his goodbyes. The final farewells to his family passed less painfully than he had feared because they too were distracted by preparations for travel. But he could never erase the memory of Elli waving him off at the station in Oldenburg with tears flowing down her face, watching his train disappear into the unknown. He travelled to Antwerp, from where he sent this postcard to his son. The writing is indecipherable and has even defeated the best efforts of a 90-year-old expert translator. Georg, forever maintaining the air of an educated, professional man,

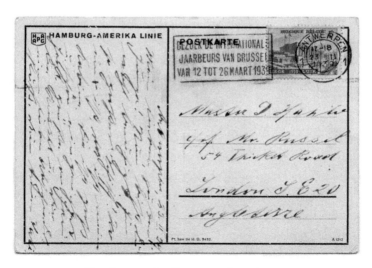

Georg's postcard to Dieter, sent from Antwerp

wrote it in historical Sütterlin script. Few people at the time could read the script and Dieter doubted that he would have been able to, describing his father's handwriting as 'almost unreadable'.

On the evening of 23 February 1939, Georg boarded SS Saarland of the Hamburg-America Line and in the night the ship weighed anchor. He had 10 Reichsmark left in his pocket, meaning he was destitute. Georg stood on deck and said farewells to Germany, his homeland no more, and to England, 'that most hospitable island'. He focused on his family: 'Will I ever see you again?' He was still thinking these same thoughts when he finished typing his account of his life on 31 March 1940. Then he would not look back anymore, only straight ahead. He trusted his own willpower to create a second homeland.[17]

Only much later did Georg become fully conscious of what it meant to be separated from his wife and children. The world did not know, when Georg embarked on his account, the full horrors of the Holocaust. He had the grace to acknowledge that they had been fortunate but at the time he must have been racked with doubt about whether it had been right to break up the family, to separate his children from their loving parents. We know now that he had correctly foreseen the dreadful consequences of remaining in Germany. We must be grateful to Georg for his clear-sightedness, his fortitude and, ultimately, for his enduring love for his family.

Georg had to process how it felt to be chased out as if he were a traitor by the country to which he had always been faithful, the country for which as a soldier he sang: 'Oh Germany, highly honoured, sacred land of loyalty.' He and his Jewish comrades had risked their lives for Germany. Twenty-five years later the country had driven these soldiers from their homeland and property, taken away their professions, their families, their homes. The Nazis had

---

[17] Did Georg sail on the Saarland? See p284

stripped them of the right to live in the country which they had defended with their blood. The Nazis had tried to take their honour but did not succeed.

Germany was no longer the sacred land of loyalty. Georg pictures the 12,000 Jewish soldiers who laid down their lives for Germany rising from their graves to bear witness, supported by their hundreds of thousands of comrades laid to rest in Belgium, France, Poland, Russia, Italy, in the Balkans and at the bottom of the ocean. Georg writes that all of them rise up and say: 'Together we suffered, together we died, in the name of our devotion to the fatherland. Does the phrase "loyalty for loyalty" no longer hold? Then woe betide you, Germany.'

In Georg's youth, people roared their commitment to Germany spontaneously – they truly believed in the greatness and glory of their nation. Years later he wonders what the young soldiers of the second great war would be thinking, lying in their trenches at Germany's border. They, too, would believe they were fighting for just cause, yet their fervour was not the same; these troops had needed years of indoctrination through education, meetings and parades to pump them full of belief in the justification of the commands they were obeying. Georg's final warning: 'You, the German youth of today, after the breach of faith you have committed, will never be victorious. First learn to be loyal. Learn the true meaning of the word.'

How right he was.

20

BERLIN, GERMANY TO HARWICH, ENGLAND, 1938

*'At the border we all grew silent as SS guards came in
and said "Which youth belongs to this case?"
I put my hand up'*

Dieter could not recall any fear at his voyage into the unknown. It was an adventure. He was largely ignorant of the seriousness of Nazi persecution and the danger his family had been in. He had already adjusted to the idea of going away due to the plans for travel to Sweden. The mood of his parents had improved with his chance to go to England, his sister Ulla was already there and his mother had assured him she too would be joining them. His only hope for the future was that he would see his family again. Like most children, he coped one day at a time, not thinking of the possibilities for grief. Dieter imagined himself speeding through England on a train and seeing Ulla from the window, waving merrily.

His optimism insulated him from reality. He didn't wonder how he was going to learn English; it didn't occur to him that knowing no English might be a handicap. He had faith that whatever course his father took, it would be the right one. He decided he would be brave for his father. He left his mother in Oldenburg, saying their goodbyes at the family home. He was wary of a prolonged farewell because his mother was prone to being tearful and, predictably, she was overcome. He wondered later at how his impatience to be away must have felt to her. His instinct was to focus on life ahead, bolstered by the thought of seeing his sister and the belief that sooner or later his mother would also come to England. His parents had been good at amplifying the positive aspects.

In later years Dieter had little recall of his goodbyes with his family. This perhaps reflects emotional suppression as well as his inability at the age of 12 to grasp the magnitude of the challenges facing his parents and himself. The mind's ability to bury the most painful experiences and preserve more agreeable memories is a coping mechanism that seems to have served Dieter well. By the time my father and I talked, sixty-four years later, any distressing feelings could no longer be retrieved. He must have been helped by his disposition, inherited from his father, which was to be optimistic and to rely on an ability to get on with people and to find a solution to even the darkest situations. Such a personality comes with some fragility; my father could be quick to anger and displayed flashes of paranoia when people didn't appreciate him in the way he expected. Both the positive and negative aspects of his character could be traces of his traumatic childhood experiences and reflect that the pain of separation never left him.

Dieter and Georg left for Berlin on 12 December 1938, going early so that they had the chance to travel around the city and enjoy parting treats. They stayed in a proper hotel, which was a novelty. They went to Berlin's enormous Christmas market. The biggest thrill was travelling on a double-decker bus. Dieter had not seen double-deckers before and could not believe the view from the front upstairs, exclaiming 'We're gobbling up everything!' as cars and people below disappeared from view. On their last evening, 13 December, they finished the day with a fine meal in a restaurant in Friedrichstrasse. The next morning Dieter and Georg boarded the train at Friedrichstrasse station for a mid-morning departure. Later transports mostly departed in the late evenings, a ploy by the Nazis who did not want ordinary citizens to witness the distress of parents being parted from their children. Later still, parents were not permitted on to platforms and had to say their goodbyes elsewhere.[18]

The suitcase was heavy and Georg had to carry it, even though only essential clothes were packed. They had strict instructions for the journey: no more than one suitcase per child plus one item of hand luggage. In his pocket, Dieter had a harmonica which he was learning to play. At the station, there was a hubbub as a large number of children milled about, it is said around 350 for this transport. It was a scheduled train with extra carriages to take the children and a few helpers overseeing them. Dieter knew no one, apart from his father. Some children had a parent or two but many did not. All were given a label on a piece of string that was put round their necks with a number on the front, permission to travel and their name on the back. There was another label for their cases. They were counted. Everything seemed efficient despite these early transports being experimental – the relief agencies did not know yet if they could successfully send several hundred unaccompanied children through Germany to Holland and beyond.

As the time of departure approached, whimpering and sobbing peaked. Mothers insisted on kissing their children over and over again. Some children became impatient, not realising it was a final parting, but some were distraught. One girl would not let go of her mother's hand. When the train started to move, she still wouldn't let go and the mother ran with her until the train picked up so much speed that the wailing girl was forced to abandon her mother. We can imagine that they never saw each other again. It is estimated that no more than 10 per cent of Kindertransport children were ever to be reunited with their parents. Almost certainly not the baby twins,

---

[18] What was the Kindertransport and how was it organised? See p286

still in their Moses basket, who were shoved onto a train at the last moment with no identification. There can be no greater sign of desperation than to send your babies away to an unknown fate.

Dieter was guided to a seat in one of the carriages assigned to the children. A dozen or so boys were crammed into a compartment designed for eight adults, knees touching. An older boy heaved Dieter's case onto the bulging rope luggage rack. Georg travelled in another carriage so as to get back to Oldenburg, staying on the train for a few hours until Hannover, almost 200 miles from Berlin. Dieter and Georg met in the corridor and stood to watch their country fly away from them. They had run out of words to describe their feelings. They saw a bullfinch from the window with its vibrant red chest, traditionally regarded as a symbol of life and joy, and Georg declared it was a good omen. There was a foray to the catering car where Dieter could have a lemonade and Georg had the chance to sit down. Theirs was a traditional steam train but Dieter was excited that they passed one of the new generation of streamlined diesel express trains going in the other direction. This was the *Fliegender Kölner* (Flying Cologne), the fastest train service in the world and part of a high-speed network started in 1933. Dieter had long been eager to see one, it was like a parting gift and a bond with his father.

Georg was anxious that he and Elli would be reassured that Dieter had arrived safely and, once in England, that life was progressing well. He presented Dieter with a small amount of English money for emergencies and several pre-written postcards with phrases such as 'I have arrived safely', 'It was a good journey' and even 'I don't know where I am'. All Dieter had to do was cross out those that didn't apply. Dieter thinks there might have been English stamps on the cards already. It was a good idea and simple to do. When the time came to leave the train at Hannover, Georg did so with the minimum of fuss, which helped to reassure Dieter. A quick kiss and Georg clambered down to the platform where he stood and waved as long as he could. It hadn't occurred to Dieter that he might never see his father again because he was confident that his father could do anything.

Dieter returned to his compartment. He was aggrieved not to be next to the window but took his hard, wooden seat obediently, his legs dangling, and tried to get some sleep despite the rattling and shaking of the train. All the children were in the same situation and there was a good atmosphere. A few seemed reflective, but most looked forward to what lay ahead. Most, like Dieter, had little concept of what they had escaped and of the dangers they had faced in Germany. There was a variety of ages with toddlers being taken care of by older children or one of the adults. Most of them were Jewish but there were a few Christians like Dieter. He was oblivious to the intricacies of the Jewish faith. Going to the toilet, he passed a compartment in which orthodox Jews wearing skullcaps were saying prayers and wrapping the straps of their tefillin around their arms. Dieter was taken aback and thought they were torturing themselves as some sort of penance. He didn't linger.

Near the border with Holland at Emmerich, the train stopped. Its doors were wrenched open and the train reverberated to the sound of heavy boots as SS guards boarded with their dogs. Everyone froze. The compartment fell silent with anxiety. No one knew what might happen. A guard in an imposing uniform came into Dieter's compartment and counted the children. Identity cards were scrutinised and permission to travel checked. He looked around. He barked: 'Which youth belongs to this case?' He was pointing to Dieter's, and Dieter fearfully put up his hand. The guard pulled the case from the rack. Dieter opened it and the man poked around in it for a while until he seemed satisfied that there were no valuables concealed. He left without conducting a thorough search and all the boys breathed a sigh of relief. Later Dieter heard that others had not been so lucky and that precious items had been confiscated and that some guards had been throwing around dolls and teddy bears to intimidate the children. The SS were looking for people flouting the rules, which limited the value of money to be taken out of the country to around ten pounds' worth. Jewellery and other valuables had to be handed in. Some guards even robbed the children of their legitimate meagre allowances of money.

At the border itself, more German guards boarded and marched up and down demanding to know, for the last time, if anyone had anything to declare. It took twenty minutes to cross into Holland and when they did, everyone cheered. Such were the attempts of countries to assert their independence before travel across borders was common that there was a time difference between the countries of twenty minutes, so the crossing started and ended at the same time, which Dieter thought was incredible. They were out of Germany at last. It was like entering paradise for the children. Suddenly, people were lining the platforms at the stations who were friendly and welcoming. None of them were soldiers. They were even cheering, which stunned the children. Tables were set up on the platforms, laden with food and drink. Dutch women and children bustled on board, handing out white bread and butter, oranges, biscuits, sweets and cakes and cups of cocoa and chocolate, at times showering them with food through the carriage windows. These were ordinary women who shared what they had from their farms and homesteads with a common language of smiles, and a few tears. Some children were even given a little English money and Dieter marvelled at the huge pennies. All were deeply touched by this warmth and generosity, which for so long had been absent from their lives. Everything was going to be all right. The children were intoxicated by the reception and became boisterous, acting their age at last. It was a good journey now, sitting back gazing at the countless windmills towering above the houses.

By the time they arrived at the port, Hook of Holland, it was late and dark. A confusion of people was jostling together on the platform. Dieter struggled to get off with his suitcase which seemed to him bigger than he was. A teenage boy who was on the transport took the suitcase and carried it for him on the long walk. Once through customs, Dieter saw the boat with its huge funnels. It was enormous, overwhelming, gleaming under the glare of floodlights. This was exciting. Children snaked up the gangplank and before long Dieter was on board. The case was stowed after Dieter had retrieved some pyjamas and he was assigned to a cabin which had around a dozen bunks. One of the helpers came in and announced that there was one boy on his own in a double berth – would somebody like to share with him? Dieter had always had sympathy for outsiders and volunteered, despite immediately regretting it. It was clear that the others would be having a much better time but he stuck with it in the double.

His mother had given him sea sickness pills and strict instructions to take them with water. So he popped them in his mouth and went to the toilets for water. There was none. By now the pills were starting to clog his mouth with a bitter foam. He went from berth to berth searching for water. Eventually he found some and, despite the water tasting foul, he drank and swallowed the pills. He made his way back to his berth and the two boys fell straight asleep, tired by the long journey.

The next morning there were orders to get up, get dressed and have a wash. Dieter dutifully washed his hands, face and neck. Elli always had a thing about him washing his neck. A woman supervising was shocked that some children didn't wash and they were told off and had to complete their ablutions. Then it was on to a brief breakfast and final preparations for England. The moment they disembarked they were surprised to be confronted by reporters and photographers with flash bulbs popping as they walked down the gangplank. Their arrival made it into the national newspapers.

Dieter was in a group that was asked to pose and, ever the performer, took his harmonica from his pocket and pretended to play. The photographer was delighted and got her shots. Dieter saw his first policeman wearing a tall helmet, who appeared satisfyingly British, and like the others, he was amazed to see people in uniform who were unarmed and who actually smiled. There were also friendly locals who had come to greet the children.

Arrivals inspection December 1938

But a cold wind was blowing across the unwelcoming space of Parkeston Quay and everyone was speaking a language he did not understand.

21

DOVERCOURT BAY, ENGLAND, 1938–39

'I felt poorly because of the cold and I was walking
with one or two people including one of the attendants
and I just found myself collapsing'

The children wore their entry visas and identity cards with a photo round their necks for checking. They were shepherded onto a bus for a short journey and Dieter peered out of the window to get his first look at English soil. He thought he might see his sister, knowing they were close to her school. He pictured her in the school playground, playing happily.

These first arrivals did not have sponsors or prearranged foster families and the refugee agencies were scrambling to find homes for them all. Near to Harwich was a holiday camp, Dovercourt Bay, which was closed for the winter. It was considered suitable to receive this sudden influx of refugees. The retired naval captain who ran the place was caught unawares and hastily recalled his summertime staff to act as hosts and cooks. Dovercourt Bay could not cope on its own and some children were sent to Pakefield holiday camp near Lowestoft. Dieter stayed at Dovercourt. He remembers five children allocated to each chalet and sleeping with all five of them in the one double bed. It had scratchy blankets which shifted around all night. There was a single chest of drawers but no other storage. The

This document of identity is issued with the approval of His Majesty's Government in the United Kingdom to young persons to be admitted to the United Kingdom for educational purposes under the care of the Inter-Aid Committee for children.

THIS DOCUMENT REQUIRES NO VISA.

PERSONAL PARTICULARS.

Name *HAHLO, Dieter*

Sex *male*   Date of Birth *11.4.26*

Place *Bad Kreuznach*

Full Names and Address of Parents.

HAHLO, George, Elly
22 Tauben...
Oldenburg

569

Arrival card and entry visa, dated 15 December on the back

children were sorted by sex but ages were mixed, in the belief that older children would look after younger ones. They spent time clustered around the stoves in the cavernous hall where meals were taken, sitting at long tables. The Jewish children conducted ceremonies and sang religious songs which were all totally new to Dieter, as was the food. Many found it challenging, especially kippers and tripe and onions. Bacon and eggs was a staple at first – someone had not done their homework on what to feed to a largely Jewish group. The menu settled into delivering typical British fare with a customary lack of variety, although Dieter was happy with the emphasis on meat and potatoes. It took him and others time to enjoy tea with milk, which one child described as 'a liquid that looked like coffee but tasted like poison'. Another declared that Marmite sandwiches with white bread were unfit for animals.[19]

Thanks to reports in the press, Marks and Spencer sent a consignment of surplus shoes and clothing and an appeal by the BBC generated further gifts. Wellington boots arrived, which were a novelty and proved useful in the mud. A butcher in Essex provided

[19] Why did the children go to Dovercourt Bay? See p294

beef sausages once a week and another donor sent cases of fruit each week. Jewish sporting clubs came to organise activities such as boxing and fencing and on Sundays some Jewish barbers volunteered their time to do haircutting. The local mayor even put in an appearance and gave a welcoming address to the children, oblivious to the fact that they could not understand a word he said.

There were attempts to instil the rudiments of English with makeshift lessons in the hall. The children sat along the tables on which were placed everyday items such as knives, forks and spoons, sugar and milk. The children had to ask 'What is this?' When they had moved on from 'Vot ist dis?', more items were introduced such as nails, screws or a hammer. There were lectures on the customs

Meal time at Dovercourt, December 1938

Weekly Menu for Jewish Children.		
	Breakfast.	Dinner.
Sunday.	Porridge. Fresh Herrings. Bread and Butter. Tea. Jam.	Boiled Beef and Carrots. Peas Pudding. Potatoes. Stewed Fruit and Custard. Bread.
Monday.	Porridge. Bread and Butter. Tea and Syrup.	Irish Stew made with all possible vegetables. Jam Tart with sauce. Bread.
Tuesday.	Oatmeal. Kipper. Bread and Butter. Tea and Jam.	Fried Fish with Chips. Green Peas. Rice Pudding with currants and sultanas. Bread.
Wednesday.	Semolina with cinnamon. Boiled Egg. Bread and butter. Tea and Jam.	Roast Beef. Mashed Potatoes. Cabbage. Treacle Roll. Bread.
Thursday.	Porridge. Fried Egg and Potatoes. Bread and butter. Tea and Jam.	Cottage Pie. Boiled Potatoes. Peas. Baked Apple Pudding. Bread.
Friday.	Semolina. Bread and butter. Tea and honey.	Irish Stew made with all possible vegetables. Apricots and Rice. Bread.
Saturday.	Oatmeal. Kipper. Bread and butter. Tea. Syrup.	Roast Beef. Green Peas. Potatoes. Cabbage. Sultana Roll. Bread.

Dovercourt Bay weekly menu

of their new country. They were told that the English admire
quietness and that it was frowned on to talk loudly in public, that
people wait their turn when getting onto buses and trains, that
younger people offer their seats to older ones and that whenever you
meet someone you have to say 'How do you do?' There had not been
time to plan what the children might do at the camp, few had books
and there was no library. Generally they were left to their own
devices. There were a few improvised activities but Dieter does not
remember being bored because there was always someone to talk to.
They played ball games and had singsongs of music hall tunes such as
'Daisy Bell' (with its chorus of Daisy, Daisy…) and 'It's a Long Way
to Tipperary'.

The holiday camp was never intended for use during winter.
There was no heating in the basic, flimsy, wooden chalets and their
only insulation was cork lining glued to thin walls which was no
match for the wind gusting in from the North Sea. The winter of
1938–39 was one of the coldest in living memory. It was bitter and it

Refugee children outside their chalets, 1938

got colder and colder. The water pipes froze and they could no longer use the basins or lavatories. The urine in chamber pots and glasses of water froze too. The children went to bed fully clothed, wearing scarves and gloves if they had them. They had to walk along an outside path in order to get to the toilets, showers or to the dining hall where there were stoves around which they might huddle. Coat on, head down and run through the wind snapping in from the North Sea. It snowed and soon deep snow lay on the path. Their toes were constantly numb. After a few days of unremitting cold, Dieter began to feel poorly. He was walking with a few children and one of the attendants to the dining hall when he crumpled in a heap. He awoke in a Red Cross hut where they had taken him because it had an electric fire. They left him there to lie on his own and he savoured the warmth and comfort. A volunteer occasionally came in with a little food or a hot drink and he started to feel better as the fevered shivering subsided. In the morning he heard lots of activity outside, followed by silence. Something was going on. He started to feel afraid. He ventured out of the hut and realised they had started to evacuate the camp and had forgotten about him! He rushed towards the nearest volunteer and only just had time to go back and gather his belongings before they all left.

Emergency measures were needed because of the extreme cold that year. The Meteorological Office report for December 1938 says:

'The most memorable feature of the weather of the month was the severe frost and considerable snow experienced during the notably cold spell from 17th to the 26th... In some areas temperatures remained continuously below freezing for several days.'

The sea froze in places and a high tide with strong winds threatened to breach the sea walls. It was a wretched beginning to life in a new country.

Various buildings were put to use to house the children, such as a boarding school and the Salvation Army Hostel, all manned by local volunteers. Dieter went first by coach to a hotel where they had to sleep on mattresses on the floor for one night. Then the group was split and Dieter ended up in the Samuel Lewis Convalescent Home in Walton-on-the-Naze, about thirteen miles away. The home put aside wards for the children, with ten to fifteen children in each ward and up to seventy in total. They each had a bed and a locker and their suitcases were put under the beds. Suddenly, life was better, although more strange food appeared such as marmalade for breakfast and smoked haddock for lunch. They had to get used to English toilet paper that was perplexingly hard and shiny. There was little to do until games and toys were donated by well-wishers, including table football which Dieter enjoyed.

By this time his mother and father had become worried about his whereabouts because Dieter had not sent any of the prepared postcards. Somehow his days were taken up with whatever was going on and activities did not include writing to home so he failed his parents, despite being an obedient son. He was just existing from moment to moment and making the best of it. His father had to send a telegram to organisers asking 'Where is my son?' before he could be reassured that his son was safe. Dieter only found out later about his parents' concern and the telegram, excusing his dereliction of duty by saying he had been unwell.

The convalescent home is where Dieter thinks he spent Christmas Day 1938, his first without his family. This year saw the deepest and most widespread Christmas snow of the century. His mother's response to learning of his whereabouts was to send a Christmas parcel. She was concerned about Dieter not having a proper Christmas so she included a small fake tree. It arrived some days after Christmas and Dieter remembers the excitement. A few boys were Christian and so they formed their own association to celebrate, which caused a bit of friction with the Jewish contingent when they put the tree up in what was, unknown to them, considered a holy room. The misunderstanding was resolved and he shared his few presents of games and food. It made him a little hero as the rest had not received a parcel from home. The food included a lovely German sausage. He took out his precious penknife and cut up the sausage and passed it round to his friends for them to share his gourmet treat. The orthodox Jews were appalled when they realised that the sausage was not kosher. Dieter was obliged to bury his knife in the garden for three days and when he went back to find it, he could not remember where it was buried. He never found it again and was very cross about that. Dieter had good memories of the home and the people there and was surprised to remember that his first Christmas separated from his parents was not too bad. Being with a group of boys of similar age, all in the same boat, meant that the absence of family was not dwelt on and, with a strong Jewish presence, celebrations were low-key.

They remained in Walton for around two months. It had been intended as more short term but somebody developed scarlet fever and the whole community was placed in quarantine for several weeks. Fortunately, Dieter didn't catch it. There were basic English lessons, otherwise they had time to kill. They played football and went for walks on the beaches which had wonderful sand and they all enjoyed jumping around in the dunes. Dieter had a gift for organising and he remembers putting on some sketches, reusing his material from Hannover and Oldenburg. Otherwise not much happened except the odd parcel of biscuits or other food from someone's home in Germany causing elation, as gifts were always shared. Something German was a special treat.

Dieter received letters from home and one or two more parcels. One letter told him that Georg had come to England, staying with Else. Georg then phoned to say he was coming to Walton, which was thrilling. Georg could not come to the home as it was quarantined, so they met in the town and Georg bought Dieter his first English cap because Dieter didn't have a hat and his father was concerned about it. Dieter was embarrassed at first but later somebody said 'You look like an English boy now' and that made him feel better. He liked that sense of belonging. The day felt strange but Dieter was happy that his father was there and hoped to see him again soon. Georg disclosed that he would have to travel and that it would be likely to be far away as few countries were accepting refugees. He told Dieter that he had started enquiries with the aim of finding him a good family home to go to. It does not seem that it was an option to lodge with Else and Richard, perhaps because they were already hosting his grandparents, possibly Leopold too. Maybe they were not keen to have more children in their home even though Ulla and Dieter were in a strange country on their own. However, they did provide significant financial support for visas, for Ulla's schooling and perhaps a guarantee for Dieter, so their support was vital. In later life, relations were cool, with only dutiful connections being maintained, and we shall see that this arose from differences of opinion about how Elli tied up affairs in Germany.

Prospective adoptive parents had been encouraged by an appeal on the BBC Home Service to travel to Dovercourt on Saturdays and Sundays to select suitable children for them to take home. Selection sessions took place in the huge dining hall at Dovercourt, to the accompaniment of encouragement from the staff. The children didn't always realise that they had to move on so that more like them could be brought over from Germany. The children were told to smile and be polite, making them feel they were parading or as if they were goods for sale in a market. The children would be sitting at the long tables sorted by sex and age, and people walked down the rows picking out the ones they liked for interview. The younger children, especially girls, were snapped up, leaving the older ones feeling even more miserable. If a foster family only wanted one of the children, siblings were separated without question. Those left at the end hated the experience and shrivelled a little inside each time they were not chosen. Among the children these displays were known as *die Affenschau* (monkey show) in the spirit of a monkeys' tea party. These recollections come from other *Kinder* and Dieter never mentioned them, suggesting they occurred while he was staying at Walton.

In time, this method of selection was stopped after the negative impacts on the children were recognised, and allocation of children to homes was then undertaken by the Care of Refugee Children Movement, which had been hurriedly set up in December 1938. Letters appeared in local press around the country, asking for offers of hospitality in private homes, usually for free although some maintenance contributions could be granted. It was believed that true home life was a necessity for happiness and that the best interests of the children would be served by merging them into the general population. Thus children were assigned to homes before they and the foster parents had met each other. The applications from prospective foster parents were reasonably thorough and Georg was satisfied by what he was told about the Russells, a respectable, professional family. There was a heavy supporting hand from the Church in providing a safe haven for refugees so organisers were pleased to have a child who could be placed easily in a Christian family.

Georg was still in England when Dieter went to meet the Russells in London. Dieter and some other children travelled by train to Liverpool Street. Dieter went to admire the engine and the driver saw him and waved and Dieter waved back. It was a comforting gesture for a boy who was growing more nervous than he had been before. The reality of not seeing his father again and living with unknown people had started to hit home. They were met by a crowd of people and Dieter was introduced with Georg to Mr and Mrs Russell. Dieter recalls his father went with him to the Russells' house but Georg implies not. Dieter's memory is muddled, I think because recollections are clouded by the emotion of his final parting from his father. Dieter saw his father once more, a couple of weeks later, staying the night with Aunt Else in Finchley in order to say goodbye. His father took him to Golders Green station to get the tube to London Bridge and a train back to his new home. Georg fell back on his natural confidence that he would work things out and he said with all the calmness he could muster: 'Somehow, my boy, I'm sure we shall meet again.' Dieter could not be consoled and for the first time he cried uncontrollably. He was distraught at the thought of his father on a boat for six weeks travelling across oceans. He was sure that Georg would be terribly seasick, as Dieter had been on his return home from his trip to Sweden. All he could imagine were huge waves crashing down on his father's boat. Added to that, his father had no idea what he would do when he arrived in his new country. Bolivia seemed such a long way off, it was completely unknown. Their parting in Germany had been different because he was going on an adventure but now his father was going so far away and Dieter's future was also uncertain.

It was a long journey from Golders Green to Penge West. Dieter sat by himself on the trains home, trying hard to pretend he wasn't crying, when everybody could see that he was. When he arrived back at the Russells', he still tried to pretend but he was only kidding himself. At dinner he kept hiding his head below the level of the table to dry his eyes. Mr Russell made no comment but took Dieter up to his room and made him kneel down to pray. Mr Russell said a prayer for Georg and for Dieter, which offered limited comfort given that Dieter hardly spoke English. He was only 12 and convinced now that he would never see his father again.

22

PENGE, ENGLAND, 1939–42

*'There's nothing like your parents. There is a difference.
I felt like a guest and that feeling never left me'*

The Russells lived at 54 Thicket Road, Penge in south-east London, or Anerley as Mr Russell liked to note on official documents, feeling it sounded better. Charles Neville Russell was a principal at a firm of accountants called Russell & Company with offices near Trafalgar Square. He and his wife were in their sixties, living with their daughter Evelyn who was aged around 32. Mr Russell was a tall, elegant, good-looking man, always dressed in a shirt and tie. Dieter found his wife dour, holding Victorian values; she was impressed by Dieter's manners when he and Georg arrived and Dieter stood aside to let his father enter the house first. They lived in a huge house opposite Crystal Palace Park, which had been the site of the Crystal Palace, originally built in Hyde Park to house the Great Exhibition of 1851. After the exhibition, it was decided to relocate the palace to an area known as Penge Common, an affluent suburb of large villas. It stood there until its destruction by fire in November 1936. The park still contains the model dinosaurs that were installed in 1854.

The Russells were motivated principally by their strong religious beliefs and it met their values to perform work of higher charity entailing personal sacrifice. They had six adult children, with Evelyn the youngest and the only one at home, and perhaps in taking on Dieter they were also attempting to bring life back into the home and thereby to stem the petrifaction of their emotions. Evelyn was Dieter's saviour, even though she seemed ancient to him. She had vitality and they got on well.

Mr Russell and Evelyn in 1947

An advantage of the Russell's address was that in the same road a home was being prepared to accommodate a dozen or so refugee children. Dieter believes that the Russells expected him to join them when the home was ready, although this is not corroborated by Georg's story. It may be that they took on Dieter temporarily but within a few weeks they offered that he remain with them. He was eager to accept because being taken in by a family was preferable to going to a hostel or some other institution and was a step up on the social scale – he had already inherited a sense of status from his parents. A few months later when Mr Russell fell and broke his leg, Dieter declared 'I shall cry all night long' and they all knew a bond had developed. He was to stay with the Russells for almost four years.

Dieter had earlier made friends with a boy named Bauchwitz and campaigned to get him into the hostel up the road, so they could be close together, as poor Bauchwitz did not have a family to take him in. Dieter remembers him mainly because the translation of his name is 'tummy joke', suggesting that his ancestors did not have the wherewithal to bribe officials at the time they were forced to adopt surnames. Unfortunately, the hostel was an unpleasant experience. Their friendship soured with Bauchwitz blaming Dieter for getting him into this terrible place. Every exchange became fraught. He and his cronies would say in a menacing tone: 'You got us into this home, now you need to find a coffin to get us out of there.' They stopped walking to school together and Dieter had to take active measures to avoid them. Eventually the boys in the hostel were placed with families or went abroad and Dieter lost track of them.

Not a great deal happened in the Russell household and the pace of life was slow. Their social life revolved around the church where Mr Russell was a churchwarden. Their religious beliefs were evident in all aspects of their behaviour. At home there were prayers morning and night and communal prayers in the evening. On his first Sunday in Penge Dieter was obliged to go to church, where he knelt down and understood that the Russells were praying for God to help young Dieter, which he appreciated. They were kind people, anxious to make him feel part of their family. He had been to church with his mother in Germany but found the different dress and ceremonies in England strange. He confided to Evelyn 'This is not the church for me Miss Russell' and she was pleased to know that he had been to church in Germany. On Sundays life was even more sedate. It was not done to read an ordinary book, it had to be a Sunday book approved by the Russells, such as the stories of Christian martyrs and scriptures, to be discussed later at the dinner table. Evelyn hosted regular bible classes which Dieter attended, taking his own copy of the bible which the Russells had given him on his arrival at their home. The Russells regarded other diversions such as the cinema and theatre as sinful.

Dieter was puzzled that they always laid an extra place at the table for meals. He thought that it must be in case Jesus were to appear, as there was a big picture of him saying Grace at the end of the dining room. Dieter thought they were so religious that they expected Christ to pop in for a meal one day but he didn't like to ask. Later, it turned out that they were in the habit of laying an extra place in case one of their children arrived.

The Russell home was an imposing four-storey, semi-detached Victorian villa but despite the apparent affluence, the house was cold. The family would sit in the lounge by an open fire but the rest of the house was icy. Dieter missed the bliss of central heating in Hannover. There were no fires in bedrooms and bathrooms and in winter he dreaded the slog up to his freezing room on the top floor. Dieter kept his vests and pants underneath his blankets to warm them up. At bath times he was allowed only five inches of water, which turned every bath into agony. He felt isolated at the top of the house and used to imagine someone nasty lurking in wait for him up the many dark stairs. He missed the warmth of an embrace at bedtimes and the affection of his parents, and regretted that the Russells did not show such emotions.

54 Thicket Road today

His room was bare and he had few mementoes from home. It looked out over the garden which contained four mature pear trees. Later Dieter took on the important role of pear harvester. He climbed up and sat in the trees, plucking pears and dropping them down to Evelyn. They were wonderful pears which were stored for eating right up to Christmas. Just after the war started, he received a letter from his father, which he left on his bedroom table but too close to his open window. The sheaves of flimsy airmail paper fluttered up and out, drifting down to neighbouring gardens. A neighbour took the pages to the police because they thought that

Beckenham and Penge County School for Boys

German planes had been dropping propaganda over London. The police assuaged his concerns and the sheepish neighbour returned the sheets: 'These must be yours.'

Everything was strange: not only the food but also the windows, the light switches, the way the beds were made, even the school hours. At first Dieter only had the odd word of English and went to school barely understanding the language. There were no special arrangements and he was expected to pick up English from home and from school. He attended Beckenham and Penge County School for Boys, a large, formal establishment with playing fields and the railway behind, which was about fifteen minutes' walk from home. He was in Bruyn House, named in memory of an ancient landowner. Dieter felt that the school made a grave mistake because he had been in the third year when he left Germany but they put him in the first year. He was the eldest in his year and felt apart from the others. He was mainly taught stuff that he already knew and therefore he failed to engage with his schooling. He grasped the language with reasonable rapidity but other aspects of English daily life were baffling, such as coinage, measurements and weights. It is questionable whether he ever had complete mastery of them. His first school report for spring term 1939 praised his adaptability, his quick picking up of the language and 'a fine start'. It was observed that he was getting on well with the other boys. A year on, spring term 1940, his report was positive, mainly B+ and A marks, except for mathematics, in which he was described as 'satisfactory' and was in the lowest set. In English he was in the top set and the comment was 'one of the best in the class'. He was reaping the benefits of reading books from the Russells' collection, working his way through classics such as Lorna Doone.

By the time of his final year, approaching the age of 16, he was becoming bored and disengaged at school. His school reports show marks that are mainly average, sometimes above. Comments in reports had become more grudging: 'can do very well when he is trying' for history; 'his logic is not always at its strongest' for maths; 'he seems to try but his ability on the science side is not great' for chemistry. The most enthusiastic is the house tutor who comments: 'Keen and active in house affairs; is capable and methodical in collecting Red Cross subscriptions.' It's not clear what activity this is, possibly evidence of his desire to support those less fortunate in life. The teachers were unmemorable, mostly recalled as the victims of various pranks. They bought chocolates for the popular French teacher and one chocolate they cut, took out the filling and replaced it with mustard. They were beside themselves with mirth as he sampled the doctored chocolate and spat it out.

Dieter started writing this postcard to his father. It says on the back in German:

Dieter's (unsent) postcard of his school

'Dear Dad, I already started a letter to you and I thought you would really like to see my chemistry laboratory from my school. I have two letters received recently. Your latest details communicated to me...'

Why it was not sent is a mystery, although Dieter had form at not sending postcards. Maybe it was because he feared it would prompt his father to inquire about his marks for chemistry.

He says he made few friends at school and that he did feel lonely. His classmates were welcoming enough but the age difference prevented real friendships and besides, the English sense of humour was mystifying. Whatever friends he made, none were lasting. He felt he could never invite anybody back to the Russells. It just wasn't done. Girls were an unknown entity and it would have been unthinkable to have brought one home even if he had been able to meet one. A German girl refugee was staying with a local vicar and they were introduced on neutral ground, but under close supervision, making the encounter feel awkward and contrived. As a result he was largely confined to solitary pursuits, such as reading and stamp collecting. His pocket stamp album, inscribed 'Started Wednesday 30/10/40. D Hahlo, 54 Thicket Road, Anerley SE20', includes a monthly tally of stamps. By March 1941 he had amassed 485.

In December 1940 at the age of 14 Dieter acquired his first pair of long trousers. This was worthy of a photograph, an

Dieter in his first long trousers, 1940

extravagance in which the Russells rarely indulged. Dieter captioned the photo of himself in his long trousers standing in the garden. At the Russells, he felt cared for but it was nothing like having his parents. He often would have loved another piece of toast for breakfast but thought it would be impolite to ask. Once he helped himself to extra marmalade, but only once, because he sensed he was imposing on their hospitality. He did not dare to ask for second helpings at the evening meal, for fear he would be considered too expensive to keep. The feeling of being a guest at Thicket Road never left him.

Despite evidence that Hitler's dictatorship was far from benign, many senior figures in the UK clung to the belief that dialogue could avert war. They argued that if Hitler's more reasonable demands could be met, all would work out well. The Munich Agreement of September 1938 allowed Germany to annexe the parts of Czechoslovakia that it believed were rightfully theirs. The response to the agreement across Europe was celebration – except in Czechoslovakia. Prime Minister Chamberlain had been committed to peace. Having lived through the first war and seen the immense suffering it had caused, it was sacred to him to prevent another disastrous conflict, only twenty years later. The British population had expected war and Chamberlain's statesman-like gesture towards peace was greeted with acclaim. Disgust with Hitler's regime had not extended to wanting a war in order to destroy it. In the days following the Munich Agreement, Chamberlain received more than 20,000 letters and telegrams of thanks and gifts including 6000 bulbs from Dutch admirers and a cross from the Pope. Everybody was an appeaser now. Chamberlain was invited onto the balcony at Buckingham Palace before he delivered his renowned 'Peace for our time' speech to crowds in London. But then the threat from Germany became more obvious and opinions changed. Chamberlain had acted from noble motives but appeasement had clearly been a flawed strategy.

In March 1939 the German army marched into Prague, disregarding the entirety of the Munich Agreement, and Czechoslovakia ceased to exist. The world stood by while Hitler argued that Germany needed to expand its territory to prevent its own population from starving. Chamberlain regarded Czechoslovakia as 'a small, far away country', showing that colonial attitudes still prevailed. Britain's, and France's, involvement in war was sparked by Hitler's invasion of Poland on 1 September 1939. Dieter was in church with the Russells at a special weekday meeting to pray for peace when they heard Chamberlain's speech:

'This morning the British ambassador in Berlin handed the German government a final note stating that unless we heard from them by 11 o'clock that they were prepared at once to withdraw their troops from Poland, a state of war would exist between us. I have to tell you now that no such undertaking has been received, and that consequently this country is at war with Germany.'

Barrage balloons over London

Within minutes the air raid sirens went off and Evelyn and Dieter rushed home. It was a false alarm but soon the sirens were a common sound and signified genuine attacks.

Crystal Palace hill had long been a London landmark, topped by its telecommunications masts. This made it an important navigation aid for German bombers as they homed in on London. The hill was heavily stocked with anti-aircraft guns and festooned with barrage balloons, creating a surreal sight over London. Dieter used to look out of a top floor window from which he could see the tower surrounded by thirty to forty balloons looking like silver torpedoes high in the sky. Many German aircraft relied on diving to release bombs accurately. Balloons tethered by heavy cables would destroy low flying aircraft, thus forcing them up into the range of anti-aircraft guns. It was then decided that the communications towers were such landmarks that they had to be destroyed. One was dismantled and the other Dieter watched being blown up. The noise was deafening as it collapsed majestically in a huge cloud of dust and smoke.

As the war got underway, the English started to take a number of German prisoners. Sometimes a train loaded with German prisoners of war would stop at a red signal as it waited to enter the tunnel by the school playing fields and Dieter would be pushed forwards: 'Go on, say something in German to them.' Dieter would mutter a few words before extricating himself from an awkward situation. He had no desire to speak to Nazis but his fellow pupils had no understanding of how he felt. One time a lad referred to Dieter as a Nazi, which upset Dieter and he raised it with the form master, who gave the boy a talking to. Dieter embarrassed himself once at cricket practice when a high ball started to drop fast and he shouted *'Achtung!'* in his agitation. The boys looked up but the incident passed without comment. He was desperate not to be seen as German, not to be regarded as a museum piece. Assimilation was preservation. Above all, the Russells 'taught me to become

English', for which he was grateful. Dieter's loyalties were in no way divided. He was as much against the Germans in the war as anybody else.

The five oldest of the Russells' children were missionaries or clergymen. When Mr and Mrs Russell received letters from their children, these were read out at the dinner table. One of the sons was a missionary and doctor in Burma. The entry of Japan into the war forced him to undertake a terrible, arduous trek to Thailand with his family. Another son was a captain in the army in the far east who was caught by the Japanese and died in prison. The letter saying he had been captured and killed was read out and everybody was visibly upset but the Russells were comforted by the belief that they would meet again in the afterlife. Captain Russell's fiancee had come to stay while they waited for news, which is how she spent her twenty-first birthday. She was utterly heartbroken when she heard about her fiance's death and Dieter never saw her again.

There were no holidays or outings, except to the Russell's kind Aunt Bertha in Bexhill, Sussex. She was deeply religious and somewhat eccentric, keeping her biscuits in her bed socks, which had become a Russell family joke. Evelyn took Dieter to the Albert Hall once or twice for a classical concert. A family friend was a Spitfire pilot in the RAF who visited and was talented musically. He used to turn up in his uniform and try to teach Dieter to play piano. Dieter was keen to learn and practised in the man's absence. He had mastered 'Silent Night' which he was eager to perform for his teacher when he was told that the man had been shot down and killed.

The frequency and intensity of air raids increased as the Nazis set about the Blitz on London. The sky above the city turned orange, purple and red, the colours of destruction. There were many nights when they heard an enormous quantity of bombs coming down, the screech of the bombs then a moment of quiet before they exploded with tremendous force and noise. This was coupled with the constant roar of the aeroplanes and of guns firing, whilst searchlights raked the sky. Even after the destruction of the towers, Penge continued to be in the firing line as a way in to London for the bombers which, if they found the shelling too heavy, would jettison their bombs and turn back. In October 1940 the headmaster, Mr Gammon, whose signature is on some of Dieter's school reports, was killed by a bomb which scored a direct hit on his house, not far away. The whole school went to his funeral. Whenever the sirens sounded Dieter was sent to sleep under the huge dining table in the lounge, along with the two maids. Everybody shared the same room, with Mr and Mrs Russell and Evelyn sleeping on mattresses. The lounge remained ready with mattresses and blankets on the floor for the duration of the war. Dieter noticed no 'Blitz Spirit'; the people had no choice. The bombing was frightening at the time but Dieter found that he could forget it the next day until one day he cycled along a road in which several houses had been hit and there was smoke, rubble and dust everywhere. Air Raid Precaution wardens were still digging out victims and Dieter stopped to look. Later, he told the Russells about it and that night he wet his bed. Dieter was hugely embarrassed but Mrs Russell said 'Never mind', realising that he had been deeply disturbed by what he had seen.

Mr Russell's office was moved out of central London and into 54 Thicket Road. There was a sizeable staff so almost every room was given over to office purposes. One night, during this period, Dieter was sick and threw up on the stairs in his attempt to get to the bathroom. When he woke in the morning, Evelyn was scrubbing away at his stains with disinfectant in amongst office people coming and going: he felt ashamed and guilty.

Dieter's main privation was sweets: 'Schoolboys do enjoy snacks.' Woolworths was on the way home from school and he had a regular appointment with its vast sweets section. Sadly, that disappeared when sweets became rationed, like much else. Everyone had their

Government campaign posters

own ration book. Every family was issued a set number of each kind of stamp based on the size of family, ages of children and income. The purpose was to ensure the population did not starve when food imports were severely restricted and local production limited due to the large number of men and women fighting or contributing to the war effort. At first, bacon, butter and sugar were rationed. These were followed by meat, tea, jam, biscuits, breakfast cereals, cheese, eggs, lard, milk and canned and dried fruit. (Beer was never rationed and pubs were kept open, to show we weren't beaten and to boost the morale of the people, although this ploy had no impact on the Russells.) At the Russells', everybody's butter was put on a little dish and marked so that there could be no dispute over whose was whose. Vegetables were not rationed and became a large part of the diet because they could be grown in gardens, parks, yards, waste ground, everywhere. People were encouraged to grow their own by the 'Dig for Victory' campaign from the Ministry of Food featuring cartoon characters such as Potato Pete and his pal Doctor Carrot. Fresh fruit was not rationed but supplies were limited and bananas were unknown. Dieter remembers that he missed fruit more than anything else.

The Russells were staunchly traditional with their food. Dieter yearned for a taste of home – dishes such as his grandmother's lentils and gherkins – but he didn't dare suggest the Russells might make them. Once, he visited his grandparents in Hendon and so enjoyed the cucumber salad with vinegar and oil, chives and seasoning, that he took some back to Penge, to delight the Russells. He announced 'My grandmother makes wonderful cucumber salad. I've brought some so you can enjoy it too.' They took one taste and declared it was revolting. Vinegar and oil! Pepper, salt and chives! No thank you, we much prefer ours, they said.

Dieter followed the war in the newspapers, collecting cuttings covering the evacuation of Dunkirk, the fall of France, the battles of El Alamein and going into Stalingrad and much else. The story that remained most vivid to him was that of Graf Spee, a trapped German battleship that was scuttled by its commander in the harbour of Montevideo after being damaged by British naval boats. He cut these out to preserve in his scrapbook, thinking that if, one day, he were to have children, they'd be thrilled to read them.

Hendon, 1941

Life was a grind during the war, with constant air raids, which meant blackouts with special paper plastered over all windows so no light escaped. Street lights were out and cars at night were allowed only a tiny slit of light front and rear, so they crawled along, if they moved at all. As soon as the sirens sounded, cars were supposed to stop and the occupants make a rush for the nearest shelter. Gas masks had to be carried everywhere, bus and train windows were blocked by safety netting. Time dragged and the war seemed interminable.

In 1942 Dieter turned 16 and now saw himself as a young man. Unlike many adult Germans in England, he was exempted from internment: 'The committee consider the alien safe to be placed in Category C', which meant he could remain at liberty as a refugee from persecution. His schooling had been disrupted and his motivation to study had dwindled. In Germany, he had been used to his parents inspecting his homework and offering advice, but without this attention he scraped by with minimum effort. He and the Russells agreed that he was unlikely to advance academically and that there was little point in staying at school now he had reached leaving age. In August he left the Russells' after what seemed to him a long three and a half years.

The Russells supported him through his subsequent college years and Dieter responded with letters acknowledging their generosity and remained in contact via occasional phone calls and visits. Mr Russell came to his wedding in 1951; Mrs Russell had died by then. Dieter had a good relationship with Evelyn and continued to visit her in Bexhill until she died in her nineties. He was fond of them all as they had been an important element in his life and part of the foundations of the man he became. But they remained unworldly, never going to the cinema or theatre, and if they had known that one day he would perform on the stage, he was sure they would have been aghast.

23

PADDINGTON, ENGLAND, 1939–45

'V-1 and V-2 rockets, when you heard them, your heart stopped
and you just hoped it wouldn't be your bad luck'

Elli had been kept busy, arranging for her husband and children to get
away. At the same time, she was hoping for her own visa to travel to
England, waiting to see what life held in store for her. After Wilhelm
and Sofie, Dieter's grandparents, and Leopold left Germany in early
March 1939 she was left to sort out family affairs on her own. The
house in Oldenburg was sold and she put the furniture and family
effects that remained into storage. She had to close down insurances
and bank accounts, duties she carried out diligently but it was tough,
as she had not before been privy to family finances and knew little
about banking and insurance. She was not permitted to take much
money out of the country and Else told her to spend it rather than let
the Germans take it. It was hard to spend large sums as a lone woman.
She bought clothes and articles for herself to bring to England and
took driving lessons. It had never occurred to her before that she
might drive.

The money enabled her to realise one of her long-held ambitions,
to travel on an ocean liner. She booked herself to go first class to
Southampton on the huge steamer SS Deutschland. It sailed with

The SS Deutschland

Elli's passport, 1939

Elli on board from Bremerhaven on 28 April 1939. It was a big event for her to travel alone, in the past all travel arrangements had been handled by Georg. Despite her nervousness, the voyage went well and she loved the ship and the experience, the attention and the pampering. Her *Deutsches Reich* passport, its front cover emblazoned with an eagle, wings outstretched, gripping a swastika in its talons, confirms her personal details:

Profession:	Housewife
Born:	Berlin
Build:	Average
Face:	Oval
Eyes:	Grey
Hair:	Blonde
Distinguishing marks:	None

She did not have blonde hair, as the photo proves. A stamp from Oldenburgische Landesbank in the passport shows that she took with her foreign currency to the value of 17 shillings (85p today).

The only way that Elli could get to England was on a Domestic Service Visa, a scheme to provide access to parents of refugee children. A sponsor and guarantee of employment were required in advance and these were arranged, with Georg and Elli's encouragement, by Ulla through the daughter of the Barrington-Wells family who attended the same school as Ulla. Elli's visa from the British embassy in Berlin is stamped with 'authorised for domestic employment' and 'leave to land at Southampton on condition that the holder registers at once with the police and does not enter employment other than as a resident in service in a private household'. It is doubtful that Elli's English was good enough to have read this accurately but she understood. She was to be a maid. On 5 May 1939, her registration certificate number 694 722 was added to her passport and stamped by the police in Chelmsford, Essex. It had been wise of her to act swiftly because movements between the two countries were stopped as soon as war erupted.[20]

[20] What was the Domestic Service Visa? See p296

Elli had never been fully accepted by Georg's side of the family.
She was not an educated woman in their eyes and she didn't have
their (Jewish) sophistication. They considered that Georg had
married beneath him and there had always been a slight atmosphere
of snobbish disdain. This came to a head when she arrived in
England. Elli was berated by her father-in-law Wilhelm and by Else
because they felt that she hadn't dealt properly with the family
money and property. They thought her first class trip was
extravagant and were furious that she hadn't managed to get more
money out of the country, even though that was not possible due to
the regulations. If she had taken the money and been searched, the
consequences in Germany would have been severe. There was an
enormous row. Wilhelm and Sofie and Richard and Else didn't need
more money and their attitude was undeserved. Elli had had to
manage everything on her own, having endured the breakup of her
family and in extreme circumstances as Germany focused on war.
They didn't understand the pressures and the trauma with which Elli
was coping. They made her few days with them unpleasant and Elli
never forgave Georg's parents and Else for accusing her of squander.
Thereafter her contact with them was minimal. The whole
experience was extremely tough, no doubt contributing to a change
in her affectionate persona from Dieter's sweet childhood memories.

The Barrington-Wells family lived in a house called Purleigh on
the London Road in Chelmsford. The head of the family was a
retired Lieutenant Colonel. As long as Elli prepared his breakfast
first thing in the morning, he was content. This consisted of two
shots of whisky with a raw egg beaten into it. The hours were long,
the wages were low and there was a multitude of tasks that were
new to her. The family was at first impervious to her situation,
giving her little attention or sympathy. Everyone called her Frau,
as if she had no name of her own, and she resented the indignity.
They had no idea what she had been through, that Elli's life had

turned upside down – from having servants of her own to working as a housemaid.

The consolation, and her motive, was that she could see her children. Dieter was able to stay with her a week at a time during school holidays, sharing her servants' quarters: a single room in the attic. In this respect, Elli was more fortunate than most, being allowed visits from her children and days off to be with them. Dieter was upset that her work was so hard and disliked the condescension with which she was treated as the servant. One impediment was that Elli spoke only basic English and the family spoke no German. She slowly overcame this but she didn't have a gift for language and spoke with a German accent for the rest of her days. Elli and her visiting children would go walking in the town and talk in German. Dieter made his mother stop talking if anybody came towards them and would start to talk loudly in English himself, saying the first random sentence that came into his head. They couldn't dare to be identified as German, such was the antipathy towards Germans, and the country was in fear of spies.

Dieter got to know the family and the lady of the house took to Dieter, on one occasion writing him a letter that he had to ask the Russells to decipher because he found it difficult to read her writing. Mrs Wells said: 'You must come again and visit your mother and us because we think you're a dear boy.' The Russells teased him about it. The Colonel had a car and he allowed Dieter to drive it into the garage, which Dieter thought was out of this world, even though he had only driven a matter of inches. Their sons were older than Dieter and they would strut around with air rifles shooting birds, which Dieter pitied so he declined their invitations to join in. In the end Mrs Wells warmed to Elli and her children and they stayed in touch after the war, with Mrs Josephine Wells writing in support of Dieter's naturalisation application several years later. In the letter she said that the Bishop of Chelmsford had asked her to take on Elli, who was escaping persecution and had 'gone through much sorrow'.

A tribunal granted Elli exemption from internment in Britain on 1 December 1939, as she had permanent employment and was considered low risk. In the following year, the level of troop movements in the Chelmsford area increased and it was felt unsuitable for an enemy alien to be working and living nearby and so, with the aid of an allowance from the Refugee Council, Elli gave up her post and she moved to Paddington. World Jewish Relief has a record of her registration in the area on 24 November 1941. She took the first room that was offered to her, at the top of a house at 57 Cleveland Square. She had to climb ninety steps up to this tiny room with a bed and a gas ring that was also used to warm the room. She had a refugee's allowance that was barely enough to live on and although other refugees lived nearby, she was never sociable and resented having to live as she did. It was winter, it was hard and it was miserable but she had no choice.

She did at least have regular contact with Dieter who saw her about once a fortnight during this period. He would cycle from Penge, or sometimes travel by bus. Whenever they had enough spare money, they went to the cinema and saw the major films of the era. Elli did not make the journey to the Russells, inhibited by her poor English as well as by her reticence to live life to the full. In August 1942, Dieter moved out of the Russells' home and into digs in Paddington, to be near his mother. He was 16 and had extremely limited experience of life. Coping with laundry, clothing and buying and preparing proper food were new challenges. As was what to do with his time – he didn't know how to handle freedom.

His first address was 19 Queens Gardens, a basement flat run by a strange lady with 'bulging eyes and Pekinese dogs' who would embroil Dieter in lengthy conversations about her eyesight and her dogs at every opportunity, which Dieter took active efforts to avoid. The flat cost 15 shillings a week (75p today), which was more than half his income. The Russells kindly sent him 10 shillings each week, which they did all the while he was a student. He also received 15 shillings a week from the Refugee Council, organised for him by Richard and Else. It was only just enough to get by and he existed mainly on Kellogg's Cornflakes and spent any spare money on the wonders of the cinema.

As soon as she could, Elli moved out of her dingy attic and found a room at 14 Devonshire Terrace, opposite Queen's Gardens, with slightly better facilities and less far to climb. She and Dieter enjoyed each other's company most days and often ate together. Elli cooked modest meals on her single ring gas burner favouring German-style food as best she could prepare in those days of rationing and little money. Elli received a work permit and eventually took an exhausting job in the laundry of a hotel nearby. This raised her income to a heady £5 a week, which meant she even had a little spare at times to give to Dieter. In those days £5 notes were huge, white and ornately decorated and when they gave one to a shopkeeper, they had to sign their name so that it could be traced in case the note was a forgery.

Paddington at the time had seen better days and was a seedy, neglected area, occupied mainly by people down on their luck and trying to make ends meet. There were innumerable boarding houses and tacky hotels and prostitutes dotted the streets. Its unwelcoming character was not helped by the war as the rail heads at Paddington and Marylebone had been prime targets and the area suffered extensive bomb damage. The Blitz itself was over but now there was the terror of V-1 and V-2 rockets, known in England as doodlebugs, that caused devastation. The first V-1 (*Vergeltungswaffe*, meaning retribution weapon) was launched at London in June 1944. At the peak, more than one hundred V-1s a day were fired at south-east England and nearly 10,000 in total. They came at all hours of the day and night, unlike the Blitz which had been at night-time only. They were aimed at London with a landing circle of seven to nineteen miles, meaning where they hit was virtually random. They had a motor at the back, which cut out when the rocket had reached its range, at which point it started a steep, fast dive. The silence after the buzzing of the motor alerted people on the ground to the impending blast. Dieter heard them often, a loud, troubling noise which stopped suddenly before impact. If you were near, you were likely to die. His heart would stop, wondering where it was going to fall and desperately hoping this time it wouldn't be his bad luck.

The rain of V-1s continued until October 1944 when the launch sites on the French and Dutch coasts were overrun by Allied forces. So the Germans developed the V-2, the world's first long-range guided ballistic missile, powered by a liquid-propellant rocket engine that was almost silent. Attacks from V-2s resulted in the deaths of an estimated 9000 civilians and military personnel. These rockets were mostly directed at London. People had little choice other than to carry on, their only comfort being that London was such a big place. It was a question of luck and for many refugees that was a much better deal than the systematic persecution and casual brutality of the Nazi regime they had left behind.

Elli was befriended by a wealthy, elderly Polish man who lived in White's Hotel on Bayswater Road, opposite Hyde Park on its north side. He would sometimes take out her out to give her a treat and in return she looked after him in little ways and did his laundry. Suddenly an explosion came from the direction of the hotel. Dieter remembers being concerned for his mother's friend and rushing in the direction of the blast. The hotel had been hit, there was lots of damage and smoke and people standing about, dazed, but the Polish man was not among them. Dieter was worried because the old man lived on the top floor so he charged into the hotel and dashed into a lift, pressed the button and as it started to move up it occurred to him that it was unbelievably stupid to take a lift in a damaged, burning building. Fortunately it reached the top floor and Dieter raced to the man's room but he was not there and Dieter was mightily relieved. He used the stairs on his way back down.

Dieter got to know London well, hopping

Dieter in London, August 1944

on and off open-back buses from the rear platforms. Buses went at a reasonable speed as traffic was light and it was thrilling to jump on and off when the bus was still moving. The windows in buses and trains were covered with strong fibre netting to stop the glass from shattering and injuring people in the event of a blast so he could not look out of the windows, save for a tiny square that allowed people to see where they were. At home, they had strips of material across the windows too and at night, there were total blackouts. Vehicles had hoods on their headlights which directed the beam downwards. Adding to the drabness was the smoke from millions of coal fires. In cold weather this often caused intense fogs known as pea-soupers that at times were so bad that people could not see and didn't know where they were. There are reports of blind people helping the sighted to get home, because they knew the contours of the route whereas the sighted were helpless when they could not even see their own feet. Dieter came into his element as he knew the area well, going out with his torch and guiding people who were starting to feel trapped and afraid. One man had lost his car and despite the two of them trying together, they could not find it. The man had to return when the fog had cleared the next day.

Having decided not to continue his schooling, Dieter had to

search for something else to do. He had wanted to study medicine but this avenue was closed by his lack of education, as well as by the cost of the courses. He discovered that a course in the new discipline of chiropody at Chelsea School of Chiropody, part of Chelsea Polytechnic, would take students who had not passed exams. The course included modules on physiotherapy, itself a relatively new discipline. Dieter was interviewed at Chelsea Polytechnic to see if he could enrol. He was 16 and normally students had to be 18 but because of the war, they said he could do the course before being called up. Dieter started the two-year course in early 1943. He failed the first year and had to repeat it. He claims it was his bad luck that his first year happened to be the most exceptionally clever class they'd ever had and that nearly all of them rose to become leaders of the profession. In fairness, they were a lot older, some well into adulthood, whereas Dieter was young and not used to the discipline of working intensely. He admits that many others were model students, doing all their homework whereas he avoided it 'like the plague'. He did manage to improve his way of working to make sure

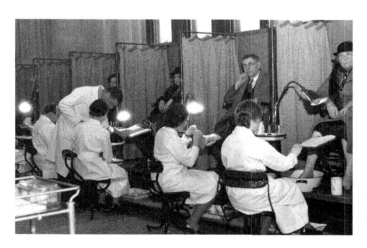

Students and patients in the School of Chiropody at Chelsea Polytechnic in 1930s

he passed his repeat year. Overall, Dieter enjoyed the course and the training. Patients sat in rows of cubicles in which students practised the art of chiropody. The course was important to him and in the end he worked hard at it, qualifying in 1945 at the end of the war.

He also found plenty to do through the students' union. By this time Dieter spoke good English and was accepted as part of the crowd. It was good for him to be involved in a slapdash production of 'A Midsummer Night's Dream', in which he played Snug the Joiner. For this part he went under the name Freddie Harlow. In most circles he still used Dieter, identifying him as German, the snag being that Germans in general were hated. The naturalisation process was suspended during the war so he couldn't apply to be naturalised. But he could volunteer to join up as a registered refugee who spoke good English. He joined the Air Training Corps and on 1 October 1944 he enrolled for the London University Officers Training Corps, which he boasted 'is much posher'. The sergeant used to call cadets 'Sir', which Dieter regarded as a bonus. This was an Army training unit to develop leadership abilities, giving cadets the opportunity to take part in military life while studying. He spent a little time at Sandhurst for training, where they enthusiastically saluted every officer they saw, who had to return the salute. After a while one of the officers came over and said 'I say chaps, do stop this won't you?' He had become fed up with all this extra saluting. In April and May 1945 Dieter attended camps or courses at Kimble, Buckinghamshire and at some point fired off 20 rounds of ammunition at a target. His scores out of 25 are given as 20, 15, 9, 9, suggesting he tired during this exercise. Dieter was proud to wear an Army uniform and although they were not classed as trained soldiers and were not deployable, he found there were lots of perks. Bus conductors weren't supposed to let him off paying but they always did when he was in uniform. Dieter felt chuffed. It made him feel English and confirmed he had shed his German background.

Chelsea Polytechnic's main site was in Manresa Road but the School of Chiropody was on the first floor of the council offices on the Kings Road, opposite the Chelsea Palace Theatre. Dieter needed to earn extra money so in his spare time he worked as a stagehand, acquiring valuable experience. The Chelsea Palace was one of many variety theatres that were a huge part of the entertainment business in those days. Performers would play on a variety bill that changed each week. It was a grand Victorian building with an imposing frontage of columns, pilasters and turrets topped with a dome and had seating for 2500 people. On Sundays it showed films, as live performances were not allowed. It was later converted into a television studio before being demolished in 1966. This site later became Heals department store and is now a branch of Metro Bank. The council offices remain, best known as the address of a chic registry office.

A favourite performer was Danny Kaye and it was a huge treat when Dieter and Elli, who loved Danny Kaye too, went to see him at the London Palladium. Whenever Dieter had time and money to spare, he went to see a film. Elli was also keen and together they saw many wonderful films. A regular haunt for Dieter was the small Blue Hall Cinema on Edgware Road that showed foreign and unusual films. On one occasion Dieter recalled sitting in a row and behind him, at the other end of the row, was an amorous couple who advanced steadily to vigorous intercourse. A man sitting behind Dieter by himself, trying to watch the film, discovered that the seats were wobbly and as things progressed the whole row shook, rocking this man backwards and forwards. When the couple finished, the man said in a loud voice 'Thank God for that' and Dieter thanked his lucky stars that his mother was not with him.

24

LONDON AND THE ARDENNES, 1939–47

'It must have been hard for her leaving again,
but children have the ability to adapt.
There was no element of choice, it had to be done'

Dieter had limited contact with his sister Ursula during these years.
The rhythms of their lives had been disrupted and they would never
recapture their early cohesion. She came once to visit Dieter at the
Russells when he was astonished at how she appeared completely
English and spoke the language fluently. Dieter had been worried
that she would not cope with the religious fervour of the Russells but
the visit passed well. After that, Ulla saw Elli and Dieter only
occasionally, not helped by the fact that Elli's room and cooking
facilities could barely cope with three people.

All aliens had to register their whereabouts with the police,
updating each time they changed address and even if they planned to
stay away for a night. The only registration card we can trace is for
Ursula. It tells a tale of dislocation. I assume that she did not feel
settled with the Northcotts and their three children, or vice-versa,
which precipitated the move to the boarding school in Clacton. It
seems that her short-term visas required her to re-enter Germany on
a number of occasions before the war, simply to obtain a new visa.
What Dieter remembered as Ulla returning for 'a holiday' was

usually an obligatory trip that must have been stressful for Ulla, as well as for her parents.

The registration card records that Ursula arrived in England on 9 November 1936, with a twelve-month visa. She returned to Germany in July 1937 and came back to England the next month with three months left on her visa, which was extended to November 1938. She went back once more to Germany in April 1938, returning to England the next month with six months still left on her visa. The next entry on her card is dated October 1939, by which time war had broken out, so the last visa must have been extended to November 1939 but this is not recorded. An Aliens Tribunal in Colchester on 1 November 1939 exempted her from internment and special restrictions applying to enemy aliens, noting that she was a refugee from Nazi oppression with no desire to be repatriated. The Secretary of State at the Home Office is recorded as 'having no objection to her remaining in the United Kingdom for the present'.

It is apparent why Dieter had little recall of contact with Ulla. She reached the age of 16 in October 1939 and finished at St Monica's at

Chelmsford, 1940

the end of the summer term in July 1940. Thereafter she is registered as living at a bewildering number of addresses:

May 1940: Holywell Manor (also called Holystreet Manor) in Chagford, Devon. It is not clear what she was doing here but it was perhaps a school excursion or work experience.

July 1940: 62 Vincent Court, Bell Lane, Hendon, London, the address of her grandparents.

August 1940: 14 Claremont Park, Finchley, London, the address of Aunt Else and Uncle Richard.

September 1940: Upwood, Shepley Road, Barnt Green, Worcestershire. This was a children's home and she described her work here as 'child care'.

19 June 1941: 50 Romola Road, West Norwood, London. It is not known why she went here.

28 June 1941: 88 Barrowgate Road, Chiswick, London. It is not known why she went here.

10 July 1941: Heath Farm, Reigate, Surrey, care of Mrs Newton. Permission was granted for her employment, subject to review by the Ministry of Labour, as a 'mother's help'.

1 December 1941: 1 Avenue Road, Highgate, London; it seems that she went to stay with the Northcotts again for a few days.

6 December 1941: YMCA in Crescent Road, Hornsey, London where she worked as a clerk. The YMCA during the war played a notable role in supporting displaced people and refugees.

17 March 1943: 9 Haslemere Road, Hornsey, London. Presumably she had a room here while continuing to work at the YMCA.

It is a mystery why she had so many changes of address within three years. The assumption might be that she was taking employment as a domestic help and perhaps this work did not suit her, or that the habitual mistreatment of servants by the middle classes of England caused her to remonstrate and resulted in the early termination of her posts. Knowing her forthright personality in later life, it is easy to imagine Ulla as a woman who would take no nonsense. Whatever the truth, this must have been an unsettling period. It is little surprise that she resented the hardships that she perceived her father to have put her through and which caused her to feel not part of the Northcotts and perhaps not even part of the Hahlos.

In July 1943, still using the name Ursula Hahlo, she enlisted in the Auxiliary Territorial Service (ATS), the women's branch of the British Army, becoming Private W/277533. All women in the army joined the ATS except nurses and medical officers. The first recruits were employed as cooks, clerks and storekeepers. As more men

joined the war effort, it was decided to increase the size of the ATS in parallel, reaching 65,000 women by September 1941. Duties were expanded and members became orderlies, drivers, postal workers and ammunition inspectors. We have to decipher her army records to know where she was, which is not easy as they are handwritten and contain a baffling array of acronyms and shorthand terms. From July to October 1943 she was in training in Pontefract, Oswestry and at Tonfanau, a camp in north Wales used as an anti-aircraft training

In uniform c 1943

facility. After training, she was posted to the Royal Artillery and worked with heavy anti-aircraft guns, trying to shoot down doodlebugs on their approach to London. From December 1944 she was switched to K Company, No. 3 Continental Group and served in Belgium, Holland and Germany. There are references in her papers to her working as an assistant financial adviser and in clerical roles; there is also mention of being at 'Gen Hosp' but it is not clear if this is as a patient or to help in the running of the field hospitals. Once, her commanding officer found her referring to some confidential papers as part of her duties. He removed them saying 'You can't look at those, you're German.' From that moment, she swore that no one would discover she was German again. It might be when she decided to stop calling herself Ursula and to use one of her middle names, Susan, instead.

Dieter recalls that in Belgium, Susan found herself in the midst of the Ardennes Offensive, commonly known as The Battle of the Bulge. The Germans had unexpectedly counterattacked in the Ardennes, a forested region of Belgium and Luxembourg, in December 1944. Susan's company was surrounded, and they would have been taken prisoner but for a contingent managing to break through the German net. Nobody except her commanding officer knew that she was German. If she had been captured, she would have been shot as a traitor. As the war ended, Dieter believes, by chance her company went to Hannover and she marched past the end of the street where she had once lived. A sidelong glance from Susan and no more. Her life had changed and she was a different person completely. [21]

When Susan came home on leave, she stayed on Devonshire Terrace close to her mother because there were often rooms available for short periods with so many people coming and going. Even

[21] What was The Battle of the Bulge? See p299

during short stays, various boyfriends came to visit. She returned to the UK in November 1946 having spent almost two years in service overseas and was discharged from the Army in January 1947. Her release papers state that her military conduct was exemplary and that she 'has been employed as a clerk/typist and has dealt with work of a confidential nature and has proved entirely trustworthy and reliable. Pleasant manner, neat appearance. Can be highly recommended.' In March of that year she was registered as living at 14 Devonshire Terrace and working as a secretary and typist at British Aviation Services in Great Cumberland Place, near Marble Arch. This would open a whole new chapter in her life, introducing her to her future husband, Alan Hunter.

She submitted her form to be naturalised as soon as possible on 12 September 1946 with the support of the Army. It took fifteen months. Part of the delay was caused by 'financial difficulties' and her inability to find the £10 fee (equivalent to around £400 today). A letter to the authorities written in May 1947 plaintively says 'I am earning only just sufficiently to keep myself.' Her commanding officer noted in unreserved support of her application that she was a normal, happy member of the company, that her service record was satisfactory and that she was assimilated to British life. Her intelligence and capabilities are described as 'average', not unkindly because it is in response to a question about whether she had special qualifications. She was naturalised as a British citizen on 6 December 1947.

There are gaps in what we know about Susan's early life and her army service. My application to see her files at the National Archives was referred to the Home Office under Section 23 of the Freedom of Information Act which deals with what are considered sensitive security matters in the national interest. In these cases, the embargo applies irrespective of content. A document in her file has only two photocopied pages, suggesting remaining pages relating to her naturalisation have been removed. Her file is closed until 2048.

Susan had not known her father through her formative years and never accepted his justification of his actions, not fully comprehending the persecution Georg had faced and how hard it had been to get his children out of Germany. She remained loyal to her mother and on good but slightly distant terms with her brother. Susan had herself endured a terrible ordeal through her forced separation from her family and the rupture of the formative years of her life. She never admitted to her trauma and it is doubtful that she recalled the details but it seems from her actions and attitudes that she never overcame the emotional impact of her experiences.

Anti-German sentiment during the war had made her ashamed of being German and appearing to be English had become an act of self-preservation. Susan and her husband Alan even had close friends who were German and when they asked if she had ever been to Germany, she said no. It seems she wanted to protect herself from confronting her past. When her mother came to visit, nobody outside the family could be present because her mother had an accent. Once Elli and Dieter were visiting and Mike Hawthorne, a famous racing driver, popped by unexpectedly (Alan was keenly involved with cars and racing). He was an important friend, so Elli and Dieter were ushered into another room and told to stay put because Susan didn't want their visitor to hear her mother talking.

Susan's son, Ian, had no idea she had been born in Germany until he was 17. She had always been good at helping him with his German homework, but he had never thought to question why and he had not identified his grandmother Elli's accent. He had applied for a job with the Ministry of Defence and been unsuccessful, making Susan think that they had checked and found out she was German. She was upset that she might have caused Ian's career to stumble at its first hurdle and told him the outline of her life story and that her father had gone to live in Bolivia.

25

PADDINGTON, ENGLAND, 1942–47

'We all went absolutely berserk. It was such a glorious day'

Dieter's digs in Queen's Gardens were a small, dim room with two beds. He could not afford the room on his own and advertised in the college for someone to share with him. An Austrian refugee called Otto Tausig replied. He was four years older than Dieter, having been aged 16 when he left Vienna in 1938, and had been permitted to enter the country on condition that he engage in war work, after his mother answered an advertisement in The Times for factory workers. He was toiling in the Lyons factory near Hammersmith, baking apples to become puree. He had to carry huge trays which he occasionally dropped in calamitous accidents. The pastry cooks, kneading the pastry by hand, were stripped to the waist because it was so hot. When they got too sweaty, Otto alleged that they picked up the dough and used it to pat themselves dry before returning it to the mix.

It was Dieter's immense good fortune that Otto was an extraordinary and talented man with a deep knowledge of theatre. They frequently lay in bed talking until 2 or 3 in the morning, helping to enrich Dieter's inadequate education. Discussions ranged from classical subjects such as Greek mythology to literature and drama. Dieter had been introduced by his father to writers such as

Schiller and Goethe but his knowledge was limited. He listened for hours to Otto and marvelled at his intellect. Dieter was naïve about worldly affairs having led a sheltered existence at the Russells', whereas Otto was ardently left-wing and Dieter absorbed that too. It was a shame that the room they shared was not as resplendent as their talks.

Otto played an active part at the Austrian Centre at 124–126 Westbourne Terrace. It was established to boost the welfare of Austrian refugees and to offer advice and support towards their settlement in the UK. Soon Otto had had enough of the shabby room in Queens Gardens and decided to move closer to the Austrian Centre. He invited Dieter to join him at 134 Westbourne Terrace which he did with pleasure in December 1942. Dieter met many Austrians at the centre, proud people with a great love for their country, their culture and their food. They hated Hitler and were campaigning for their country to be independent. Dieter loved it all. As soon as he finished his chiropody course for the day, he went to the Austrian Centre to take part in whatever they had to offer. He took to eating there because it was heavenly to reconnect with food such as sauerkraut, which had been decidedly off limits at the Russells'. He relearned to speak German. He adored the artistic life that the centre promoted. At one party they played games and one of the girls, as a forfeit, had to kiss a man. The fellow licked his lips in anticipation. Dieter thought 'How disgusting!' but was shocked to observe that the girl rather enjoyed it. It took him time to overcome his inhibitions but it was where he came of age and cast aside the conservatism of the Russells and of his mother.[22]

The Austrian Centre had a small theatre for shows and music called Das Laterndl (The Lantern). One reviewer praised the intimate venue and estimated the stage as about ten feet wide by

[22] What was the Austrian Centre? See p301

eight deep, 'the size of a postage stamp'. Otto was a key member of Young Austria Players, one of the dramatic groups fostered by the Austrian Centre and so, through Otto, Dieter developed his interest in the theatre. At first, he put his know-how as a stagehand to good work and found himself helping out in areas such as the lighting, ignoring the fact that he had no practical experience. He approached tasks with enthusiasm and eagerness to please, even when he didn't know what he was doing. He didn't know that he had to keep one colour of wiring separate from another so that when he tried to join two wrong wires, he caused a blackout of an entire block of Westbourne Terrace. He vowed to do better and borrowed books from the library to learn what to do. He had found his tribe and it inspired him. The reviewer of a January/February 1945 production mentioned the 'ingenious lighting'. The standard of the productions was high as among the exiles were professional actors and others well known in Austria. Dieter started to realise that Otto Tausig was a brilliant actor who only had to walk on stage for something to happen. As Dieter spent more and more time at the centre, he didn't take long to find an excuse to get on stage himself, playing small parts, such as the gardener in a fairy tale called *'Der Verschwender'* (The Waster) in January 1943. It became a full-time social life.

Otto had met Johanna Pick, known as Hansi, at the Austrian Centre and they moved together into a nearby flat but the house was damaged in a bombing raid. If they were not wed, they could not get another place to live together, so they married quickly and Otto asked Dieter to find somewhere else to live because his wife was going to move in with him. At the end of the war Otto was one of the first to return to Austria and Dieter lost touch with him, although was aware that he had risen to prominence. A few years after the war, Dieter went on holiday to Vienna with his new wife and on the spur of the moment Dieter looked in the telephone book and found Otto's name. Otto remembered him and invited them to

*Otto Tausig
with Hansi,
London 1942*

see a play in which he was appearing. It was a comedy of mistaken
identity and Otto played two parts, the director of an important
company and an ordinary man who happens to look like him. It was
always apparent to the audience which character was which, even to
Dieter's wife who couldn't understand a word of German, and they
thoroughly enjoyed it. They had a pleasant meal afterwards with
Otto and Hansi but the magic of their friendship had gone.[23]

In June 1943 Dieter moved from the flat he had shared with Otto
into a room in the same house as his mother at 14 Devonshire
Terrace. It was convenient, saved him a little money and had the
benefit that his mother would often cook for him. Their landlord
was a comical, tiny man and they strained not to offend him because
rooms were hard to come by and landlords had power: if they didn't
like you, you could be chucked out. It was easier to find another
tenant than it was for a tenant to find a room. The landlord's wife
was extremely large and Dieter used to joke with friends about how
they managed their sleeping arrangements. Which side of the bed
does he sleep? Does he have to climb over her to get out if the bed is
against the wall? They lived across two floors and if the wife needed

[23] Who was Otto Tausig? See p303

her husband, she would stamp her foot on the floor and shout 'George!' and he would run up as fast as he could. It was a great source of amusement. Unfortunately he monitored comings and goings. Despite creeping in as quietly as he could, Dieter seldom evaded his watchful eyes. In the mornings George would confront him: 'A very young and attractive lady came in with you last night.'

The war ground on. It was assumed that Hitler would have to give up but he hung on in his bunker until suddenly the German army capitulated. Everyone clustered around radios, leaning in to hear the news, hardly managing to breathe. Dieter read the News Chronicle, a liberal paper, and saw pictures of Germans surrendering and the headline that Hitler had committed suicide. There were pictures of Russian soldiers climbing the Reichstag and raising the red flag and on 8 May 1945, they heard the momentous broadcast: Peace in Europe. Dieter was in a big crowd of fellow students at the time. They went berserk, jumping around and embracing people they knew and people they didn't. It seemed incredible that peace, in Europe at least, could finally be grasped. He joined his Austrian friends and together they walked to the Russian embassy. The Russians had liberated Berlin and everything Russian was regarded as good and noble, especially to socialist Austrians. There was madness in the air as years of repressed emotions and of curfews exploded in a riot of elation. Dieter was dazzled by the exuberance in the streets, the feeling that life could be good again. Complete strangers hugged and kissed and people sang and danced in Trafalgar Square. People tore down blackout material and mesh netting as a celebration of no more bombs. Lights went on. Bus windows were cleared and Dieter was able to sit on the top deck and see where he was going. Woolworths soon had counters with a few sweets and little novelties that Dieter had never seen before. With joy coursing through him, Dieter felt fully English. He no longer thought in German.

The fly in the ointment was the ongoing war in the Far East – a lot of personnel were still fighting out there. People could not celebrate the end of the entire war until the surrender of Japan in August of the same year.

Life in the country tried to return to normal. This included going ahead with the scheduled general election in July. In one of the greatest-ever swings of public confidence, Labour won overwhelming support and Churchill was stunned by a crushing defeat. The greatest factor in Labour's dramatic win was its policy of social reform calling for nationalised healthcare, expansion of state-funded education, National Insurance and new housing. The Conservatives had been confident of victory and based their campaign on Churchill's popularity, rather than new programmes but voters distinguished between Churchill and his party. Another blow to the Conservative campaign was the memory of appeasement by Chamberlain, which with hindsight was condemned for allowing Hitler's Germany to become too powerful. Clement Attlee was invited by King George VI to form a government and, building on his landslide, Attlee nationalised much of the economy, including coal, railways, road transport, the Bank of England, civil aviation, electricity, gas and steel followed by the creation of the National Health Service.

Dieter and Elli enjoyed the liberation as far as they could in their straitened circumstances. They bought one of the few lifestyle gadgets that was affordable for the man in the street – a Brownie camera. There are snaps of short breaks around the country and of close to home, such as Hyde Park in the snows of winter 1946–47. One of their first trips was to Dovercourt Bay, allowing Elli to see for the first time where her son had been during the early years of the war, although they chose to stay in a hotel rather than in the holiday camp. There are breaks taken with Elli to Bournemouth in 1947 and 1948 recorded in Dieter's albums.

One of the new government's welfare schemes was to help people enjoy holidays at home. Most people were unable to go away on holiday due to a lack of money and because there were few places to go. Many seaside towns still had beaches with mines and barbed wire which were taking a long time to clear. As part of the government scheme, the Young Austria Players toured venues with Dieter an enthusiastic member of the troupe. They wanted to enlighten people about Austria as many still thought it was part of Germany. They performed reviews, sketches and songs, particularly Viennese songs. St Albans was the furthest they went and the venues were mainly local clubs, sometimes a hotel, in inner London communities such as Kings Cross. Dieter was the compere and occasionally part of the show. He had responsibility for lighting as well as dealing with the venue in terms of managing the queues, seating, finish times and so on. It was all done in English and now Dieter didn't speak German at all. He sometimes won applause because the audience admired his clear and fluent English. One club at Elephant & Castle had the latest electric switchboard with dimmers. Dieter enjoyed himself, ceaselessly dimming and changing lights during the show just because he could – there was no dramatic necessity.

Caricature of the compere, 1946

He appeared regularly at Das Laterndl's final home, at 69 Eton Avenue, near Swiss Cottage, and was paid for compering the cabaret and sketch shows. By now he was using an anglicised stage name,

Peter Harlow. On Sunday, 29 September 1946 the bill for a 'Grand Cabaret' presented a number of guest artists including Peter Harlow and the Young Austria Players who performed a number of sketches. The evening was billed as 'Produced by Peter Harlow' and he was the compere. A busy man,

Beyond compere, New Year's Eve 1946

with sufficient standing among his peers to be rewarded with a caricature of himself at work. There were special cabaret shows on Boxing Day and New Year's Eve 1946 in which, they claimed in publicity, well-known artists had agreed to appear. Among them was Nicholas Parsons, on the verge of a long and glittering television and radio career. On Boxing Day 1946 the Grand Xmas Show featured a one-act comedy, 'The Boor' by Chekhov, with Peter Harlow acting and producing. Another of the cabaret acts was Andre and his Wonderdog. The New Year's Eve programme kicked off at 6pm with the Sylvester Cabaret followed by dancing to a live band from 10.30 to 1.30am. Tickets were 3 shillings and 6 pence (17.5p). The compere for the evening was Peter Harlow who was paid 10 shillings, which he considered a fortune for doing something he loved. He was billed this time as Dieter Harlow, which might have been a mistake by whoever compiled the programme, having known him under both names. Dieter had arrived, and he felt terribly important.

26

LA PAZ, BOLIVIA, 1939–57

'One day he just wrote to her "I'm sorry but the
situation is so hopeless, I've decided to divorce you"
and that was it. She was very upset'

On his voyage to South America, the first time Georg touched land
again was in Panama. As soon as he could, on 11 March 1939, Georg
sent this card to his son. It is from Gatún Locks, the first locks
encountered which raise southbound ships thirty metres from
Caribbean waters to Lago Gatún. The three sets of double lock
chambers stretch for almost two miles and each chamber could have
accommodated the Titanic with room to spare. This time Georg
used for the most part his typewriter and we can read what he says:

'In front of the Panama Canal.
My dear good boy. In 2 days we will be on the Panama Canal, for the
first time near land and there I can post. I wrote a long description
of my journey that first goes to Uncle Richard who will give it to
Mutti, but I want to send you warm greetings and tell you that I had
a good journey and I am doing very well. It was quite boring, but
now it is getting more interesting as we are now mooring a lot.
Above all, I'm looking forward to going through the canal. You will
then get to read my description. In about 2 weeks I am in Peru and

*Georg's
postcard to
Dieter from
Panama*

then I take the train to La Paz. Can you imagine that it is so hot here
that you can lie outside in your pyjamas at night and (not) only
during the day. Hopefully I will get some post from all of you soon
and hear that Mutti is also in England.'

Georg wrote regularly from Bolivia: long, long letters. He deeply felt
the pain of separation from his children and his wife. Dieter believes
he wrote fewer letters to Ulla, if any, and relied on Dieter to keep her
informed. Georg believed his parting words to his son: 'Somehow
my boy we shall meet again' and had inner belief that he would
succeed in Bolivia, that he would make a living, he just couldn't be
sure how. Georg assumed that one day his family would join him in
Bolivia, the rough intention being that they would reach Bolivia via
his sister Lotte and her husband Julius, who had settled in Texas after
leaving Berlin in 1936. This plan was partly fuelled by the belief that
it was only a matter of time before Hitler and his forces would arrive
in England. They had taken Holland, Belgium and France, and the
Allies had been compelled to evacuate their troops from Dunkirk.
The worst was thinkable. Hitler believed it too and it is said that
detailed plans were drawn up, including identifying the art deco
office blocks that would become Nazi headquarters (Senate House

in Bloomsbury) and Hitler's personal offices (Ibex House at
Tower Hill).

Dieter started off believing he would eventually go to Bolivia, to
the extent of feeling he should learn Spanish alongside his school
studies, although he never actually did. He expected that his mother
would go too but was doubtful that his sister would. She had become
anglicised and estranged from her father by the time of his
emigration. But the first letters from Bolivia indicated that Georg
had realised with dismay that there was no future there for his
children. La Paz was the highest capital city in the world at around
3,650 metres above sea level with an unusual subtropical highland
climate, meaning rainy summers and dry winters. Daily life was a
struggle, even climbing stairs left people out of breath and their
health suffered due to altitude sickness. Cooking also has its
complications at high altitude because water boils at a lower
temperature so foods need longer to cook. It could take several hours
to cook a pan of potatoes.

Everyday life, its rules and regulations, were vastly different too.
Bribery and corruption were rife and it was important to know
whose palms to grease. There was a community of refugees in La Paz
from Germany, Austria and Czechoslovakia whose mindset was that
they would leave as soon as they could to go to more prosperous
countries such as Argentina or Brazil where academics and
professionals might do well. But these countries had already received
so many refugees that they had closed their doors. The future was
bleak and they had no idea what it might be. Dieter's interpretation
was that 'It was just a hopeless dump.'

Dialogue about the future was difficult because post was conveyed
by steamer and letters took six weeks to reach La Paz and another six
weeks for a reply to come back. There was no continuity to
exchanges; Dieter would receive a letter and feel unsure from his
father's answers what his questions had been in the first place. Georg

tried to tempt his wife to join him and Dieter thinks that she had expected to do so but when she received his letters describing his life, she was not prepared to take on the challenge, which is not surprising as she had always been fearful of strange situations. When war was finally declared, Elli's priority was her children and she elected to stay with them in England, leaving Georg disappointed. Nonetheless, it was a complete shock to Elli and Dieter when towards the end of 1940 a letter arrived out of the blue that said: 'I'm sorry but the situation is so hopeless, I've decided to divorce you.' That was it, a blunt, even brutal, way to end a loving relationship.

Georg had arrived at his decision without prior discussion, hampered to an extent by the struggles with communications. He had researched the process and discovered that in Bolivian law, he could divorce his wife without her consent, unlike in German or English law. So that is what he did. Dieter learned more about his thinking later but the reason given in the letters was simply that a man needed a woman in order to live and work in La Paz. He needed a woman to cook and manage the home while he strove to earn a living. There were few women in the immigrant population, so for Georg to find a partner was a major triumph. In those days a woman would not live with a man without being married, so that is what he decided to do. In his view, his survival depended on it. The war seemed interminable and by now he knew that his wife would not join him in Bolivia. His chances of returning to Europe seemed non-existent. It was not a good way to behave towards his faithful wife, but in his mind the situation had become so desperate and detached from the ambitions they had once shared that he felt it was his only option.

Georg's new wife was a German refugee called Margot Pincus, born in Berlin on 18 October 1902. They married on 20 December 1940. It must be true that together they helped each other to overcome the devastating loss of friends and family. Together, they had a better chance of starting a good new life. We know little about Margot but it seems she had not been married before. She was Jewish and converted to Lutheran in 1965. We know almost nothing of their shared life in La Paz. There were no postmen or women (still true today) and letters went to postal box numbers. The written word was introduced by the Spanish and the culture had no history of letter writing. The only recorded address for Georg is on Dieter's naturalisation application and is given as Calle Genaro Sanjinés (no number), which is in the old quarter of the city.

Bolivians exhibit little appetite for record keeping. In 1986 I visited the German embassy and the German cultural club in La Paz and they had no records. The immigration office was renowned for claiming that its records were destroyed in a fire and nobody knows if this is true. I visited the law college, the Tribunal and the Courts of Justice, none of which had records, and I was told a register of practising lawyers was only started in 1979. Perhaps a hefty bribe would have solicited more help somewhere but there is no certainty that any further searching would have been successful. I found Georg's post box, 'Casilla 1020', in the old post office where he would have come often with his little key to open his box and scoop out letters from his wife and his son, for a while probably his most important and pleasurable experience in La Paz. This building has since been demolished and the chances of feeling a connection to Georg in La Paz have effectively been expunged.

Life in La Paz was not uncivilised. Public transport was good and cheap, with electric trolleytrams and lots of buses. Because of the uneven terrain, hardly anyone used bicycles. The few cars were mainly taxis and were old models because new parts were unavailable and everything had to be repaired or remade, hence Bolivians were expert mechanics. Only a few rich individuals owned newer cars for which they paid exorbitant prices. The road system outside the capital was chronically underdeveloped. On paper Bolivia had a

democratic government with officials elected by popular vote. In
practice a coup which changed the president happened almost every
year. These mini revolutions were mostly bloodless and staged with
the help of the military. A few tanks would drive up to the
presidential palace, a few shots would be fired and then everyone
would go home for their tea, the papers reporting the next day that
there was a new president.

La Paz had some attractive districts although most accommodation
was extremely primitive. Old colonial buildings in the centre of town
were well maintained, mostly as government buildings around the
central landscaped square. There were a few upscale businesses and
restaurants in and around Plaza Murillo. These included the Café
Paris, a European-style establishment where the immigrant
community met on Sunday afternoons. They had coffee and cake
while a small band played light music in the background. Another
restaurant had white tablecloths, uniformed waiters and a pianist
playing semi-classical music.

Georg found work at first
as a secretary and interpreter
in a lawyer's office before
going to university to learn
Bolivian law, eventually
receiving the local equivalent
of a doctorate. This grainy
photo from a Bolivian
national or local paper, sadly
undated, shows four men
recently qualified in law at
the Higher University of San

EL DIA DE AYER RINDIERON EXAMEN DE LICEN-
CIATURA, en la Escuela de Derecho de la Universidad Mayor
de San Andrés los señores Guillermo Asturizaga, Juan Loba-
tón, Mario Bueno y George Hahlo, quiénes fueron aprobados
sobre tablas. — Cabe destacar que el señor George Hahlo, en
2do. lugar del presente gráfico, ha obtenido la revalidación
de su título de Doctor en Ciencias Jurídicas de Alemania,
siendo, de consiguiente, la primera vez que una de nuestras
Universidades otorga revalidación de tal género luego de ha-
ber calificado de "excelente" el examen del señor Hahlo. —

*Clipping from a Bolivian
newspaper, date unknown*

Andrés. This is the leading public university in Bolivia established in 1830, making it the second oldest, and one of the most prestigious academic centres in the country. The clipping, sent with pride by Georg to his son, highlights the achievement of Dr George Hahlo (second left), as it was the first time a Bolivian university had revalidated legal qualifications from another country, due to the excellent exam performance of Dr Hahlo. This was an exceptional feat for someone working in a new language (which he did not learn at school) in another country with different laws and approaching the age of 50. In one early letter to Elli, Georg had enclosed a photograph of himself standing in front of a microphone at the presidential palace with the comment: 'What do you think of me as president?' It was a joke but Elli believed that is what he had become. She was naïve, but it shows the strength of legend of a man who had managed to spring his family from Germany and who had succeeded against the odds in countless testing situations. Elli had unshakeable faith in his abilities, and she took it badly when Dieter convinced her that the photo was a hoax.

There had been a handful of practising Jews in Bolivia in the 1930s but the rise of persecution bolstered the Jewish community with the arrival of around 12,000 German immigrants. A lot arrived on agricultural worker visas but, being from cities and given no tools or help with which to farm their parcels of land, they gradually migrated to the cities, mainly La Paz. With his new qualifications Georg became a legal adviser to the organisation representing the

Georg c *1942*

German immigrant community, helping people to settle in the city. He received Bolivian nationality, which helped him in his studies and work. There was an association for German immigrants and he became its president and was a board member of the German Democratic Union in La Paz from 1941 to 1953. He wrote a newspaper column in Spanish for a leading Bolivian paper. By the time Hitler was defeated, he had established himself in La Paz and started to feel at home. The thought of returning to Germany didn't occur to him until after the war ended and the immigrant community started an exodus to Europe or went to find a better life in the Americas. His law practice dwindled because his clients were leaving the country.

In the late 1940s, Georg travelled to Germany with Margot, funded by a refugee scheme from the German government, to see if they could establish a life back home. There seemed no opportunity for work in the legal profession. The best he was offered was a job as legal adviser to the Employers' Federation in Nuremberg, which he felt obliged to take despite being over-qualified. Dieter jumped at the chance to visit him, having last seen his father when he was a child. Georg talked about life in Bolivia and it was obvious that he was comfortable with Margot. There was no 'difficult' talk. After all this time, Dieter could see no point in recriminations. Dieter never forged much of a relationship with Margot who remained rather withdrawn and dour in the face of Hahlo reunions.

It was clear to Dieter that they were struggling back in Germany, which was a broken country where food and basic necessities were in short supply. They were boarding in accommodation that didn't have a flush toilet, just a cesspit below a toilet seat in an outhouse. Georg had been reduced to being a pen-pusher and the prospects were so dismal that Georg and Margot decided to go back to Bolivia. Having been excited on the journey to see him, saying goodbye to his father again was extremely upsetting because Dieter feared that they would not meet again. Georg had painted a bleak picture of Bolivia, and made it clear there were no jobs or prospects for a young man such as his son. The train journey back to London was long and dreary. Tears fell. The only consolation was in the dining car where they served lentil soup. It was the first time Dieter had had proper lentil soup since leaving Germany and it was just as his mother used to make it, with meat and sausage. It was delicious, and the only thing that could cheer him up.

Georg and Margot came to London in March 1953, staying with Else and Richard Hochfeld. Dieter brokered a meeting between Georg and Elli at Victoria Station. Georg strove to make it easy for her by greeting her with the words that he had used the first time they met in Berlin, lifetimes ago: 'I am honoured, gracious young lady.' Despite the emotions, it was good for Elli to see him. It seemed to exorcise some of her demons when she realised he was living a respectable life. She felt that he had deserted her, but he felt that she had deserted him. They even met once more a few years later, when Dieter and Elli had a short break in the Harz Mountains. Margot and Elli never met.

Georg and Margot returned to Bolivia in 1955 but once back, the situation deteriorated further and there were even fewer foreigners. His law practice was more or less non-existent. The atmosphere had become problematic too. Several Nazis had arrived via ratlines, notorious escape routes organised by the Catholic church and US intelligence agencies, which used the fugitives as assets during the Cold War. This created an unlikely jumble of competing ideologies in La Paz and even less cohesion among the immigrants. Everyone had become wary. Georg stayed for a short while before realising he had no choice but to return to Germany.

This time, in 1957, he had the foresight to get in touch with the students' union, a source of help in Germany. His university in Jena invited him to a dinner with a number of ex-students. By chance he sat next to a lawyer who was beginning to specialise in the restitution laws and needed a specialist to help him. Georg had valuable experience through his work in Bolivia such that the man offered him a job on the spot. And so the final part of Georg's career was working for the Compensation Bureau on the legal process of restitution for the tribulations suffered and the earnings lost during the Nazi era. He and Margot settled in Hannover where the practice was based, living in 1960 at Sedanstrasse 56–57. At the end of his life their address is recorded as Am Jungfernplan 5A. Georg worked until 1975, retiring at the age of 80, which is good going after such a strenuous and draining life. And lots of cake.

Susan felt bitter at the manner in which Georg had ended his partnership with Elli, seeing him as a traitor to the family. After Georg left England in early 1939, he only saw his daughter once more in 1981 when he was nearing the end of his life. It is not known how much persuasion she needed from her brother. Susan's children, Ian and Penny, first found out that they had a grandfather who was alive and in Germany when Susan announced she had to go to see him as he was in frail health. They were then aged 30 and 27.

Margot, Georg and my father, May 1970

They insisted on accompanying her, despite her misgivings. Ian drove and they travelled with Ian's wife-to-be, Tina. When they arrived at the slightly squalid, tiny apartment in Hannover, Susan refused to allow Tina into the bedroom as she was not yet family. Ian and Penny's only sight of their grandfather was his tiny, immobile frame clinging to life. Penny hugged him and said 'Hello Grandad.' Ian shook his hand and said 'How do you do?' Ian offered to translate because his schoolboy German was fairly good but to everyone's amazement Susan gabbled away in German as if she had never left, despite not having uttered a word of it in over forty years. Margot stayed at the margins, seemingly resentful at the reunion. She was starting to suffer from dementia and was prone to throwing her food and other odd actions.

Georg was delighted to see Susan; he had found the separation hard to bear and had always been concerned to hear what she was doing. He must have been relieved to have a final reconciliation and there was warmth as they sat holding hands, but they could not reknit a bond after a lifetime – wounds could not be instantly healed. Georg died at his home on 18 August 1982, aged 86. Susan refused to talk about her childhood afterwards and Ian and Penny realised that questions caused discomfort, even pain, and were reluctant to probe. Their mother's silence was too loud. They were sad that Susan did not want to go to her father's funeral to pay tribute to a brave, formidable man who overcame the odds to ensure his family survived and who then rebuilt his own splintered life.

Margot died on 22 February 1984 at her apartment at Haeckelstrasse 6. The will stated that after the death of them both, their housekeeper, Frau Schmidtke, was to receive 20,000 Marks (value just over £17,000 today) plus the entire furnishings of the apartment and Margot's jewellery. The remainder was split between the two children, with Dieter receiving seven-tenths of the estate that was left after the bequest to Frau Schmidtke and Susan three-tenths but there cannot have been much left to distribute.

Elli started work in the 1950s as a cook and housekeeper in Sutton and learned to live independently at 10 Western Road and then at 38A Worcester Road before moving to Mayfield, Sussex. In 1965 she applied for reparation payments following the Anglo-German Agreement of 1964, which issued compensation to British victims of Nazi persecution. She had been encouraged by an appeal by Clement Attlee in the Daily Express on 27 February 1965. She wrote in a fine, spidery hand that she had been happily married for eighteen years (her marriage is recorded as 'dissolved' on her naturalisation certificate of 1952) and that from 1933 they had been 'forced to move from one town to another' and could never settle. She says she came to England thanks to the Society of Friends (Quakers) and stayed because she could not bear to be separated from her children. She acknowledges that she had already received a small compensation of £400 but says that she now needed money to help cope with her arthritic and rheumatic pains. The appeal failed. The official reply states that she was not deemed a victim of persecution because she had not suffered detention in a camp 'designed to inflict suffering, torture or death'. It seems a harsh verdict and would have intensified her anguish.

Elli was not a loving and tactile grandmother to me and my brothers and seemed to find it hard to relate to us. It perhaps shows how her challenging life had damaged and hardened her. She was prone to get emotional when talking about family and at such moments she sometimes would lapse into German. Or perhaps not, it was hard to know because her English came with a thick accent which made it difficult for us children to communicate with her. We were slightly in awe of her makeup, her refined and upright air, her heavy smoking. We found her a little sour but she had plenty to be sour about. Until you have had to say 'Here, please take my adorable children' it is impossible to understand what she went through before, during and after the war and to judge the mental and emotional impact on her.

Elli is another hero of this story. Although she was a timid, nervy, middle-aged woman used to being guided by her husband, when the crisis came, she found the courage to put her children on trains to an unknown country and to see her husband board a boat to a distant continent. It was only after helping to secure safety for others that she finalised arrangements for herself. She had intended to reunite with her husband and his actions had felt a devastating betrayal. That it was all decided and arranged without her knowledge after she had stood by him seemed cruel and she never fully accepted his reasoning. Elli died in a nursing home near Sutton on 17 February 1977. Susan died on 13 May 2011 aged 87, a good age given her lifelong devotion to smoking.

27

SUTTON, ENGLAND, 1945–50

*'I sat there confronted with the most extraordinary thing,
what looked like gravy on a big plate and nothing else'*

Dieter decided to call himself Peter Hahlo at all times from now on
and his stage name Peter Harlow disappeared. It was easier to have
an English first name but he had no intention of losing his family
name. This was a brave choice given the times, which I think can be
interpreted as a tribute to his father and the trials they had both
endured. In the family history, there have been many name changes,
as people have striven to blend in, to assimilate somewhere new. It is
understandable given the strained times in which many were living
and their need to secure a future. Few seem to have reverted to their
original name with the same pride as Peter.

With the cessation of war, he needed to earn a more reliable living
than through occasional theatre work. With his qualification in
chiropody under his belt Peter took a job with Scholl, a company
founded in Chicago in 1906 as specialists in footcare and a brand
that still exists today. In the period after the war the company had its
own shops selling its products and offering treatments, primarily
chiropody. Peter started work at the clinic in Regent Street, which
was the main branch in London. He got on well and liked the
company, feeling that they encouraged people to develop their

abilities. It was evident that Peter had received good tuition at Chelsea Polytechnic and it was not long before patients were asking for him to treat them, more so than for other members of staff. His work was valued because he was more medically orientated than other chiropodists and interested not only in conditions and their treatment but also in the causes and their prevention. This was noticed and one day in 1947 Peter was summoned to head office and asked what he thought about taking a managerial position. He agreed and was given the opportunity to see how management worked by being sent to branches around the country to perform chiropody and to fill in for absent managers.

He claimed it was a lonely life doing stints in different towns and cities lasting several weeks at a time and that he was still hampered by his upbringing with the Russells, who had not helped him develop his social skills and confidence. But he didn't lack for company. In his photo album is a record of his 'relief tour'. There are tiny, grainy photos of him in York with Mr and Mrs Lofthouse and their daughter, and with Kathleen and Muriel and Lillian and other friends by the River Ouse. He goes walking with Phyllis near Middlesbrough. He pops up in Bolton with Pauline and Brenda but Brenda seems to gain the upper hand, also featuring in a photo from Manchester. He takes Eileen rowing in Northampton, striking an athletic pose by gripping the oars and clasping a pipe in his mouth. Kitty Smith merits a photo of her own and one of her with her mother in their garden. He was invited occasionally by colleagues to go for a meal and to meet their families but he found it hard to develop relationships with people he had little in common with. He had a big surprise when he went to his first Yorkshire home and was given an extraordinary meal that looked like gravy on a plate and nothing else. He had no idea what to do with it and had to follow his hosts as they tore into the Yorkshire puddings and lapped up the gravy. They followed the meal with a cup of tea that they poured into the saucer and drank from the saucer. He was agog and it took concentration not to laugh. He was seeing real life: 'there was nothing wrong with these people, it was just the way they were'.

In his white coat, on tour in Birkenhead

In his spare time Peter went to the theatre, mainly to see variety shows which were all the rage, feeling he was making up for lost time. He felt liberated after life with the Russells and the war. Every town had a variety theatre which showed a different programme

In Northampton

every week. The chances of having seen a show before were negligible and at 1 shilling and 6 pence (7.5p today) the financial risk was small. Sometimes it was boring but mostly it was highly entertaining. In Huddersfield he saw the singer Helen Clare for the first time. She had been a darling of the airwaves during the war and was now a star of the variety circuit. She came on stage looking stunning in a ballgown and sang so beautifully that it took his breath away. A performer of that quality was a rarity. Peter became a fan and saw her perform a number of times. By sheer coincidence, several years later, she walked into his surgery in Wallington for treatment (under her married name, Helen Riddle). They talked at length about the theatre and it was not long before she was roped in to perform in one of Peter's productions. They became long-time firm friends.[24]

In 1947, after managing both Kilburn and Oxford Street branches temporarily, Peter was asked if he was interested in becoming a manager full-time. He was offered Sutton, despite still living in Devonshire Terrace. This attracted him because it was a small branch where he could practise chiropody as well as managing the branch, whereas the West End managers had to spend too much time on sales and management rather than on treating patients. He knew he was good at his work and was starting to practise more physiotherapy which he didn't want to give up. This interest was thanks to a lecturer at Chelsea Polytechnic, Mr Coombs, who spoke about physiotherapy and massage as well as about legs and feet. Mr Coombs was an osteopath and was also engaged by Scholl to give talks to the staff. Peter questioned him after one of his talks and decided to train in the emerging discipline of osteopathy.

Peter went to see the branch in Sutton before committing. It was in Grove Road, near the station and Post Office and he was relieved that this was the better side of Sutton so he took the role. Peter was moving up in the world and he volunteered to Mr Russell that he no longer needed his payments, thanking him for his help with genuine warmth. Peter was now earning about £5 a week, a salary with which most factory workers would have been delighted.

The next task was to find accommodation and it was agreed that he, his mother and Susan would share a flat, Susan having been recently demobbed. It was a wrench to leave central London and the Austrian Centre and all the connections Peter had made but that era was waning as many Austrians returned to Austria. They moved in

[24] Who was Helen Clare? See p304

With Barbara in London 1947

to their first flat on 26 February 1948, on the first floor at 7 Egmont Road, walking distance from Scholl's. Elli and Susan had one room, sharing a double bed, and Peter slept in the living room on the sofa. They shared the bathroom with other people. It was hardly ideal but it was good to be together again and they could use the rear garden. There are photos of them sitting in the sun, at times accompanied by Barbara Bracher, whom Peter was keen on. She too was involved in the theatre. The flat proved too small and in June 1949 they found another at 54 Sutton Court on Brighton Road, a big block of flats near the station. It was brighter, more modern and Susan had a room of her own, although Peter remained on the sofa. They spoke in English, despite Elli's being not as good. Her English gradually improved although she never lost her accent and complex matters had to be explained to her in German.

Peter enjoyed the work. There was one other chiropodist and a receptionist, with whom Peter bonded, sharing meals at each other's houses with her and her husband. They were helpful in getting Peter and his mother established in Sutton, as was the estate agent, Philip Saint, who invited Peter to join Round Table, which is a non-political, non-sectarian association founded in 1927 open to men aged 18 to 45 from any profession or trade. Its aim is encouragement of ethical standards in commercial life, the promotion of fellowship among young professionals and businessmen and to empower them to make a positive impact in the community. This was Peter's much-wanted introduction to mainstream English life and respectability. It opened a new world and enabled him to mix and socialise on a level he had not enjoyed before. It fed his gregarious nature and his compassionate tendencies, through its support of local charities.

Elli did not work again until Susan and Peter met their future spouses and looked to move away. In 1949 Susan started work as an air hostess at Croydon Airport, the UK's main international airport, before it was supplanted by Heathrow and Gatwick. She worked on short haul international flights, such as to Paris. Some of these flights used large, lumbering planes in which a few passengers sat in wicker chairs at little round tables like a cafe and were served coffee. If you wanted fresh air before takeoff, you simply opened a window. On some routes, these old planes were being replaced by sleeker, faster aircraft. It was a good job and a glamorous life. She and a colleague were featured in a diary piece in The Star, a London daily evening paper, with a photo of them in their uniforms as 'air girls who are the only official hostesses at Croydon Airport', noting approvingly that they are '25-year-old brunettes'. The piece remarks that their duties included being receptionists, booking clerks, taking charge of freight and transport arrangements, preparing aircraft papers and answering 'hundreds of queries'. It says that they both had nursing experience and could deal with patients being flown to hospital, experience that Susan must have picked up during her time in the ATS. She was an attractive, spirited young woman and not short of boyfriends. She met Alan Hunter, an aeronautical engineer and an archetypal English man. Susan embraced this, becoming stereotypically English herself. She and Alan married on 15 March 1950 in Croydon. She changed her name, moved out of the shared flat and erased all remnants of her German life, until the encounter at her father's deathbed. The past was pushed away and not discussed: it was her means of survival. She strove hard to provide a stable, loving environment for her children but as Jews persecuted by the Nazis know better than most, you can never entirely escape your past.

After Susan moved out, Peter was earning enough money to take responsibility for the rent. Elli looked after the home and the housekeeping expenses took all the money she had. They used a dense, austere 1929 German cookery manual, Dr Oetker's School Cookbook, to give themselves an occasional taste of home. The bookmarked page has recipes for salads: healthy, green, tomato, celery, potato, mushroom, sauerkraut, herring, fish and meat salads are listed, alongside Peter's favourite, cucumber. It suggests that his kitchen skills were limited and that he found it useful to have guidance on how to mix together peeled cucumber, salt and pepper, oil and lemon juice or vinegar, scattered with chopped parsley. A simple cake recipe has been written out by Peter in English with evidence he was still getting to grips with the language: he lists among the ingredients '500g of flower'. It also shows he still wasn't at ease with pounds and ounces.

Aside from Round Table, Peter's social life centred on the Tavistock Repertory Company based in Tavistock Square, Bloomsbury. The Austrian Centre had emptied of talent and he had searched for a new theatre group. The Tavistock was not professional but was prestigious, staging as many as twenty separate productions in a year. Peter started working with them in October 1947 as a member of the background cast. In four years with the Tavistock he worked on twenty-one productions, despite the long commute from Sutton. For many plays, he is credited as the electrician, which confounds his children who have the impression that he could barely change a plug. Peter would have been in his pomp, with an irrepressible energy and zest for life. As children, we are deprived of seeing our parents in their prime.[25]

---

[25] What was the Tavistock Repertory Company and what was Peter's involvement? See p306

In 1948 a young woman named Mavis Foley was also starting out in chiropody. She later became my mother. At school she had excelled, securing a coveted place at University College London to study biochemistry, with a grant too. But her parents didn't want her to go to university because they believed that it was only worth educating a son, despite the gulf between Mavis and her brother Alan in academic ability. Mavis's mother suggested her daughter study chiropody because she went to a chiropodist herself, and Mavis consented. In those days if your parents said 'do this', generally children complied, especially after the war when life was difficult. Mavis applied to Chelsea Polytechnic but was too late: entry for the course had closed. But when she appealed and the college saw her exam results, they accepted her straightaway, exempting her from the first term of general science that she already knew.

One reason for accepting chiropody was that she could work around the country. She'd always had an urge to explore, as well as to escape her stultifying suburban home. She worked in Weymouth and Oxford before returning to London and getting a job at Scholl's in Regent Street. She liked working there and treated well-known actors and musicians who were working nearby at the BBC. It was where she acquired the nickname Fay – her colleagues balked at calling her Mavis and she was delighted to shed her old name.

Fay's parents moved from Petts Wood to Epsom in 1949 and she wondered if she could get a job at the Scholl's branch in Sutton, the nearest to Epsom. She mentioned this to a colleague who recommended talking to the Sutton manager. There were meetings at Caxton Hall in Victoria Street, where employees attended talks once a month. At the next one, she asked someone to introduce her to Peter Hahlo. They had not overlapped at the Polytechnic but Fay had seen his name on record cards as having treated patients before her and it stood out as unusual. She sat next to him for a lecture and shyly introduced herself. They didn't speak much and afterwards she met a friend from the Polytechnic. Over coffee she said to her friend 'Did you see that chap sitting next to me, I'm thinking of trying to get a job with him?' The friend replied in jest 'I thought he was your husband!' Fay laughed it off: 'I'm not getting married; I just want a job.'

In January 1950 Scholl held its annual New Year party and dance at the headquarters in St John Street, London EC1. A copy of the invitation was kept in Fay and Peter's folder of mementoes. Fay went with a crowd from the Regent Street branch. Peter was there and Fay said she was interested in working in Sutton and they started talking and later danced together. Early in the conversation Peter asked 'Do you like the theatre?' and Fay truthfully answered yes. Fay liked him, he was amusing, a good dancer and he was interested in the arts and cinema. The job vacancy never arose and they never worked together, for which we should probably be thankful. But the next chapter of family history had started.

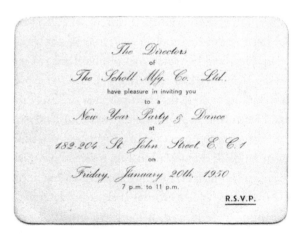

Invitation to the Scholl party, January 1950

28

SUTTON, ENGLAND, 1950–53

*'He was out of the mould of the suburban middle class
and I wanted to escape from that. I soon discovered
he wanted to be middle-class suburban English
because he'd been an outsider'*

Peter grew to admire Fay's intelligence and was encouraged by her
genuine interest in theatre and cinema. She and Peter got on well
and talked easily about the arts, medicine and many other subjects.
He gave her a tough introduction to theatre work. The play was
Heartbreak House at the Tavistock in March 1950, for which Peter
was electrician. He asked Fay to do the sound effects from the other
side of the stage, using marked records which had to be cued in with
a handheld stylus at precisely the right place, at precisely the right
time. It was a Heath Robinson approach but despite no experience,
she coped. That was not enough to earn her a credit in the Tavistock
archives but in terms of their relationship, it sealed the deal.

Fay liked this new life, travelling into town wearing her brother's
trousers held up by one of her brother's ties around her waist and a
baggy old jumper. Her parents didn't approve but she loved the
Bohemian style and wanted a break from the suburban middle-class
men that she normally met. She didn't want to follow the set pattern
of life that her parents had. Although Peter was not from the same

mould, she discovered later that he had other ideas. He wanted to be received into middle-class English society because he'd been an outsider, so much so that Fay felt it affected his personality. He was desperate to be one of the gang, because he wasn't the type who normally belonged to Round Table. Foreigners were a novelty and he had to work to be accepted, trying hard to entertain with a stock of yarns and to put himself in the spotlight. He wanted the conventional life from which Fay was trying to escape.

Fay's parents were underwhelmed. They were shocked that he was German. Her mother had been vociferous about her hatred of Germans during the war, even though opposition to Peter was illogical because he was a refugee. They were perturbed by the idea of their daughter courting somebody from a different background. They were bemused by his devotion to theatre, which was not part of their experience. Fay remembers her mother saying, after Peter had left following one stilted afternoon tea, 'Well, at least the dog seems to like him.' But before long, Fay's parents realised that Peter regarded himself as English and that he was a lively and approachable young man. He started being invited to Sunday tea, which was the done thing at weekends, and eventually he was introduced to various relatives, the ultimate badge of acceptance.

Peter also introduced Fay to his relatives in North London. Everybody thought she was charming and educated, always important to this branch of the family. Fay was self-effacing, reluctant to take the limelight. Her charm and tact helped relationships with Elli and Susan. She went to Sutton Court for meals and for tea with Elli, which could be difficult. Sometimes Fay could not understand what she said; the rest of the time, Elli couldn't understand what Fay said. It took time and effort before Fay endeared herself. Elli was not part of the support networks set up after the war to help escapees as she was not Jewish and had become isolated and a responsibility to Peter. She had no interests apart from watching television and it wasn't easy to find ways for her to make friends. She was 45 when she arrived in England, having led a cosseted, male-dominated life. Being a stranger in a country where she didn't speak the language was hard and Elli never fully acclimatised, possibly never accepted her fate. She appeared older than her years, aged by her experiences. She envied the finality for women who had lost a partner whereas being abandoned by a living husband seemed to prolong her pain.

Within six months or so of serious courtship, Peter proposed to Fay. He had always wanted a wife and children. The swiftness most likely reflects his need for security and reassurance, common in refugee children. Fay was only his second serious girlfriend after he had been rejected by Barbara as a possible husband, which had left him heartbroken. But Fay was perfect in every way. The proposal didn't come as a surprise to her. The occasion was prosaic, in his flat in Sutton, and the ring was cheap, as Peter had no spare money. The big step was to tell her parents. Despite the groundwork, Fay dreaded it. She was lying in bed one night, fretting, when her mother came in. Fay blurted out 'we might get married' and burst into tears. They were not used to talking about feelings and Fay had seldom had the courage to stand up for herself. Her mother offered no comfort, simply saying 'I must tell your father' and left the room. There was a lack of closeness with her parents.

Peter received a letter from Fay's uptight mother who was concerned that Peter was still German and who was not keen on the match. Peter wrote explaining that it not been possible to get naturalisation during wartime, and that he had started the process as soon as he could. Britain had come to his rescue and this was his life now. He praised the country for its religious and cultural tolerance and for its respect for democracy. He received a conciliatory letter in return saying that they hadn't understood the problems he had faced. Such was the couple's confidence now that they sent an official

December 1950

portrait to their families for Christmas 1950. Naturalisation started
with announcements in three local papers: The Sutton & Cheam
Advertiser, The Croydon Times and The Surrey County Mail. The
referees for his application in November 1950 were Mr Russell,
Mrs Wells, John Francis, whom he knew from the Tavistock Theatre,
and a family friend from Hendon, Frederick Bracher, presumably
the father of Barbara. He died during the process and his wife
stepped in to vouch for Peter. The good character of Peter and his
referees was confirmed in reports from MI5 and Special Branch.
His file was to be kept closed until 2058 but became viewable at the
National Archives under the terms of the Freedom of Information
Act. His address was given as 11A Meadway, Epsom and his
occupation as chiropodist. He swore his oath of allegiance, 'by
Almighty God', in the offices of Copley Clark, solicitors, in Grove
Road, Sutton, on 2 March 1951, three weeks before his wedding.
He was proud to be British.

Fay's parents were uneasy about Peter's devotion to the theatre. Her
mother asked her: 'Are you going to be able to live with that?' Fay
admits it was difficult in the early years of marriage and parenthood
to accept that Peter was often out in the evenings, taking on acting
parts or directing plays. Occasionally, it made Fay unhappy but she

Guernsey
1950

could see that it was core to who he was. He had to be busy. As ever, Fay remained stoic and accepting; she was right to be so. Peter loved and needed to be part of a theatrical family, to revel in the friendship and the humour. One of Fay's qualities was her empathy and she started to participate in productions with Peter at another company, the Epsom Amateur Operatic and Dramatic Society, although she would always shun anything more than a crowd scene role.

Fay and Peter had a quick holiday in Guernsey in 1950 to celebrate their engagement, sleeping in separate rooms. Those were the rules. Peter wrote to his father to tell him the good news. He enclosed a photograph of himself and Fay on the beach in Guernsey with Peter sitting on a deckchair and Fay sat next to him on the stony beach. Georg quipped in reply 'I see, just like a pasha. You take the comfortable chair and make her sit.' Georg did what he could to contribute to the union, sending a cheque for a small sum that would have cost him a lot, given the poor exchange rate of the Bolivian peseta. Peter appreciated the gesture. Georg did the same for Susan when she was married but, not comprehending his challenges, she had been offended by the amount.

Fay and Peter were married on 24 March 1951 at Christ Church, Epsom Common, around the corner from her parents' house at

105 Hookfield. There were thirty-seven people in attendance in the main group photo. The reception was at a small tearoom/restaurant nearby, the Dorking Gate,

Wedding day, 24 March 1951

which is now a branch of Pizza Express. Fay didn't want a traditional white wedding and she still needed scarce coupons to buy clothes. She bought a new dress and hat; Peter bought a new suit and all went well. The report in the Epsom & Ewell Herald on 30 March says that the bride wore a lemon, grey and white figured silk dress with grey hat and

Outside the church: Mr Russell, Elli Hahlo, Bill Marney, Peter and Fay Hahlo, Gillian Remes, Doris Foley, Wilfrid Foley

accessories and carried a bouquet of white lilacs and yellow and blue irises. The bridesmaid was her cousin, Gillian Remes, and the ushers were Alan Hunter and Fay's Uncle Arthur. Georg could not attend and Elli is accompanied in photos by Mr Russell, now known as Uncle Russell by Peter and Fay. (Mr Russell was also a guest at Susan's wedding, which was a nice touch.) Leon Eagles, a fellow actor/director at Tavistock, was due to be best man but two days before the wedding he developed a boil and had to pull out. They had to find a new best man at the last minute and asked a guy they had met on their holiday in Guernsey called Bill Marney. They hardly knew him, but they knew few people well. Peter had little history of lasting friendship after his scattered upbringing. Their connection with Bill and his wife petered out after a few years, as did that with Leon Eagles.

They took off that evening for Ventnor on the Isle of Wight where they stayed for a week. The local paper informs us that the bride travelled in a grey suit with blue blouse, grey hat and accessories. There are several happy photos in the album each merrily captioned by Fay. However she appears coy, headlining the section as:

Post Wedding Recreational Furlough
(or honeymoon)

Three months later they had what seemed a proper honeymoon: they took the train to Bacharach on the Rhine, where they stayed at the Hotel Gelber Hof for two weeks from 23 June to 7 July. Peter showed Fay his beautiful homeland: it was her first time abroad. They visited his home town and Peter enjoyed the nostalgia. They gazed at the block in which he had grown up and discovered that Frau Knaul still lived next door with her two daughters, the father having died at Stalingrad. The reunion was joyful and they accepted an invitation to stay the night. The next day they enjoyed a nostalgic

Bacharach, 1951

row on the river and visited the chalet that the Knaul family owned in the mountains. Peter found the house with the unusual triangular mirrors in the centre of Bad Kreuznach; the name Michel was still underneath the bell. He rang and announced his name. After a moment of disbelief, there was a scream of joy and Frau Michel rushed down to greet him. She was delighted to see him, quite overcome with emotion. Herr Michel had not survived: he had been arrested in the last months of the war and had died in a concentration camp.

Peter feasted on a frankfurter in a roll with mustard from a vendor on a station platform. It was the old flavour he loved but he couldn't finish it – he no longer had a hearty German appetite. Reminders of the war were everywhere and Peter and Fay were moved by the effects of the obliteration of Cologne. They were uneasy to think that many of the people around them must once have been Nazis. There had been millions of Nazi party members and many still wore the caps that had had swastikas removed recently – Peter could make out the pattern on the cloth. It was extraordinary that Nazis seemed to have disappeared and no one knew about the atrocities. Peter had left Germany twelve years earlier and had gone through more than the normal maturing process. It had been a metamorphosis from German boy to English married man. He tried to be English even when having to speak German. Not to be thought of as German felt equally important to him in Germany as in England.

Back in England, they at first lived at his lodgings in Epsom, five minutes' walk from Fay's parents. Fay dutifully noted the recipe for German lentil soup in her recipe book. Peter never grew to be adventurous with food, hankering always for meat and potatoes in various forms, partly a connection with his briefly happy childhood. He described Fay's attempts to vary the diet as 'vegetarian muck'. Within three months of the wedding, Fay was pregnant. On 4 March 1952 Peter went to work as usual on his bicycle and Fay cycled to hospital as she could feel it was time for her baby to be born. At the end of the day Peter cycled to Sutton hospital to see if there was news and found he had become a father to my elder brother, Michael. On his way to work he had often told stories to his imaginary children, just like his father had told him stories when they went wandering together. He wanted to give his children the happy childhood that had been taken from him.

Peter and Fay were no longer able to stay in their rented rooms with a baby. With so many displaced people after the war there was a long wait for council housing and nobody wanted to let rooms privately to people with a baby. Fay's father, Wilfrid Foley, stepped in with financial help and they bought a house at 13 Fairview Road, Sutton for £2500 (equivalent to £71,000 today but house inflation is way ahead of general inflation). There was also a loan

April 1952

13 Fairview Road, Fay at upper window

from Alan Hunter, and Peter's Round Table friends realised they were struggling and made a collection which raised £9, a valuable sum. Leopold arrived with a glass drinks cabinet strapped to the roof of his car as a belated wedding present. He also brought the dark wooden chest with ornate carving which had been in the family for many years and had travelled from Oldenburg (both cabinet and chest are still in family possession today). They let out the top floor, with a shared front door, to help with the cost of loan repayments. Living downstairs, they had an outside toilet and no bathroom. The weekly wash was taken in a tin bath in front of the stove. The garden had a pear tree and a shed and, at the bottom of the garden, two passenger steam trains an hour would rumble past in each direction on the line between Sutton and Crystal Palace. The road was at the top of a rise to the east of Sutton from which its name derived but any hope of a fair view had long been obscured by the terraced housing all around.

Peter trained as an osteopath, mainly by correspondence course, and opened a surgery in Wallington at the time of severe post war austerity and competition from the new National Health Service. There was opposition to osteopathy from the medical profession, so it was a struggle getting his own practice established. Fay worked for a year at a local umbrella factory, packing up orders, while Michael spent the day at a nursery. Their disposable income was around £4 per week, barely enough. The arrival of Fay's parents' first grandchild meant that all resistance to the union disappeared. They adored baby Michael and frequently drove over from Epsom. They were in their mid-fifties and their energy and willingness to help out were a blessing to Fay as she worked and managed the household. At weekends, Fay's father would come to take them out in the car. He liked motoring.

Peter had worked hard to be genial to them. It hadn't been easy because Doris and Wilfrid Foley didn't talk about their feelings and could become stiff and uptight if someone did. Baby Michael made the difference. They were good, kind people, typical of the British middle class of the era. Doris became focused on her expanding family and Wilfrid remained a calm, ordered man who extolled the virtue of regular, early morning bowel movements and struggled to understand those who could not follow this simple regime. Peter had to be careful not to espouse more liberal views in their earshot and there were occasional disagreements about politics around the dinner table.

In March 1953 Georg and Margot came to England on their way to or from Germany and spent a few days in Finchley with Else and Richard. They came to Peter's home in Sutton where Georg met Fay for the first time, as well as baby Michael. Georg had visited Oldenburg and Hannover and managed to secure token reparation payments from the German government for his family. Their possessions had been auctioned on behalf of the state police on 28 October 1941 in Brüderstrasse,

Fairview Road, March 1953

Oldenburg. The sale was promoted with a newspaper advertisement and supported by a neatly-typed list of thirty-five 'items to be auctioned regarding Jewish removals belonging to Frau Hahlo, formerly of Taubenstrasse', from boxes of porcelain and the furniture to carpets and the piano. Peter never recovered his beloved electric train set. The compensation money was not much in comparison to what had been lost but it was a godsend, enough for Fay and Peter to go to Shinners, the department store in Sutton, to buy their sitting room furniture.

It was unfortunate that the English occupying administration had put the process of reparations in German hands. Core roles went to people with experience in justice and government, many of whom were ex-Nazis. It was in their interest to dispose of evidence and suppress records. Thus truth and justice were denied to many people. Nothing and no one could bring back murdered family or compensate for childhoods lost, friendships not allowed to blossom, education denied and chances of carefree lives lost for ever.

As his chiropody and osteopathy practice started to build and Peter was establishing himself in Sutton he splashed out on a motorcycle, one which had been dropped by parachute into France at the start of the invasion. It had no gears, just a throttle. One icy day as he drove round a roundabout, the machine slid one way and he went the other. He got up unhurt as a funeral cortege was passing. The driver of the cortege tipped his hat – it was a friend from Round Table. Much ribbing was endured at the next meeting. He later bought a second-hand motorbike with sidecar and family outings were taken with Fay crouched alongside and Michael on her lap.

The impact of his childhood and adolescent experiences could be observed throughout Peter's life. He strove to provide a loving, secure family home, similar to that from which Fay had been looking to escape. He wanted his children to have the childhood he had missed, not to suffer the privations he had endured. Like his father, he wanted to belong, to be accepted at the higher levels of local life, to better himself. He needed to be the centre of attention, always entertaining, borne out of a fear that people might ignore him. Once, his mother had seen a play in which he appeared and queried afterwards why he had not been more centre stage; he was always striving to live up to parental expectations. Perhaps we'd be the same if we had been uprooted and cheated out of our childhood and education. In his own words:

'The feeling of in-between has never left me. To be where I was or where I would like to be seems always better than where I am now.'

Despite this, Peter was never bitter about the hardships he endured. He knew he was lucky. It would have been so much worse had his parents not acted bravely and promptly. He would stand silent and sombre as the bells pealed on Remembrance Sunday, aware that so many had not had his luck. He had no time for recriminations and grudges. His experiences gave him a keen sense of justice and an instinct to support the underdog. He took the road less travelled and showed himself to be a champion of the alternative. He stood up for what is right. He was generous to those less fortunate than himself. He was open to ideas, fair and honest. He dedicated himself to work and family with energy and humour. He wished only that his three boys would never experience anything similar to what he had. A happy, comfortable life was an achievement. Tinkling bells, flaming candles and the magic of Christmas, the family together.

A book published in 1966 called 'We Came As Children' contains the recollections of their experiences from 234 unnamed *Kinder*. It was anonymous to allow the *Kinder* freedom to express the distress or guilt that they had always been supposed to hide, having been told previously that they were expected to express only gratitude. There are four contributions from Peter and he has the very last word in the book:

> 'I am no longer a refugee since I married and have my own home, friends and family.'

He regretted having minimal contact with other *Kinder*, to share how they dealt with their experiences. He did try but, because he wasn't Jewish, he didn't feel part of their community and contact petered out.

This book has been written in the shadows of Brexit and Trump with much talk about keeping out immigrants. Antisemitism is on the rise in Europe, on both the right and on the left and reports of antisemitic acts in Britain are rising. The children of the Kindertransport only survived due to the kindness of strangers. Thanks to them, many have made a significant contribution to our cosmopolitan society. There are statistics about how refugees do better in school, are more productive and create more jobs than the average person. It's hardly surprising, from people capable of such desperate journeys. They do not take citizenship and education for granted. It contrasts to the callous rejection today by people who claim our prosperity is under threat from refugees. They have forgotten that it was refugees who helped to build our prosperity in the first place. Many more people, I believe, would be willing to repeat the generosity shown to Kindertransport children, if only politicians would rise to the occasion.

In this context, writing about the family is not self-indulgent. We've always known that we would not exist if the Nazis hadn't happened and without the suffering of Georg and Elli, Peter and Susan. In their eyes, I think, we are the explanation for what they did. At one stage, the Hahlo family had virtually nothing left, except its spirit. Like a story being played out upon the stage, in an epic tale of love, hope and community overcoming darkness and evil, the boy on the train had come a long way.

END NOTES

Historical context

1 Why did the Hahlo family convert from Judaism? Antisemitism in late nineteenth century Germany

The formation of the German Empire in 1871 promised to be good for the country's Jewish population. It heralded emancipation of the half million or so Jewish minority, or at least of its men, and their days of being seen as social, political and economic pariahs were officially over as they won equality before the law and equal civic rights. Liberalisation of attitudes towards marriages between Jews and the Protestant majority and between Jews and Catholics meant Jews started to decline as a proportion of the German population.

Historically, Jews had been prevented from acquiring landed property that had meant many of them made their living in commerce, as moneylenders and as traders, like the Hahlo family, and thus contributed to the expansion of the Empire's economy. Education was no longer beyond their means and Jews embraced learning. Germany had an excellent education system in which scientific research was at a higher level than in other countries and by 1913, more books were published in Germany annually than in other countries. Those German Jews who did not enter their fathers' firms after schooling would go into professions such as law and into the press. This gave them high visibility, although their opportunities for senior appointments in education, the military, the civil service and the judiciary were limited. Antisemitism still existed among upper classes and nobility who considered Jews to be socially inferior and unsuited to be invited to court and into their clubs.

Segments of the lower classes and peasantry also harboured deep-rooted antisemitism that was encouraged, or at least not opposed, by the church. The Jewish minority had long been blamed when harvests failed or for other disasters and as the German Empire flourished, those not finding success needed scapegoats to avoid having to confront their own shortcomings. Those who were left behind by or feared the rapid changes associated with industrialisation were apt to strike out at groups they regarded as different and the Jews were a small and easily identifiable group to be thrust into this unhappy role.

In October 1873 the stock market crashed and tens of thousands of middle-class and aristocratic families lost everything. The antisemitic scapegoat syndrome was activated because so many stockbrokers happened to be Jews or were prominent in the press. In 1880 a prestigious official Prussian state historian published a paper which formalised antisemitic ideology, describing the Jews as 'our misfortune'. By the 1890s the populist *Völkisch* movement was established with a romantic focus on folklore and a naturally grown community. They viewed Jews as a race that could never be properly assimilated into German society. In 1893 candidates who made antisemitism their main platform won several seats in the Reichstag and one party's policy was to oppose 'obtrusive and corrosive Jewish influence on our national life'. Open antisemitism had become respectable.

Some Jews responded to attacks in the press and elsewhere by converting but most did not convert and wanted to be integrated into German society whilst preserving their identity as an ethnic group. Around 15,000 Jews converted to Christianity between 1871

and 1909, relatively few out of half a million. More than 100,000
Jews participated in the First World War, a higher percentage of their
number than among all other ethnic, religious or political groups in
Germany. Around 12,000 died for their country.

2 Why was Germany so confident? The Franco-Prussian war 1870–71

Prussia had already created a myth of military invincibility with its
victory in the Seven Years' War (1756–63), when it whipped the
Austrians and the French into submission, albeit with the help of an
alliance with Great Britain. It was a conflict that involved most of
the world's superpowers of the time and resulted in Prussia
maintaining an army of disproportionate size and might.

A hundred or so years later, Prussia's defeat of Austria in the Seven
Weeks' War in 1866 had confirmed Prussian leadership of the
German states and threatened France's position as the dominant
power in Europe. The French emperor, Napoleon III, declared war
on Prussia in 1870, assuming a victory that would restore his
declining popularity in France. The French were convinced that the
reorganisation of their army made it superior to the German armies.
They had great faith in two innovations: a breech-loading rifle, with
which the entire army was equipped, and the *mitrailleuse*, an early
machine gun. French generals, blinded by national pride, were
confident of victory.

The German states saw France as the aggressor and, swept along
by patriotic zeal, rallied to Prussia's side, providing troops that gave
superiority of numbers. A huge asset was the Prussian army's General
Staff that was responsible for mobilisation and the rapid, orderly
movement of troops to battle zones. It was distinguished by its
selection of officers on grounds of ability, intelligence and merit,

rather than of patronage or wealth. Rigorous training produced a body of professional experts with common methods and outlook and gave German armed forces a decisive strategic advantage. The French, meanwhile, tended to place members of noble or royal households in command of army units irrespective of suitability or experience.

Despite the population of France being greater, the Germans had more soldiers thanks to conscription of every male Prussian of military age. The General Staff used the railway system, which had been partly laid out by them, for efficient mobilisation. The French military had no control of the railways, which had developed from commercial pressures and was run by competing companies. Troop journeys to the fronts in Alsace and Lorraine were long with frequent changes between trains meaning many units arrived late or with inadequate supplies. The French army had lost 100,000 stragglers before a shot was fired.

There was also the matter of the *mitrailleuse*, their prototype machine gun. It had been developed in such secrecy that little training had occurred. Once the small number of gunners who had been trained became casualties, there were no replacements who knew how to operate it. The Prussians had guns with a longer range and a faster rate of fire, two features which had been discouraged by the French army in the belief that it wasted ammunition. The French were outthought, outmanoeuvred, outnumbered and outgunned. They never stood a chance.

The swift defeat of France astounded Europe. A heady wave of nationalist fever swept Germany as centuries of French hegemony were blasted away. It resulted in a punitive peace treaty and Germany's annexation of Alsace-Lorraine. France had to pay an indemnity of 5 billion francs and cover the costs of the German occupation of its northern provinces until the indemnity was paid.

The Franco-Prussian War led to 'a united Germany, but a more

divided Europe' and laid the foundations of the catastrophe of the
First World War. It established both the German Empire and the
French Third Republic, mutually hostile powers in rival alliances. It
changed the balance of power in Europe and confirmed a united
Germany as the major player on the continent. The harsh terms of
the treaty aroused a deep longing for revenge in the French people.
In a final twist, the superior organisation of the German railways set
the template for the efficient deportation of Jews by the Nazis more
than half a century later.

3 Did the Germans achieve their objectives? The Battle of Langemarck, 21–24 October 1914

This period is commemorated by Germans as the Battle of
Langemarck, which was early in a sequence of fighting known by the
Allies as the First Battle of Ypres.

It started in early evening when the men of six regiments,
including Georg's, entered the little town of Bikschote. From 21 to
23 October German reservist regiments launched mass attacks at
Langemarck, suffering losses of up to 70 per cent of their men and
making only minimal gains. The British used buildings to snipe at
the Germans as they struggled to overcome hedges reinforced with
wire. A German officer commented in his diary that the first day at
Langemarck had been a shambles, few people had any idea what they
or the enemy were doing and casualties were overwhelming. The
next day the Germans, surprisingly, renewed their attack, and the
outcome was identical meaning heavy losses for little or no advance.
Positions won at heavy cost during the day were lost again at night. It
was an exercise in futility.

Neither side had moved forces to the area fast enough to obtain a
decisive victory and by November both sides were exhausted. Armies

were short of ammunition and suffering from low morale. The battles in Flanders had become static, attritional operations, as the Allied troops in their improvised field defences proved able to repulse German attacks for several weeks. The defensive use of artillery and machine guns dominated and the ability of armies to supply themselves and replace casualties prolonged battles. As the weather worsened and set in, the First Battle of Ypres petered out, resulting in an Allied victory. German forces sustained heavy losses whilst failing to make a strategic breakthrough on the Western Front or to capture the British ports. Allied forces profited from being faced by ill-trained German reservists, such as Georg. He was undoubtedly better off out of it.

Langemarck now has a mass grave and a huge memorial to the German war dead in Belgium. There is a monument in the garden of the University of Berlin, in honour of those who died. Its inscription is: '*Invictis victi victuri*' (overcome, undefeated) but German tributes to the 'Spirit of Langemarck' are based on myth. Tens of thousands of men perished to little advantage.

4 What were they fighting for? The Gorlice–Tarnów Offensive, May–July 1915

This was the chief offensive effort of 1915 for Germany and Austria-Hungary, a series of actions from early May that were ended by bad weather in October by which time they had caused the collapse and retreat of the Russian lines.

The Austro-Hungarian army had started to attack the Russians but had suffered heavy casualties and needed reinforcements. The Germans formed a new army made up of eight divisions already trained in assault tactics on the Western Front, led by General von Mackensen. They were brought east on 500 trains with 159 heavy artillery guns. Once there, each division had 200 wagons with drivers to help cope with the poor roads. The German field telephone service advanced with the attackers enabling frontline observers, supplemented by aeroplanes, to direct artillery fire. The siege mortars and German light artillery supported the infantry, crushing Russian fortresses within days. The Russians had only four pieces of heavy artillery, one of which malfunctioned and blew up as soon as battle began.

The Russians sent two additional divisions to stem the tide, but they were annihilated before they could even report back to headquarters. On 3 May they started a limited withdrawal. By 9 May the attackers were through all the Russian lines and had met their objectives. Having said that, Germany committed 126,000 men to the campaign (backed up by 90,000 from Austria-Hungary) and 69 per cent were killed or wounded, which is 87,000 men.

The Germans decided to continue to advance. It required meticulous organisation: relieving surviving but worn-out infantry, moving forward artillery, ammunition and other supplies along roads and rail lines that had to be repaired as they advanced. Replacement soldiers brought the depleted ranks back close to their initial strength. This is where Georg came in.

On 3 June the victors marched into Przemyśl and the victorious troops were cheered by its citizens, triggering high-spirited celebrations throughout the land. The Galician oil fields, crucial to the German navy, were swiftly back in production and 480,000 tons of badly-needed oil was captured. Soon Poland was in Austro-German hands.

Lemberg (modern day Lviv, in Ukraine), the Galician capital and the fourth largest city of the Austrian Empire, was the next objective. After a short-lived attempt to defend the fortress by outnumbered Russians, German forces entered the city on 22 June. It was, both politically and in terms of planning and resources, a crowning moment of the campaign.

5 The Iron Cross

The Iron Cross 2nd Class is the most common
variant of the medal, awarded for 'a single act of
bravery in the face of the enemy'. The commitment
and self-sacrifice of soldiers had to be rewarded,
especially when the battles of the First World War
involved such heavy losses. For survivors, the
decoration was a gesture of consolation and social
recognition. By the end of this disastrous war,
almost one in three German soldiers had received
the Iron Cross, that is over 5 million combat
soldiers. The Iron Cross 1st Class was awarded to

The Iron Cross

around 200,000 men. Exact numbers are not known because
archives were destroyed.

The Iron Cross united pride in the individual's achievements with
the nation's sacrifice and loss of lives. The Iron Cross 2nd Class came
with a ribbon and the cross itself was only worn on the first day after
award or when in formal dress. For everyday wear, the ribbon was
worn from the second buttonhole.

6 Who against who in the German revolution of November 1918?

The November Revolution arose from the extreme suffering of the
population during the war, the impact of defeat in that war on
Germany and tensions between the population and the aristocrats
who held power but had lost the war. War-weary German troops and
the population at large were longing for a speedy end to hostilities
when revolution sparked, in the navy. The German naval command
in Kiel planned a battle against Britain's Royal Navy in the North

Sea, acting on their own initiative. The battle never took place because, instead of obeying orders, German sailors mutinied in the first days of November. The sailors had no intention of risking their lives so close to the end of the war. This precipitated civil unrest across Germany that swept aside the monarchy within a few days. The proclamation of a republic on 9 November 1918 led to Emperor Wilhelm II abdicating and fleeing the country. The Prussian Empire was consigned to history.

Many revolutionaries were inspired by socialist ideals and looked to hand power to Soviet-style councils that were appointed spontaneously and arbitrarily and had no management experience. Many councils came to arrangements with the old administrations so that law and order could be restored. The Social Democratic Party of Germany (SPD) opposed their creation, opting instead for a national assembly. Fearing all-out civil war between militant workers and reactionary conservatives, the SPD sought to integrate the bourgeoisie into the new system. This allowed the army and nationalist militias to suppress communist uprisings by force at the time of the elections and again in January 1919. The revolution ended in August 1919, when the Weimar Constitution was adopted. By this time all twenty-one regional monarchs had been dethroned.

7 Why did Germany lose the war?

Germany should have won. Its industry gave it a vital edge, developing new war technologies such as poison gas, flame throwers, heavy artillery, long range bombers (zeppelins), submarines and machine guns. But calamitous decision-making created disasters which turned the tide against them.

By 1916 the Russians had been exhausted by offensives against the Austro-Hungarians, and wanted a quick route to peace but

Germany's insistence on creating an independent Poland enraged the Russians sufficiently to ensure their continued participation. In 1917 the Bolshevik revolution in Russia established a new leader, Lenin, who wanted peace so he could consolidate his power. A deal with Russia would have enabled Germany to free up a huge portion of its army to fight the advances of Britain and its allies in the west. But the leadership had grand plans to smash the new regime and establish Russia as a puppet state of Germany and so its resources were stretched beyond breaking point. By the end, German armies were exhausted.

The decisive blow was the entry of the US into the conflict three years after its start. Germany had foolishly goaded the Americans into the war by targeting merchant shipping in the Atlantic with its submarines and by attempting to form an anti-America alliance with Mexico. This dragged America into a war which most of its citizens and politicians would have gladly sidestepped. Its vast industrial resources became available to beleaguered Allied forces and fresh US troops arrived in France at the rate of 10,000 a day, which tipped the balance.

Germany ran out of allies and its economic resources dwindled to nothing. Support among the population had begun to crumble after half a million Germans died at the battle of the Somme in 1916 and the war itself turned into a quagmire. By mid-1918 only diehard monarchists and conservatives wanted to continue. Retreat and defeat at hand, the army told the emperor to abdicate because it could no longer support him. However, generals Ludendorff and Hindenburg soon proclaimed that it was the defeatism of the civilian population that had made loss inevitable and nationalists blamed the civilians for betraying the army and for the surrender. This was the 'stab-in-the-back' myth according to which revolutionaries stabbed the army in the back and turned victory into defeat. That was widely believed and ensured that many conservatives would not support the ensuing government. The German military command avoided acceptance of responsibility for defeat and political parties were left to cope with the turmoil.

Jews were the traditional scapegoat. They were accused of sitting on the sidelines even though 12,000 had given their lives for Germany, hugely disproportionate to their number in the population. In October 1916, by which time 3000 Jews had already died, the war minister had ordered a census to determine the number of Jews at the front. This revealed that 78 per cent of Jews who served saw frontline duty, refuting the rumour of non-participation. Jewish soldiers suffered a crisis in morale when the results of the census were withheld and the ministry continued to be flooded with complaints about Jewish draft dodgers. In total over 100,000 Jewish soldiers served in the German army and more than 30,000 were decorated for their bravery. They considered themselves Germans, rather than Jews.

On 11 November the armistice was signed in a railway carriage in the Forest of Compiegne by German representatives. It ended military operations and amounted to German capitulation. A naval blockade would continue until peace terms were agreed at the Treaty of Versailles in June 1919. Germany had to accept mass reduction of its military and confiscation of territory. The War Guilt Clause said that Germany accepted responsibility for causing the loss and damage sustained by the Allies as a consequence of its aggression and was forced to pay compensation. National disgrace was felt throughout Germany at the humiliating terms imposed by the victors, which fuelled the rise of extreme nationalist movements. Hitler later repeatedly blamed the new republic and democracy for accepting the oppressive terms of the Treaty.

8 Why would Georg want to become scarred?

Duelling scars were seen as a badge of honour among upper-class Germans, thanks to the status of duelling societies at the universities. The practice of duelling was common in the German military. The duels between students were ritualised. In some cases, protective clothing was worn, including padding on the arm and an eye guard.

It was important to show duelling prowess but more important to be able to stand and take the wound that was inflicted, to be seen as showing courage. In fact, the victor was seen as the person who walked away with the most obvious scar. Because most duellers were right-handed, scars were usually targeted to the left profile. The wounds were usually not serious, the swords were razor-like and cut without bruising, leaving no great disfigurement. I cannot remember if my grandfather still sported duelling scars when I met him, but he may have done.

As scars were associated with elite status and an academic institution, they showed that the person not only had courage and but also was good husband material. Ladies admired them.

Roughly 300 fencing fraternities still exist in Germany, Austria, Switzerland and a few other European nations. If the practice of inflicting scars sounds shocking, remember that we still do this today. We call it having tattoos.

9 Why was Georg involved? The Spartacist uprising of January 1919

After four years of war and famine, German workers were worn out, physically diminished and dispirited. Lost industrial exports, the restriction of supplies of raw materials and foodstuffs, the loss of German colonies and worsening debt to pay for war reparations created an economic crisis that left millions disenchanted with capitalism and hoping for a new era.

Two of the perceived paths forward were social democracy or a council republic similar to that in Russia, primarily a power struggle between the moderate Social Democratic Party of Germany (SPD) and radical communists under Karl Liebknecht and Rosa Luxemburg, who had led the Spartacist League, its name derived from the rebel gladiator, Spartacus. The Spartacists concluded that their goals could be met only by forming a party of their own, thus they joined with other leftist groups to found the Communist Party of Germany aiming to establish a Soviet-style republic.

Rosa Luxemburg presented their programme on 31 December 1918. She said that the communists would not take power without the clear will of the majority which they hoped to gain by continued agitation in the factories and from pressure in the streets. On 5 January, with hunger and unemployment rampant and returning soldiers everywhere, hundreds of thousands of people poured into Berlin, many of them armed. By the afternoon, train stations and newspaper offices were occupied. Some of the middle-class papers called for the raising of more militias and for the murder of the Spartacists.

The next day saw another mass demonstration, with even more people. Most of the army were not willing to support armed revolt and remained loyal to the Government. Negotiations were broken off and the Spartacist League called on its members to engage in armed combat. On 9 January government paramilitaries violently quelled an improvised revolt, brutally clearing several buildings and executing occupiers on the spot. Others surrendered, but were still shot.

On the same day, militias made up of former soldiers started to attack the protesters using the weapons and equipment they still had from the war, and with this formidable advantage quickly re-conquered blocked streets and buildings, forcing many of the insurgents to surrender. On the evening of 15 January, Luxemburg and Liebknecht were discovered in a Berlin apartment, arrested and handed over to the largest militia unit. They were questioned, beaten unconscious and shot in the head. In total, 156 insurgents and seventeen soldiers died during the fighting and the revolt was quickly over.

Elections were held on 19 January 1919, the first of the new Weimar Republic. It was the first free and fair German election, using proportional representation with women's suffrage and a voting age lowered to 20.

10 Why was inflation rampant and what happened to the Weimar Republic?

The National Assembly elections of January 1919 gave a solid majority to moderate democratic parties. To avoid ongoing sporadic fighting in Berlin, the National Assembly convened in the city of Weimar, giving the Republic its unofficial name.

From its beginning, the Weimar Republic was afflicted with the stigma of military defeat. In its fourteen years, it faced numerous problems, including political extremism and contentious relationships with the victors of the First World War. The main problem was hyperinflation. To fund the war, Germany had borrowed money from its own people at unfeasibly high interest rates, planning to pay it back by taking money from the conquered enemy. In order to pay its debts the Government started printing new money because the economy was too fragile for tax rises. The more they printed, the more the value of the Reichsmark sank, hence the more money they had to print. Inflation grew at a staggering rate: in 1919, a loaf of bread cost 1 Mark; by 1923, the same loaf of bread cost 100 billion Marks.

In 1923 the Republic could no longer afford repayments. In response, French and Belgian troops occupied the Ruhr region to enforce delivery of reparations, mainly in the form of coal. This was Germany's industrial heartland and the final blow to the economy and to national pride. The Government encouraged the response of passive resistance by promising to pay the wages of workers who downed tools, which meant it had to print even more money when production was crippled and the tax-take reduced. A new currency, the Rentenmark, stabilised the situation in 1924. People who owned property survived because their property retained value and low-paid labourers and workers didn't suffer because they had no money to lose in the first place. But millions of people saw their life savings obliterated and respectable families were reduced to penury. They sold their possessions simply to survive and could no longer afford the services of doctors or lawyers, even teachers. The middle class in Germany was wiped out and felt abandoned by the republic.

Nationalist groups were outraged by the terms of the Treaty, which they considered treacherous and humiliating. It was galling to the officers and soldiers who had fought in the war that Germany was forced to reduce its army to 100,000 men and that the General Staff was dissolved. There was resentment at the revised borders and abandonment of territory in France and Belgium. Monarchists and militarists claimed that the democratic republic had been forced on Germany by foreign powers. The elites from industry, landowners, military, judiciary and administration never accepted the democratic system and still hankered for an authoritarian state similar to the Empire with all the privileges they used to enjoy. The fact that the constitution had been drawn up by a Jew, Hugo Preuss, made him and his work an obvious target, added to which they blamed socialists and Jews for Germany's defeat in the First World War.

Left-wing extremists accused the ruling Social Democrats of

having betrayed the ideals of the workers' movement by suppressing the revolution and unleashing militias upon the workers. Minor rebellions broke out in Berlin, Hamburg and Frankfurt. A Soviet-style republic was declared in Munich before being brutally quashed by right-wing paramilitary groups. In March 1920 a general strike was called and over 12 million people refused to go to work which had an immediate economic impact. Transport ground to a halt and electricity, gas and water suppliers were unable to provide services. It didn't last long but the events revealed a country deeply divided between left- and right-wing factions. Both sides worked to bring down the Weimar Republic.

The Government implemented a programme of progressive social change, introducing reforms such as a maximum eight-hour workday, the release of political prisoners, abolition of press censorship, increases in workers' pension, sickness and unemployment benefits, and the right to organise into unions with committees composed of workers' representatives to safeguard rights. Exemptions for domestic servants and agricultural workers were removed, making it harder for estates to sack workers and to prevent them from leaving when they wanted to.

The 1920s saw a remarkable cultural renaissance in Germany. During the worst phase of hyperinflation in 1923, clubs and bars were full of speculators spending daily profits before they lost their value the next day. Berlin intellectuals, influenced by a brief cultural explosion in the Soviet Union, presided over an era of great creativity in German literature, cinema, theatre and music. Weimar Berlin became the intellectual and artistic heart of Europe. Innovative street theatre brought plays to the public, and the cabaret scene and jazz bands became hugely popular. Young women broke with traditional mores, wearing makeup, having short hair and smoking. They could vote. No one was conscripted. Gay nightlife flourished. Art, especially film, was daring and imaginative and the capital's theatres became renowned worldwide for their experimentation with expressionism. A new type of architecture taught at 'Bauhaus' schools reflected these new ideas. The arts scene was a source of pride and put Germany once more at the heart of Europe.

The Wall Street Crash in 1929 brought economic disaster to Germany again when it lost its major source of investment overnight. The majority of loans that had rescued the country had come from US banks, which only a few years before had eagerly lent money to the Weimar Republic, but now called in loans, which the country was unable to pay. The bubble burst and the consequences were catastrophic as unemployment spun out of control.

The Jewish position in Germany had advanced under the Weimar Republic as universities opened their faculties to Jews and the arts; journalism and publishing were enriched by Jewish participation. But scapegoating of Jews became rife when hardship hit, far right political groups blaming them for the economic collapse and the misery in which Germany now found itself. Hatred was intensified by belief that Jews held the levers of power, either through prominent political positions (some ministers were Jews) or because they pulled the strings behind the scenes. Jews' propensity to own stores gave them prominence in daily life and led to the misperception that they were 'everywhere'. In reality, Jews were 1 per cent of the German population.

In the end, right-wing extremists succeeded, ushering in the ascent of Hitler. The reparations that Germany was made to pay by the Treaty of Versailles were so crippling that they set up the conditions for radicalism to succeed. In 1933, Adolf Hitler was appointed Chancellor as part of a coalition government. Within months, normal law making was replaced by emergency decrees, wiping out constitutional governance and civil liberties. The seizure of power was enabled without legislative participation, bringing the republic to an end. Democracy collapsed and the single-party Nazi era began.

Hitler was a genius at encapsulating the feelings of those who felt they had been betrayed and had lost too much and at expressing the wrath simmering in people at the injustices foisted on Germany.

11 How did Hitler rise to such power, and so quickly?

The elections of 1928 gave the Social Democratic Party, centre-left as its name suggests, a chunky 30 per cent share of parliamentary seats. Hitler's National Socialist German Workers' Party had 3 per cent. Two years later the Nazis were the biggest party and by 1933 they were in power. In between there was the global stock market crash of 1929 but it was the support of the Prussian elite that helped to create a nationwide movement. Hitler appealed to the old guard which gave him access to wealthy sponsors and political respectability and gifted Hitler control of a huge swathe of the press and of cinema newsreels that were in Prussian corporate hands. Hitler knew how to use powerful imagery and simple messages in a new age of mass media (sound familiar?) and promised to bring back the good old days, to restore the glory of Germany (sound familiar?). And although he was indebted to the old aristocrats, he was careful not to be seen as one of them and part of the old system and many Germans were ready to go for someone fresh and charismatic who was unsullied by the old structures of government. Someone who promised to put things right, now. The Protestant population flocked to him in support, still in the mindset of an aristocratic society that defers to the military and to those in authority. Many believed that Germany was inherently unsuited to democracy.

In February 1933 a fire erupted at the Reichstag, supposedly caused by arson on the part of a young communist. The truth is still unknown but it was seized as an opportunity. Hitler, already Chancellor, pressurised Hindenburg to suspend civil liberties in order to protect Germany from communists. The Nazis could now arrest people simply for being opponents. The next elections in March 1933 were preceded by communists being rounded up and the anti-Nazi vote being forcibly suppressed. As soon as he was in power, Hitler proposed that he be allowed to govern without the constraints of parliament because the country was in crisis. This still needed to be debated and voted through but outside the Reichstag MPs who had voiced opposition to these extreme powers had to endure the jeers and jostling of Nazi supporters and their henchmen. Even so, many voted bravely against the motion but Hitler won the majority he needed. In January 1933 Hitler had stood before Hindenburg and solemnly sworn to uphold the German constitution and to maintain parliamentary rule. Fifty-two days later the Enabling Act marked the end of the Weimar Republic and gave Hitler the right to rule without the Reichstag. Democracy had been snuffed out.

Nazi propaganda pitched wholeheartedly for the middle ground, supported by the wheels of the governmental machine. In the background, Nazi thugs made electioneering almost impossible for liberal and left parties. Before long, most people believed Hitler was the only one who could stop the communists and deliver national renewal. His was a potent message in a seething brew of unemployment, malnutrition, stock market panic and hatred of the Treaty of Versailles. Hitler was not bringing original political thought; he was bringing originality of leadership. He made sure he looked and sounded like a leader, burning with passion to do right for Germany.

Hitler consolidated his hold on power in mid-1934 by ordering the summary executions of potential rivals and critics of his regime. This was the Night of the Long Knives in which at least eighty-five people were killed, presented as a preventive measure against an imminent coup. Some had been among Hitler's long-time supporters. More than 1000 perceived opponents were arrested. The purge strengthened the support of the armed forces and provided a grounding for the Nazi regime, as the courts swept aside centuries of legal prohibition against extrajudicial killings in order to demonstrate their loyalty. It established Hitler as the supreme administrator of justice for the German people and enabled his pursuit of the Jews to slip quickly and smoothly into place.

12 Why was Georg Hahlo, a God-respecting Protestant, classed as a Jew?

Before the 1790s Jews in Germany who converted to Christianity were few and far between. After this, the steady arrival of Jews fleeing antisemitism elsewhere in Europe saw clergymen and the nobility encourage conversions by handing out gifts and money to new converts. Special entries were made in church books describing the baptisms and who attended. When a Jewish convert eventually married a Christian, the marriage record usually added a reference to the conversion. The Nazis were aware that conversions were recorded in church books and discovered that the Christian population with Jewish ancestry almost equalled that of the Jewish community of around 500,000.

The Nazis pushed 'Positive Christianity', a unique form which rejected Jewish origins and the Old Testament. It portrayed Christianity as fighting Jews and depicted Jesus as an Aryan. Germans were required to prove an Aryan background in their *Ahnenpass*, a Passport of Ancestors, in which information on at least three generations of ancestors had to be given. Genealogical research flourished in Germany as every German was obliged to toe the line in order to get his or her *Ahnenpass*, and had to continue to be an ardent Nazi supporter for fear of losing it. There was underground resistance against the Nazi government and its demolition of democracy but the risks were immense. Even listening to foreign radio stations or passing on news of Nazi crimes of violence could carry the death sentence.

Converts and their children and grandchildren were not considered Aryan. Decrees in April 1933 required all public servants to be of Aryan descent. The Reich Citizenship Law, announced at the Nazi party annual rally in Nuremberg in 1935, marked an escalation in persecution. declaring that only Aryans were Reich citizens, legitimising inequality of rights. Anyone with Jewish ancestors, even only one grandparent who had converted as a child, was defined as a Jew. Lots of people who had previously not thought of themselves as Jewish became targets of persecution. A second law banned marriage and intercourse between Jews and Aryans and forbade the employment of Aryan women under age 45 in Jewish households. Anybody breaking this law would be guilty of racial defilement and faced imprisonment.

The Nuremberg laws were complex in trying to define who was or was not to be considered a Jew. In this official diagram, only people with four pure German grandparents (four white circles – left column) were considered to be full-blooded Aryans. German nationals with three or four Jewish ancestors (at right) were Jews. Columns two and three show the *Mischling* grades (half-breeds) depending on the number of Jewish ancestors. Classification of Jewishness became dependent on the religion of grandparents, regardless of whether the persons identified themselves as Jews, Christians or atheists.

Further decrees issued regulations such as dismissal of Jewish officials, even though many governmental posts had been given 'for life' to those who had fought for Germany in the war in recognition of their service. There was suspension of employment of Jewish physicians, dentists, pharmacists and lawyers, dissolution of Jewish organisations, exclusion from public welfare and state schools, loss of

Classification under the Nuremberg laws

citizenship upon leaving Germany and the collection of property in the event of departure or death. Jews could now only go shopping at certain times, could not take taxis, could not visit coffee houses or cinemas or other events, had to travel in designated carriages on the trains and were even barred from some parks. Most Germans welcomed the measures, although some did offer support or sympathy to beleaguered Jews. In August 1938 it became mandatory for Jews with non-Jewish names to identify themselves as 'Israel' if male and 'Sarah' if female to make it easier for officials to distinguish them. Eventually the concept of Jewishness caught up with everyone, including third generation descendants such as Ursula and Dieter.

It wasn't only Jews. The persecution of Gypsies became genocidal, the Nazis believing they were non-Aryan with genetically-inherited criminality. They believed that disabled people were genetically impure and were a burden on the state and a law forced anyone with one of nine disabilities to be sterilised, proclaiming it would allow

Germany to achieve racial purity. Thousands of disabled people were murdered in a euthanasia programme. Gay bars and publications were closed down. The law allowed the authorities to arrest men suspected of homosexual activity, who were then tortured for the names of partners in an attempt to create a register of all gay men. They were subjected to medical experimentation, such as castration. Lesbians, Jehovah's Witnesses and those deemed to be 'work-shy' were also persecuted.

As a footnote, Hitler himself could not prove pure Aryan blood. His father Alois Hitler was born illegitimately in 1837 to a 42-year-old unmarried peasant, Maria Schicklgruber: his paternity was never established. When Alois was promoted in the customs service, he applied to be legitimised in the name of his stepfather Hiedler, in order to be eligible for inheritance. His name was entered in the register as Hitler, for unknown reasons. Following rumours that his paternal grandfather might have been a Jew, in 1931 Hitler ordered the SS to investigate but naturally they found no evidence of Jewish ancestors. After the Nuremberg laws came into effect Hitler ordered publication of his genealogical tree, which showed that his family were all Austrian Germans and that he had an unblemished Aryan pedigree.

Hitler made documentary proof of Aryan ancestry a matter of life and death for millions of people although he himself possessed no document to prove who his grandfather was.

13 Who produced Der Stürmer?

Der Stürmer was a weekly German tabloid-format newspaper published by Julius Streicher, leader of the Franconia branch of the Nazi party from 1923. It was a significant part of Nazi propaganda and was vehemently antisemitic. It was published privately by

Streicher and was not an official publication, hence did not display the swastika.

The official Nazi party paper had a serious appearance, whereas Der Stürmer depicted Jews as ugly characters with exaggerated facial features and misshapen bodies. It furthered medieval stereotypes, such as that Jews killed children, sacrificed them and drank their blood. There was also sexually explicit, anti-Catholic, anti-Communist and anti-monarchist content.

The first copy was published in April 1923. Der Stürmer's circulation reached a peak of almost half a million in 1937, as well as being made available in public spaces for German citizens to read as they went about their daily lives. Most towns had special noticeboards erected for displaying the latest copy with a permanent sign above saying 'With Der Stürmer against Judea'. It was also distributed in several other countries, especially in the Americas, and it made Streicher a multi-millionaire.

As early as 1933, Streicher was calling in Der Stürmer for the extermination of the Jews. During the war, Streicher regularly authorised articles demanding the annihilation and extermination of the Jewish race. After the war, he was convicted of crimes against humanity and executed.

14 How did the Nazis manage the Berlin Olympic Games?

The Games were Hitler's event. He saw it as an opportunity for him to be glorified, as well as to promote his ideals of racial supremacy. He declared initially that Jewish and black people should not be allowed to compete but was forced to relent when threatened with a boycott by other nations. To appease them he allowed one token Jew on the German team, a woman who had a Jewish father, but excluded several of the country's top athletes, including world record holders.

The lavish opening ceremony included a flyover of the Olympic stadium by the airship Hindenburg. All did not go according to plan, however, when they released 25,000 pigeons followed by the firing of a cannon. This scared the pigeons and the crowd was treated to pigeon droppings falling on their hats and in their hair.

Berlin was prepared for visiting officials and athletes by the removal from the tourist areas of signs stating 'Jews not allowed' and similar slogans. They cleansed the city by arresting Gypsies and keeping them in a camp beyond the city boundaries. Olympic flags and swastikas bedecked the monuments and houses. The Games was more than a worldwide sporting event, it was a show of propaganda. The Nazis promoted a new, strong, united Germany while masking their racist policies and growing militarism, bedazzling foreign spectators and journalists with an image of a peaceful, tolerant Germany. The forty-nine nations who sent teams legitimised Hitler in the eyes of the world and strengthened his popularity in Germany. The New York Times reported that the Games put Germany 'back in the fold of nations' and made them 'more human again'.

Germany was the most successful country, winning eighty-nine medals in total, ahead of the US with fifty-six. To Hitler's dismay, Jesse Owens from the US won the four most prestigious sprint gold medals and was acclaimed as the most successful athlete. He was black.

Normal service was swiftly resumed at the end of the Games and signs forbidding Jews were restored. Two days after the Olympics, Captain Fuerstner, head of the Olympic village, killed himself when he was dismissed from military service because of his Jewish ancestry. Hitler pressed on with his plans for German expansion, which included taking over the Olympics and holding them in Germany forever.

15 How did Sachsenhausen fit with Nazi ideology?

The first concentration camps were set up in Germany in March 1933 after Hitler became Chancellor and his party was given control of the police. They were used to hold and torture political opponents and union organisers. Their role steadily expanded to hold 'undesirables' such as Jews, Roma/Sintis, Serbs, Soviet prisoners of war, Poles, disabled people, clergymen, Jehovah Witnesses, Freemasons, homosexuals and persons accused of asocial or deviant behaviour.

A camp in Oranienburg, twenty miles north of Berlin, was used mainly for the persecution of political opposition. It was cramped and too public because it was in the centre of the town and so in 1936 a new camp was constructed by prison labour in the forest around the parish of Sachsenhausen, a couple of miles to the north. The new camp set a standard in both its design and its treatment of inmates. The headquarters for all German concentration camps was transferred from Berlin to the site. Training grounds and barracks for *Schutzstaffel* (SS) officers were established opposite and here recruits

The main gate at Sachsenhausen in 2020

would pledge allegiance to the goals of the SS and its motto: 'My honour is my loyalty.' It was a cult of hardness and any recruit showing the slightest sign of sympathy towards prisoners was ousted.

The Sachsenhausen site covered 1000 acres. The machine gun placement above the main gate dominated with watchtowers on the perimeter. The entrance tower had an enormous central arch and forbidding metal gates with a welded steel sign spelling out *Arbeit macht frei* (work sets you free). The slogan appeared on the entrances of many Nazi concentration camps. The authorities believed that work allowed prisoners to discipline themselves and so enable them to withstand better the demoralising effects of their imprisonment. It seems not mockery but more a mystical declaration that self-sacrifice in the form of endless labour brings a spiritual freedom. The sign was seen by all prisoners, all of whom quickly learned that they would likely only be freed by death.

The radial layout of prisoner accommodation in a semicircle with a system of watchtowers ensured that there were no spaces in which prisoners could loiter unobserved, embodying the goal of total control. The perimeter consisted of a three-metre-high stone wall. Inside that was a space patrolled by guards and dogs bordered by a lethal electric fence and a gravel death strip that prisoners were forbidden to enter. There were few successful escapes. Any prisoner venturing onto the death strip would be shot without warning. It was at least an effective method of suicide. A survivor recalled:

> 'In their despair some of the Jews ran into [it] of their own accord and almost every day eight to ten Jews could be seen hanging lifelessly on the wire. Some in their despair simply let themselves be shot by the SS.'

Rewards such as extra leave were offered to guards who killed a prisoner in the death zone and they would sometimes force prisoners on to the strip at gun point so they could shoot them.

The parade ground had at its apex the gallows. Foiled escapees or those guilty of misdemeanours would be hanged in front of assembled prisoners. There was an execution trench in which resistance fighters, conscientious objectors and people sentenced to death by Nazi courts were shot. The Nazi's 'Final Solution' was three years from being formalised and so Sachsenhausen did not have gas chambers. There is a distinction between concentration camps and extermination camps, which were established for industrial-scale murder.

Around 30,000 persons were arrested in Germany following Kristallnacht and around 6000 of them were sent to Sachsenhausen. The camp did not have enough capacity, so a small camp was built to the side of the main semicircle for the incarceration of Jewish prisoners. The huts of the small camp had sleeping and living quarters at each end with the lavatories and washrooms in the middle. The huts were built to house 120 prisoners but up to 400 were crammed together. The three-tiered bunk beds were removed and prisoners had to sleep pressed together on the floor. The worst luck during the winter of 1938–39 was to require the toilet during the night. There would be no way of regaining your space in the huddle and you'd be condemned to shiver on the edge until morning.

The washroom comprised two central basins with cold water springing, like a fountain, from the middle. Prisoners were woken at 4.15am and had forty-five minutes to wash, make their quarters tidy and to collect and eat their breakfast, usually a piece of dry bread and lukewarm, ersatz coffee, before roll call at 5am sharp. Prisoners not on parade by this time were beaten. Guards would delight in tripping or otherwise delaying a few inmates and meting out punishment as a result. Competition for places to wash and use toilets was intense as each person only had a few minutes to do so. Prisoners were only allowed to use the toilets in the mornings and evenings and such was the rush that sick, weakened or older inmates were prone to fall and be trampled on the floor which was covered in excrement. There was no soap or toilet paper. Prisoners could lift lice off their bodies by the handful.

In 1940 the camp commandant Rudolf Höss, later to command Auschwitz, ordered prisoners to stand on parade for twenty-four hours in freezing weather. No movement was permitted and medical treatment was refused. Fingers and toes froze and had to be amputated. When a representative came forward to say that people were dying, Höss replied: 'They are not people, they are prisoners.'

Life in a camp that was so overcrowded was chaotic. The treatment of inmates was dependent on the whim of individual guards, who would apply rules arbitrarily or make up new rules on the spot. The only constant was brutality. The mental strain was increased by the Nazi policy of never stating the length of a sentence so that prisoners never had an end date to focus upon, only uncertainty about whether freedom would come tomorrow, next month or next year.

A key role for the camp was to perfect the most efficient execution method. At first prisoners were shown into a small room, with music playing to relax them, and told they were to be fitted for a uniform by having their height and weight measured. As they stood in front of the height measure and a little triangle of wood was slid down to the top of their head, they were shot in the back of the neck through a small sliding door. Over 10,000 were executed this way, mostly Soviet prisoners of war. However, this method was considered too time-consuming, so officers tried an execution trench, for shooting en masse. This created too much panic, making prisoners harder to control. So they started small-scale trials of gas chambers. These facilitated the means to kill the largest number of prisoners without excessive initial alarm and in September 1941 gas chambers were put into use at Auschwitz.

Detainees were put to work in an area outside the camp perimeter that contained a brickworks and workshops. Local industry took on platoons of slave labour for which they paid a paltry sum to the camp or to guards with whom they had an arrangement. Well known industrial concerns such as AEG and Siemens turned a blind eye to the treatment of this workforce even though the bruises, the thinness, the pallor, the shaved heads and the ragged clothing were giveaway signs that they were captives. Heinkel, the aircraft manufacturer used 6000–8000 Sachsenhausen prisoners on the production line for their bomber aircraft, some of which crashed around Stalingrad and it is suspected nowadays that prisoners had sabotaged them.

The working day was up to sixteen hours before an evening meal of gruel made from decaying vegetables. Competition was fierce to be in the middle of the food queue. Too early and you only got the thin soup. Too late and you risked everything having gone. In the middle you might get a scrap of actual vegetable. Bedtime was at 11pm before the next day repeated, seven days a week.

Punishments were varied. The 'Sachsenhausen salute' was where a prisoner had to squat for hours with his arms outstretched. Another punishment was to be assigned to the shoe walking unit. These prisoners were forced to spend their entire day walking along tracks that had nine types of surfaces to test the endurance of different military footwear. Each day they had to wear new shoes and march about twenty-five miles over a track of cement, cinders, broken stones, gravel or sand. A torture was to make prisoners walk in shoes one or two sizes too small while carrying heavy sacks. Prisoners of war were made to run up to twenty-five miles a day with backpacks to test the effectiveness of performance-enhancing drugs such as cocaine, as the Nazis endeavoured to increase their soldiers' stamina.

About 200,000 people passed through Sachsenhausen, mainly political prisoners. At least 30,000 died from overwork, disease, malnutrition or pneumonia, from execution or as a result of medical experimentation. Gold teeth were extracted from the corpses, which were then accumulated in a pile and incinerated.

With the advance of the Red Army in the spring of 1945, 33,000 inmates were evacuated on 21 April and taken on a death march that ended on 2 May, by which time only 18,000 survived, the rest having collapsed en route and been shot. On 22 April 3000 inmates who had been left behind were liberated by the Red Army.

After the Second World War, Sachsenhausen was in the Soviet occupation zone and used as a detention camp where the Soviet secret service also indulged in brutal treatment of inmates and summary executions until 1950. In the 1960s work was begun by the East German government to convert the site into a memorial of its victory over fascism. Since the reunification of Germany what is left of the camp has become an official memorial and museum with an emphasis on its historical context and displays to communicate what happened in the very place where it happened.

The last words go to two people who experienced Sachsenhausen:

'In the whole of someone's life it can never be worse than in a concentration camp. One no longer need fear death.'

'Hell is still a paradise compared to a concentration camp.'

16 Background and aftermath: Kristallnacht 9–10 November 1938

In June 1938, the Nazis arrested some 10,000 people they classified as 'averse to work and asocial' or otherwise undesirable and sent them to concentration camps, among them at least 1500 Jews. This was the first time that the Nazis had targeted a significant number of Jews for incarceration. In October 1938 around 18,000 Polish Jews were expelled from Germany, but when they arrived at the border Polish guards turned them back. They spent days without food or shelter. On the morning of Monday, 7 November a Polish Jewish teenager called Hershel Grynszpan shot a German diplomat at the German embassy in Paris. His parents had been expelled from Germany and he said this was an act of protest. Anti-Jewish riots broke out that same evening around Germany, news spreading by word of mouth and by telephone.

Hitler's doctor was flown to Paris to treat the patient, who conveniently died on 9 November and instantly became a martyr for the Nazi cause. Later that day the Nazi leadership gathered in Munich's old town hall to observe the anniversary of their failed coup in 1923. Minster of Propaganda Joseph Goebbels addressed the assembly, ordering that Jewish businesses and synagogues be destroyed in retaliation for the death. The police were not to interfere and the fire departments were to protect only Aryan property. Goebbels noted in his diary:

'I go to the party reception in the Old Town Hall. A gigantic event. I describe the situation to the Fuhrer. He decided: let the demonstrations continue. Withdraw the police. For once the Jews should feel the rage of the people... I issue corresponding instructions to the police and the party. Then I speak briefly to the officials of the party. A storm of applause. They all rush to the telephone. Now the people shall act!'

Nazi officials rushed off to disseminate orders by telephone. Their subordinates passed the instructions down the ranks to different Nazi auxiliaries throughout the land. The pogrom was both orchestrated and improvised with differences in intensity according to local factors. It reached all parts of the Reich, from cities to small towns and villages and as evening fell on 9 November 1938, Germany erupted into widespread violence. Many German and

Austrian citizens proceeded to terrorise their Jewish neighbours with a ferocity that few could have anticipated, sanctioned by the Nazi leadership.

Disciplined, equipped squadrons of men in civilian clothes set about destroying anything that was deemed Jewish. They burned and destroyed around 1400 synagogues. Rabbis were forced to desecrate the torah themselves, to tear it up and to dance on the remnants, while their precious books and relics were drenched in petrol and set alight. The fire brigades confined their activities to preventing fires from spreading until the synagogues were merely a heap of smouldering ruins and then they left, job done.

The mob invaded homes, brutalising thousands of men, women and children. Possessions were looted or strewn outside for people to trample. Pianos, ornaments, tables, sideboards and furnishings were taken into the street and smashed. Thousands of Jewish-owned businesses were vandalised with people gleefully helping themselves to whatever they could carry. After the areas were cleaned up, Jewish shops were sold to Aryans who ran them as if nothing had happened: there were no Jews left on the streets to protest.

The events of 9–10 November are known as Kristallnacht which means 'The night of the broken glass', reflecting the devastation left in its wake. Over 100 Jews were killed and an unknown number succumbed to injuries or died by suicide in the weeks and months following.

Various humiliations were heaped on the Jewish population after the night of violence, such as being forced to clean up on the basis that they were blamed for inciting the riots. Accounts relate old men and women on their knees in the streets surrounding the synagogues having to scrub the cobblestones with toothbrushes, to the jeers and laughter of spectators. Contingents of Nazis in their uniforms would turn up, occasionally booting the cleaners to make them work harder, which added to the crowd's entertainment. From 10–16

November, the police rounded up more than 30,000 Jewish men of all ages and backgrounds and deported them to concentration camps. Families had no idea where they had been taken. Some women were also arrested and there are reports of violence against them including sexual assault and rape, also of women being forced to dance and high-kick, naked.

This nationwide outburst towards Jews was unprecedented. There was almost no public opposition, although some individuals quietly helped their neighbours. The Nazis felt emboldened by the public support and intensified their persecution. They imposed a one billion Reichsmark fine, called 'The Atonement Levy', on the Jewish community to pay for damage and demanded the surrender of insurance payments, causing increased deprivation for Jews.

It had taken almost five years for the persecution of Jews to reach fever pitch. The pogrom was a landmark moment for Jews and made it clear that there was no place for them in Nazi Germany. Release from the camps was often conditional on a commitment to emigrate. Despite the desire to force Jews out, measures to prevent them from taking anything of value hindered attempts to leave. It was decreed that no one could take more than ten Marks with them, a pitiful sum. Nazis could be counted on to check if possessions were being 'smuggled' out of the country.

For the Nazis, Kristallnacht was justified as 'the rage of the people', claiming that the Jews had started events and the crowds were only defending themselves. Everyone knew this was the fake news of its day but Jews were expelled from schools, no longer entitled to welfare, had restricted access to public spaces and buildings and had driving licences confiscated. There had once been 50,000 Jewish companies in Germany but by 1938 only 9000 were left.

There was worldwide condemnation. For those who had backed Hitler's new Germany, it was a shocking revelation. It destroyed the argument for appeasement and showed that the Munich Agreement, signed only six weeks earlier, had been a sham. In Britain the Jewish community and Quaker organisations persuaded the Government to allow a visa waiver scheme for children and intensified efforts to help people escape with schemes such as the Domestic Service Visa. The British Government did not finance these efforts and they didn't change the rules – they simply allowed it to happen. Germans would place ads in newspapers advertising their services in return for someone to sponsor their exit. The employment pages of The Lady, a popular magazine among middle class women notable for its advertisements for domestic service and child care, had an increasing number of people applying for work in return for sponsorship of a passage to England. Doctors and lawyers were reduced to offering themselves as servants or gardeners. In total around 120,000 German Jews left Germany between Kristallnacht and the outbreak of the war, including almost 10,000 unaccompanied children on the Kindertransport.

In the UK and countries that comprised the Allied forces, 11 November commemorates the day the armistice was signed to end the First World War. It receives less attention in Germany because early November, by coincidence, marks several catastrophes that overshadow Germany history, such as the German revolution 9 November 1918, the Beer Hall Putsch 8–9 November 1923 and Kristallnacht 9–10 November 1938. More pleasingly, the fall of the Berlin Wall started on 9 November 1989.

17 Did Georg sail on the Saarland?

Ships were the main form of inter-continental transport in 1939, when Heathrow was still a small airfield. The Hamburg-America Line was one of the 'packet companies' criss-crossing the high seas. Its main routes were Hamburg to New York, via Southampton, and

to Philadelphia.
There were also
routes to the Far
East and Australia
via the Suez Canal.
Georg's boat
travelled from
Hamburg via
Bremen, Amsterdam
and Antwerp, where

SS Saarland

he seems to have embarked even though Hamburg or Bremen would
have been much more logical. The boat went through the Panama
Canal to the west coast of South America, where it made several
stops. The main business was cargo but there was accommodation
for forty-seven first class passengers.

The Steamship Guide of 1939 lists a departure from Antwerp on
21 February, arriving at Mollendo on 24 March but it gives the name
of the vessel as SS Amasis which conflicts with Georg's account. His
postcard from Antwerp is postmarked 23 February so there is little
doubt about the date of the sailing. He spent almost five weeks on
board and within a year of his voyage he had completed his journal.
It seems impossible to me that he would have been mistaken about
the name of his ship. Therefore I am inclined to accept what he says.

SS Saarland was launched in 1923 and worked ceaselessly until
September 1940, when she was sold to a Japanese shipping company
and put into service as the Teiyo Maru. She was confiscated by the
Japanese navy when Japan joined the war and used for troop
movements. On 2 March 1943 she was to the north of West Papua
when the convoy was attacked by US and Australian aircraft. The
Teiyo Maru sustained direct hits from four bombs and two
torpedoes, burst into flames and sank with the loss of 1918 lives.

18 What was the Kindertransport and how was it organised?

The Kindertransport (German for 'children's transport') was an organised rescue effort that took place during the nine months prior to the outbreak of the war. It was not widely known as the Kindertransport until the 1980s when efforts were made to recognise the feats that resulted in the escape of so many children and to record their experiences.

The rise of antisemitism had been signalled by the boycott of Jewish businesses in April 1933. World Jewish Relief (originally Central British Fund for German Jewry) was set up to support Jews in Germany and Austria and started campaigning for lenient treatment of those fleeing persecution and it pleaded for Jewish children who were being victimised to be admitted to Britain. The issue was not new when it intensified in 1938.

The Nazis were willing for Jews to leave Germany and Austria but countries around the world failed to solve the problem of where they might go. A conference was convened by President Roosevelt in July 1938, at Evian in France. He was hoping for commitment from the thirty-two invited nations to accept more Jewish refugees, and to deflect attention from American policy that limited the quota admitted to US. The conference failed to come to an agreement. The British delegation claimed that Britain was fully populated and suffering unemployment so it could not take refugees. There were plenty of pious platitudes but in the end, the world was unwilling to intervene or to help. Only the Dominican Republic volunteered to take more refugees. The remaining countries, having heard the extent of the crisis, departed with resolve to strengthen their border controls.

On 15 November 1938, five days after Kristallnacht, a delegation of British, Jewish and Quaker leaders appealed, in person, to Prime Minister Neville Chamberlain and Home Secretary Samuel Hoare to request that the Government permit the temporary admission of Jewish children. The Cabinet debated the issue on 21 November. Chamberlain wasn't keen but Lord Halifax, the Foreign Secretary, believed this positive action could help to bring the US on board as allies. He thought it politically advantageous after the embarrassment of Kristallnacht coming so soon after Chamberlain's blunders of the Munich Agreement. A bill stated that the Government would allow entry for unaccompanied children, from infants up to the age of 17, as long as there was no recourse to public funds. A special travel permit would be issued to eliminate the need for formal documents. No limit on numbers was announced. The Foreign Office confirmed arrangements in a circular dated 23 November 1938.

Permission was granted only to children aged up to 17. To assuage public concern, the Government stated its intention that the refugees were to be repatriated when they came of age. Despite knowing the scale of the problems and the numbers clamouring to leave, the Government refused to allow the parents of children to accompany them and were assured that parents were prepared to face the ordeal of parting for the sake of their children. It was optimistically expected that most children would return to their homeland within one to two years.

The agencies planned for up to 15,000 children to arrive, pledging to find homes for all of them. They promised to fund the operation and to ensure that none of the refugees would become a financial burden on the public. On 25 November, British citizens heard an appeal for donations and for foster homes on the BBC. There were 500 offers and Refugee Children's Movement (RCM) volunteers started visiting possible foster homes and reporting on conditions. They did not insist on Jewish homes for Jewish children. They did not probe the motives and character of the families, or if they were capable of caring for children. They simply checked that houses and families looked clean and respectable.

The RCM sent representatives to Germany and Austria to establish systems for choosing, organising and transporting children aided by Jewish organisations and the Quaker Society of Friends which provided much of the financial support, supplemented with funds raised by Jewish aid groups in Britain. Initially, no sponsor or guarantee was needed but from February 1939 each child needed a British sponsor to cover the costs of hosting them and a guarantee of £50 to finance his or her eventual re-emigration (equivalent to £3300 today). Many families trying to escape were penniless, meaning that those who were well-connected or had their own funds were more likely to find space on the transports. Families who did not have contacts in UK resorted to newspaper adverts to find a placement for their child. The RCM also advertised for families who were willing to take a refugee child or two and were prepared to stump up the guarantees. Adverts did not give people a lot to go on, for example: 'Two sisters brought up in a nice family. Will somebody give them a home?'.

Organisers worked around the clock to make lists of children most in peril: teenagers in concentration camps or in danger of arrest; children threatened with deportation; those in orphanages; those whose parents were too impoverished to keep them; those with a parent in a concentration camp. Children who were ill or had physical or mental disabilities or special needs were subjected to medical examinations and not likely to be selected, because of fears that they would be unable to find a family for them in UK or because they could become reliant on public funds for treatment. The British Government had indicated that they expected all children to be in good health, for fear of a burden of care on the state. Thus the fates of children were in the hands of many different agencies, voluntary organisations, foster families and sponsors. There are stories of the agony of some parents who could only choose one of their children for transport, and had to decide which

Female   PARTICULARS OF CHILD   **CH.** No. *K6f*

Full Name: *Kvansova Liza*

Address in Germany: *Pilsen (now) Jodermageroova 7/II C.S.R*

Date of Birth: *1. 4. 21*

Sex: *Female*

Nationality: *German (Czech)*

Religion: *Jewish.*

Correspondent in England

Full Name: *Mrs Boyle*

Address: *c/o New Light Attings Ltd 67 Banker St.*

Telephone: *or Mrs Wittkauer 25 Clarendon Rd Park 9318*

Fathers Profession and Circumstances: *Sudeten German now - Everything gone - Escaped to Pilsen - no future for girl.*

General description of situation under which child is living: *Girl knows 5 languages - Shorthand & typewriting - willing to do anything.*

Index card from Hampstead Garden Suburb Care Committee for Refugee Children. The notes suggest that skills were important as well when considering an application

to select – the cleverest, the fittest or the most vulnerable? There is no definitive account of the selection process or of the demographic composition of the children who travelled on the transports.

Parents had to send an application with a photo and a health certificate to Berlin with a signed agreement that their child could be placed in any home. A charitable Jewish group, *Reichsvertretung*, in Germany selected Jewish children from lists and non-Jewish children were selected by a Christian body, *Paulusbund*. The lists were then sent to the RCM in London which made travel arrangements after permits had been granted by the Home Office and passed by German police. Frequently parents learned only days before departure that their child or children had been offered a place and so families were separated with rushed goodbyes. Children could only take a small suitcase with no valuables and a maximum of ten Marks in money. The early days of the transports were frantic for the volunteers but they succeeded in extricating around 2000 children from Germany and Austria in the first four weeks of operation, including Dieter. It is little wonder that how it was organised for him remains opaque. Thousands of families applied for spaces on the transports but were unsuccessful. In the words of one: 'The children were thrown around by the tides of history.'

The German government said that evacuations must not block its ports, so most transport parties went by train to the Hook of Holland and on to a British port, generally Harwich. The first Kindertransport left Berlin on 1 December 1938, three weeks after Kristallnacht, and arrived in Harwich on 2 December with 196 children. Most were from a Berlin Jewish orphanage burned down during Kristallnacht, others from Hamburg. Dieter was probably on the second train from Berlin, which left, we think, on the morning of 14 December. The first train out of Vienna left on 10 December. Most of these children did not have prearranged foster families and went to temporary holding centres at summer holiday camps such as Dovercourt Bay and Pakefield in Suffolk. Later, when homes had mostly been arranged, trains took children straight to Liverpool Street Station and its reception centre set up in the staff gymnasium. This had a rope across it: children on one side, foster parents on the other. The name of each was called out and they met at the rope and walked off to start new lives together.

In nine months the UK took 9,354 unaccompanied children from Germany, Austria, Czechoslovakia and Poland. Three-quarters were Jewish, the remainder being of other religions, ethnicities or members of persecuted groups. The precise number is debated but it is agreed that the total is just under 10,000. The RCM ran out of money at the end of August 1939 and decided it could take no more children. A group left Germany on 1 September 1939, the day Germany invaded Poland. Two days later Britain, France and other countries declared war on Germany. The last party left Prague on 3 September 1939 but was sent back by the Germans.

The Kindertransport was an act of child rescue, and an act of family separation. The children went through extreme trauma in parting from parents. There are many accounts of tears and screaming at train stations. The government decree that the programme be privately funded and that the welfare of the children be overseen by non-governmental agencies was disastrous in many respects. These agencies were ill-equipped and the children lacked emotional support and guidance. Having to learn a new language and having to live with strangers who only spoke English was traumatic. At school, English children would often view them as enemies. One family reported having to remove the whistle from their kettle because it alarmed their refugee child, reminding him of police rounding up Jews.

The organisations and foster families expected that the children should be grateful for being rescued and that Britain should be regarded as heroic for its efforts. Hence *Kinder* were under pressure to present a favourable version of events and to regard themselves as fortunate. This denied their emotional hardship. It was thought that they should not be mollycoddled and most homes lacked the affection and warmth that these bewildered children so desperately needed – typical English reserve was not what they required.

There is evidence of casual discrimination in that many bright and able *Kinder* were denied opportunities. Several were refused entry to prestigious educational establishments despite clear abilities. They were directed to learn crafts and trades. One child, when asked what he wanted to be, said a doctor. A woman filling in a form said: 'I can't put that down. You must remember that you are a refugee.' A number went on to have successful careers after the war when freed from these shackles on their development.

It seems that the Government did not want concentrations of refugees in urban centres, in case of antisemitism being stirred up, so *Kinder* were scattered across the country. Their dispersal meant that they had no community, no camaraderie to provide comfort and support. This was at a time when fascism seemed to be on the rise. Oswald Mosley and his British Union of Fascists remained popular and his Britain First rally at Earls Court in July 1939 was the biggest indoor political rally in British history, with a reported 30,000 attendees.

In London there were ample Jewish families willing to accept children but a shortage of Jewish foster homes outside the capital. Some children had the added pressure of not being able to practise their faith, or of being indoctrinated in Christianity and were expected to suppress their true identities.

The treatment of the children in their new families varied from highly positive to surprisingly common physical and economic exploitation. Some adoptions were opportunistic, with foster parents seizing the luxury of having unpaid domestic help. Many of the girl refugees found themselves working as maids, housekeepers, cooks or nannies. In some cases there was discrimination such as having to eat separately from the family, or only being allowed margarine while the family enjoyed butter. One girl collected blackberries for her foster mother to make jam but was not allowed to taste it because it was for the family. Some foster families received weekly maintenance money and then relinquished responsibility for their charges when the war ended and the maintenance was discontinued. These children suffered a second trauma of abandonment.

Some children never recovered. Many survivors were unable to speak about their experiences for many years, if ever. Most of their parents were murdered by the Nazis and they knew they had become orphans only when the rest of the country was celebrating the end of the war. Many were the only members of their families who survived. Few of the children were left unscathed by their experiences amid tales of depression, mental illness or uncontrollable anger. For many, nothing could heal the wound of separation.

The agency attempted to keep track of all 9,354 children and their circumstances. Home visits occurred sporadically but interviews tended to be conducted with foster parents and child together, meaning that children could not express any hardships or abuse that they faced. The volunteers were keen to record how they were doing and to rejoice in successes. World Jewish Relief has thousands of case files for children who came with detail of the support given, from medical help to repairing shoes or providing cinema tickets, through to providing education, training and employment as well as religious education. Sadly, there are no records of Dieter. Many files from the aid committees were lost in the tumult of moves and evacuations whilst London was being bombed. The case files of the Refugee Children's Movement are embargoed until 2051.

Many *Kinder* went on to serve in the British armed forces, and their language skills were put to good use during the D-Day Invasion and as the Allies progressed into Germany. Several thousand remained in Britain when the war ended and there was no attempt to return refugees to their countries of origin, as had been planned. The Government recognised that it would be cruel to compel Jews to return to the scene of such unimaginable crime. Two-thirds of Europe's Jewish population was murdered in the Holocaust.

Many *Kinder* founded their own families in Britain and as adults made considerable contributions to Britain's services, industries, commerce, education, science and the arts, for the defence, welfare and development of their country of adoption. Four of the escaping children went on to become Nobel prize winners, one for every 2500 of them, far ahead of normal expectations.

As a footnote on Dieter's journey to England, it is curious that Georg and Dieter do not agree on the departure station. Georg writes that the train left in the morning from Schlesischer station and I'd expect his memory to be clear given that his account was written not much more than a year later. Dieter was adamant that his departure station was Friedrichstrasse and led his family there for a nostalgic visit in the 1980s. Schlesischer station is unlikely because it was the station that served Silesia to the south-east and long-distance destinations in east and south-east Europe (now called Berlin Ostbahnhof). My guess is that they are both right and that refugees were boarded at a feeder station and were already in place by the time the train pulled into Friedrichstrasse for its scheduled departure. Records from Berlin were lost in the war and there is much else we don't know. What was the date of departure? Was it in the morning as Georg states or evening as Dieter recalls, and which was most common for Kindertransport trains? How many days and nights did the journey take? Did Dieter's train cross the border at Emmerich (most common) or at Bentheim, which was also used? Why did Georg and Dieter go all the way to Berlin if the train stopped at Hannover and almost certainly at Hamburg? I guess that it was to be certain that Dieter would be able to take his precious place on the transport.

19 Why did the children go to Dovercourt Bay?

In January 1937 forty acres of land between Low Road and the sea shore were leased by Harwich Council to the Dovercourt Bay Holiday Camp & Lido, run by Mr Butlin and Capt. Warner. The site soon became Warner's Holiday Camp. There was accommodation for 1500 guests and facilities included a dining room, bars, ballroom, swimming pool, putting green, tennis courts and a boating lake. The location was attractive, on the cliffs facing the North Sea with a view of Dovercourt Bay. Publicity from the era describes a fashionable and delightful seaside resort, going on to say, somewhat optimistically, that the views could be compared to those of the bay of Naples.

The camp had only been open for one season when it was taken over by the Refugee Children's Movement as short-term accommodation for refugee children. Anna Essinger was asked to manage the reception camp, a German Jewish educator who had been influenced by the Quakers. She had founded a school in Germany only to be forced by the Nazi threat to move it and its sixty-six children, who were mostly Jewish, to England where she set up Bunce Court School in Kent. Essinger, who was nearly 60 years old, worked with three teachers, her cook and six of her older pupils to establish the camp. They found it difficult to find teachers and helpers who could meet the challenges and needs of refugee children.

She met the transports with her first objective to instil calm and confidence that people would now be kind in hundreds of homesick and anxious children. A good first meal eased their concerns, as did settling them in their sleeping quarters. British committees sought placements for the children by inviting prospective foster parents to Dovercourt. This appalled Essinger, who likened it to a cattle market, where attractive children were chosen and less attractive ones were not. The experience of running the reception camp and placing the children was so difficult that Essinger refused to talk about it afterwards.

A report on a visit by N. de Selincourt of the Women's Voluntary Services, dated 12 January 1939, praises the staff and helpers: 'The camp leaders are very keen, full of human kindness, vitality and emanating a cheerful atmosphere. Great efforts are made to stress the future hopes of the children and so help them to forget the past. They seem wonderfully happy, considering all they had been through.' However, it would seem that the report put a gloss on arrangements with no mention of the extreme cold. And no mention of the scandal when some of the boys allegedly discovered Harwich's red-light district. I think we can assume Dieter was not in the party at the tender age of 12.

The camp was used to greet the first three transports, after which it was realised that it was completely unsuitable in such harsh conditions. After the cold snap eased it welcomed further refugees until March 1939 when it was transformed into a military base before being used as a prisoner of war camp. Once the war was over, the camp resumed welcoming holidaymakers. At its peak the camp entertained 11,000 visitors a year. Dovercourt Bay's last season was 1990 by which time the popularity of holiday camps had dwindled. Eventually it was demolished and replaced by a housing estate, called Hightrees. Before this, the camp was used for scenes in the popular BBC situation comedy Hi-de-Hi. The cast even had the joy of staying on site.

20 What was the Domestic Service Visa?

Between 1933 and 1939, around 20,000 Jewish, non-Aryan or politically active refugee women from Germany, Austria and Czechoslovakia fled to Britain by getting jobs as domestic servants. They accounted for a third of all refugees to enter Britain before the war, twice the number of children who arrived on the Kindertransport. The conditions for receiving a domestic permit were formulated to control the numbers of applicants: women had to be single, divorced or widowed and between 18 and 45. Married women were only accepted if the husband was already in the UK and married couples were allowed entry only if both were employed in domestic service – single men were excluded. Elli must have been granted her visa as an exception because her children were already in England and she had her job confirmed through a schoolfriend of her daughter.

At first, women were only accepted if they had a job arranged. A British family had to show that they had advertised locally for a maid and been unsuccessful. Then the job could be offered abroad and the vacancy matched to an applicant, who had three months to organise their exit visa. There were rudimentary tests to ensure applicants were fit for domestic work and sometimes an inspection to ensure an aptitude for maintaining a clean and respectable home. A medical certificate would be issued, assuring Britain that the applicant was capable. Most of those who arrived were under 30 and many tried to get their mothers accepted too but were often unsuccessful due to age or doubts about suitability for domestic work.

The first arrivals were mainly Austrian, after the Anschluss, and then Kristallnacht precipitated an influx of German refugees. As events unfolded rapidly the requirements had to be relaxed and the organising committee, mostly women in the British voluntary sector supported by the Jewish Refugee Committee, arranged for 400 visas a month to be sent to Germany for distribution to applicants with or without jobs arranged. The holder of a visa had a priceless ticket to evade the calamity caused by the Nazis.

Britain was not entirely altruistic. It was an opportunistic response to a shortage of servants that the scheme conveniently helped to address. The burgeoning middle class wanted to assert their status by employing servants just as working-class women were increasingly rejecting domestic labour because the work was underpaid and exploitative. Managing a household in 1930s Britain was arduous. In contrast to Germany, modern conveniences such as central heating were rare, meaning that even in modest homes coal fires had to be cleaned and relit each day. Families that now had indoor toilets still used chamber pots at night and these had to be emptied and cleaned. Washing up was done by hand and there was an endless round of scrubbing, polishing and cleaning. The British middle class believed it appropriate for a servant to spend large amounts of time on their hands and knees to perform the daily drudgery, rather than use new-fangled devices such as mops. It kept them in their place. The middle class wanted things to be done as they always were and liked to show off their servants as status symbols and as examples of their benevolence.

A pamphlet called 'Mistress and Maid' was issued to those coming over on a Domestic Service Visa. It encouraged new servants to 'adapt yourself as quickly as possible to your new surroundings'. It carried a warning to be alert to the cultural nuances of the English: 'You will notice that the mistress usually states her requirements in the form of a request but this should be carried out at once as an order.' It contains the line: 'English houses are often colder than continental ones and you must expect to guard against the cold by wearing thick underclothes and woollen indoor coats.' The advice would have been little comfort to women far from home, doing jobs that made them unhappy and dealing with unsympathetic, emotionally frigid people. But becoming a servant did save lives.

Many women who had previously employed servants in their own households now found themselves cooking, cleaning, making beds and scrubbing floors for the first time in their lives. They were discouraged from speaking German and expected to assimilate into English culture at the expense of their personal identity. People thought that their maids should be grateful. A great many of the domestics were more educated than the people they had to serve. And they were much more aware of events in Europe. As one said:

'I had to work from 8am to 11pm with an hour's break, cleaning and scrubbing and looking after the house, with half a day off a week. After a few weeks I complained, saying it's too hard. The lady of the house said, "If it's too much for you, I'll send you back to Hitler." '

Some of the women were well treated by the families they served, but most were underpaid, sometimes maltreated and subjected to undeserved class discrimination or antisemitism. They were excluded from family life and expected to eat and live separately. There was scant understanding of what they had gone through. There were no allowances made for mothers who wanted to have their children close to them. Even the agencies are reported to have told hysterical mothers who could not see their children that they had nothing to complain about. The loneliness could be paralysing, they had no one with whom to share their unhappiness and humiliation. The emphasis was on conformity, as stated in the 'Mistress and Maid' pamphlet which said: 'In this country it is good manners to speak and walk quietly, both in the house and in the street and public places.' They were expected to bottle up their feelings and carry on.

When war was declared on 1 September 1939, Britain no longer allowed immigration from Nazi-controlled countries. A great many maids lost their jobs as homes were closed down, especially in coastal areas (from which aliens were excluded) and in cities such as London. Most domestic servants had left their jobs by 1941 and thus they found other work or joined the war effort in whatever capacity they could.

There has subsequently been a veil of silence over their experiences, especially compared to the large number of stories of the Kindertransport. This speaks to the marginalisation of these women and the trauma of separation they struggled to come to terms with for the rest of their lives.

21 What was The Battle of the Bulge?

The Battle of the Bulge in the Ardennes was the last major German offensive on the Western Front, the name coined by the contemporary press to describe the bulge in German frontlines on wartime news maps. It started on 16 December 1944 and was intended to stop the Allies' use of the port of Antwerp and to split the Allied lines, allowing the Germans to encircle and destroy several Allied armies. The plan and timing for the attack sprang from Hitler, against the advice of his generals. He believed a critical fault line existed between British and American military commands, and that a heavy blow on the Western Front would shatter their alliance. Planning for *Unternehmen Wacht am Rhein* (Operation Watch on the Rhine) emphasised the commitment of overwhelming force.

The offensive was planned with utmost secrecy, with minimal radio traffic and all movements of troops and equipment carried out under cover of darkness, rendering the Allies virtually blind to German troop movements. Foggy weather prevented reconnaissance aircraft from assessing the ground situation. German units were even issued with charcoal instead of wood for cooking fires to cut down on smoke and reduce chances of Allied observers deducing a build-up of troops. Orders were conveyed using landline communications and motorised runners. During the liberation of France, the resistance had provided intelligence but it did not operate beyond the French border. Previously radio messages relayed within the German army had been decrypted by codebreakers at Bletchley Park and German radio silence had not been foreseen.

Hence the German attack achieved complete surprise due to a lack of intelligence. It involved around 450,000 troops and 1500 tanks and assault guns. The battle severely depleted German forces and the Allies managed to block access to key roads so that the Germans were largely unable to replace them. This, along with forbidding terrain that favoured the defenders, delayed the German advance and allowed the Allies to mobilise reinforcements. Improved weather conditions allowed air attacks on German forces and supply lines that defeated the offensive by 25 January 1945.

American forces bore the brunt, suffering 89,000 casualties of which 19,000 were killed, out of a peak deployment of 610,000 troops. Up to 98,000 German men were killed, wounded or captured. The battle was the largest and bloodiest fought by the US in the war and the second deadliest in US history.

22 What was the Austrian Centre?

The Austrian Centre was established in March 1939 by Austrians who had arrived in London seeking refuge. By the outbreak of the war 30,000 had reached Britain. Its mission was to promote the welfare of refugees and to offer advice and support towards their settlement in the UK. Its first President was Sigmund Freud. Headquarters were at 124–126 Westbourne Terrace and there were branches across Britain. It developed into a comprehensive organisation that offered support and practical help to refugees trying to overcome their sense of loss and hardship and organised social, political and cultural activities. The Centre's restaurant offered Austrian specialities such as *Fridattensuppe* (broth with sliced pancake), *Faschiertes mit Spinat* (minced meat with spinach) and *Polsterzipf* (sweet pastries), all of which pleased Dieter. It worked for the re-establishment of an independent, democratic Austrian state and

The Lantern

Das Laterndl

Wiener Kleinkunstbuehne in London

124/126, WESTBOURNE TERRACE,
:: W.2. ::

The programme for 'Vienna Cabaret in London'

endeavoured to gain British support for the cause. There was a faction that had a socialist, almost communist, agenda.

Its theatre was Das Laterndl, founded by refugees who wanted to keep alive the traditions of Austrian cabaret, drama and literature, in particular of *Wiener Kleinekunstbühne* which were small theatres producing inexpensive shows that concentrated on wit, topical satire and had a progressive outlook. The founders saw Das Laterndl as preserving one of the characteristic forms of Austrian culture and intellectual life, as well as a way of relieving exiles' homesickness. The shows were mainly political, satirical and socially critical. The name denoted a beacon of hope for the future.

The actors had limited space in which to perform and the auditorium held seventy seats. The first production in June 1939 was a revue of nine short sketches that performed to full houses almost sixty times between June and August. The theatre received praise in reviews in leading British newspapers and attracted prominent patrons and supporters, such as authors HG Wells and JB Priestley.

Activities were curtailed by the outbreak of war in September, when theatres and places of public entertainment were forced to close. The rules were relaxed when the danger of bombing raids receded and in January 1940 Das Laterndl reopened in larger premises at 153 Finchley Road. One sketch spread fame for Martin Miller (born Rudolph Muller) whose spoof Hitler speech on April Fools' Day 1940, in which Hitler claimed that Columbus had discovered America with the aid of German science thus giving Germany territorial claim, led to an invitation to broadcast on BBC radio. It was the start of a notable acting career for him.

From mid-1940 the company faced the problem of internment of enemy aliens. One production saw the principal role played by three different actors, as the first two were interned. It became too difficult to continue, and Das Laterndl closed for fifteen months.

It reopened at the house of a supporter at 69 Eton Avenue in November 1941 until closing for good in 1947. It had been founded as an assertion of Austrian cultural identity and with the re-establishment of the country, its raison d'être had disappeared.

23 Who was Otto Tausig?

Otto Tausig was born in Vienna in 1922, the only child of parents whose lives had been disrupted by antisemitic activity. His father was a lawyer who had been reduced to working in the wood trade and his mother was an author who found herself having to run a sausage stall. When German troops marched into Austria in March 1938, the situation for Jewish citizens became even more threatening. At the age of 16, Otto fled to the UK after his mother answered an advertisement for factory workers which had been posted in The Times. In Britain he worked in odd jobs before being held in a detention centre on the Isle of Man as an enemy alien for twenty months before becoming a factory worker. His parents managed to escape to Shanghai in April 1939. His father died in Shanghai but his mother returned to Austria in 1947 to see her son for the first time in nine years.

After the war, Otto returned to Vienna and studied at the prestigious Max Reinhardt Seminar, a school of drama. He worked at the Vienna New Theatre in the Scala until its closure in 1956. He worked from 1957 in east Berlin, including with the Berliner Ensemble founded by Bertolt Brecht. He refused a well-paid individual contract and requested a standard contract without privileges and benefits. After this followed engagements in Zurich, Vienna, Cologne, Hamburg, Frankfurt and Munich, mainly as a freelance director. He was a theatre and film actor, usually appearing in German language films but also in English and French films. He wrote and directed several German television films and became a professor at the Max Reinhardt Seminar.

Otto Tausig is remembered as 'One of the most outstanding actors in Austria who understood how to captivate the audience with his voice.' He saw his life as an assignment to help people for whom escape was the only way to survive, was politically active and understood art as a means of changing the world. He founded an Amnesty International group in support of politically persecuted actors and artists. When filming in Bombay (now Mumbai), he became aware of poverty and donated his fees to support exploited and abducted children. He financed a 'theatre hotel' to support Indian quarry children, as well as a home in Austria to care for young refugees. His motto was: 'Do not complain, just do something.'

He was renowned for having a little dog that he idolised. The dog sat in its basket backstage when he was performing and would know from the applause when to get up and wait for its master as he came off stage.

Otto had one son born in 1950. He divorced Johanna Pick in 1953 and married Lilly Schmuck. He died in Vienna in 2011. A square in Vienna has been named after him and he is remembered by an honorary grave in the central cemetery.

24 Who was Helen Clare?

Helen Clare was born in 1916 in Bradford as Helen Harrison. She was an actress and singer who became a household name through her BBC broadcasts, recordings and live tours. Helen's earliest memories were of Australia, where the family went to live when she was four. Young Helen had a gift for singing that led to her touring Australian theatres and concert halls, billed as Little Nellie Harrison – Child Wonder.

The family returned to Yorkshire following the Wall Street crash. After her debut with her brother Tom's dance band in Bradford, she began getting bookings all over the north of England, keeping her busy from as early as 1933. In 1936 she joined one of the UK's leading bands, Jack Jackson & his Orchestra, at the Dorchester Hotel in London, singing the hits of the day. Hundreds of BBC broadcasts

Helen Clare

and commercial radio performances followed, plus some early television. After war was declared the BBC asked her to relocate to Bristol. The idea that Bristol would be safer was shattered by horrific air raids and when the BBC Variety department was bombed out she moved with it to Bangor in North Wales.

Helen became a freelance singer in 1941 and toured variety theatres up and down the country. She worked with the stars of the period including her friend Vera Lynn and they became 'forces' sweethearts', giving concerts at army bases, aerodromes, naval stations and factories. The BBC still included Helen in an array of programmes including 'Calling Forces Gibraltar' in which Helen sang requests and 'It's All Yours' in which servicemen would ask to hear their children on air. One day a little girl came into the studio to send a message to her uncle serving in North Africa. The broadcast was delayed by an air raid. The producer requested that someone perform, to settle the jittery audience. The girl volunteered, receiving an enthusiastic response. It was the first radio broadcast for 9-year-old Petula Clark.

While travelling back from a troop concert on an overnight train, the train lurched and Helen was thrown against the basin mirror, breaking her nose. She had to do an edition of 'It's All Yours' live from London Zoo the next day. The doctor advised her to keep her nose safe but she sat on a camel with a child under her arm and a microphone in her other hand. These location broadcasts were pioneering and linked children with relatives in the forces all over the world. Her voice offered comfort, hope and distraction.

After the war, radio and television broadcasts kept her in the limelight. She married the renowned violist Frederick Riddle and they had a daughter called Elizabeth who inherited her mother's voice. After leaving broadcasting and the concert platform Helen gave singing lessons and appeared with the Wallington Operatic Society until the age of 90. In November 2016 Helen celebrated her hundredth birthday and was invited back to the Dorchester Hotel. She was at Alexandra Palace, the location of her early television broadcasts, to mark eighty years of BBC Television. A highlight was being reunited with Petula Clark on the BBC One Show. In 2018 Helen released an album of her best recordings shortly before her death aged 101.

25 What was the Tavistock Repertory Company and what was Peter's involvement?

The company was founded in 1932 at the Tavistock Little Theatre in Tavistock Square, Bloomsbury (nothing to do with the town of Tavistock in Devon). In 1952, it moved to Canonbury Tower in Islington which included the 156-seat Tower Theatre. The company remains active, staging as many as twenty productions a year.

Although non-professional, a host of well-known actors appeared early in their careers, notably Alec Clunes, Tom Courtenay and Michael Gambon. Richard Baker, who for many years was President of The Friends of the Tower Theatre, was a prominent actor and newsreader and appeared in productions with my father, which explains why my father was able to call on his help when seeking publicity and funding for the building of the Secombe Theatre in Sutton in 1983.

Dieter, using the name Peter Harlow, started working with the Tavistock in October 1947 as a member of the background cast and stayed involved until October 1951, by which time he was married. The company archive lists him as working on twenty-one productions. He was clearly enthusiastic, despite the long commute from Sutton.

Here is a list of his contributions:

Acting roles:
October 1947: Beggar on Horseback: character in the dream
May 1948: Misalliance: Bentley Summerhays
June 1948: Lysistrata: Strymodorus
May 1949: Androcles and the Lion: call boy (and assistant electrician)
June 1949: Macbeth: a servant (and lighting)
November 1949: Volpone or The Fox: Nano
May 1950: The Taming of the Shrew: Grumio
June 1950: Struts and Frets: unspecified
October 1950: A Merry Death: Pierrot
January 1951: The Drunkard or The Fallen Saved: second loafer

A summary of some of Dieter's more notable parts:

Misalliance by GB Shaw is an inventive comedy about class and feminism and the mating instincts of a varied group of people gathered at a wealthy man's country home on a summer weekend. Romantic interest centres on the host's daughter, Hypatia Tarleton, who is engaged to Bentley Summerhays, an intellectually bright but physically and emotionally underdeveloped aristocrat. It is a substantial part. By the end of the day, eight marriages have been proposed. But which are the misalliances?

Volpone (Italian for sly fox) is a comedy by Ben Jonson first produced in 1606, drawing on elements of fable. A satire of greed and lust, it is ranked among the finest comedies of the Jacobean era. Nano is a dwarf who is a companion of Volpone. The review said that 'Peter Harlow's miming, mumbling dwarf provided laughs', which can be imagined from the photo.

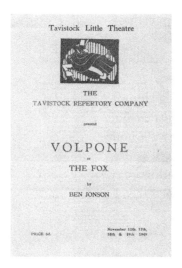

As Nano, 1949

As Grumio, under the table, 1950

The Taming of the Shrew by Shakespeare depicts the courtship of
Petruchio and Katherina, the headstrong, obdurate shrew.
Initially, Katherina is an unwilling participant in the relationship;
however, Petruchio 'tames' her with various psychological
torments, such as keeping her from eating and drinking, until she
becomes a compliant bride. The subplot features a competition
between the suitors of Katherina's younger sister, Bianca, who is
seen as the ideal woman. Grumio is Petruchio's old servant and a
comic figure. He tends to misinterpret his master's speeches and
commands in literal and ridiculous ways, requiring an actor with
comic and rhetorical skills. A cutting of the first night review
praises the production as compact, always enjoyable, bold and
with obvious zest. Peter Harlow is mentioned as 'bringing his own
mercurial qualities to the part'. This play, which my father later
directed at Polesden Lacey, featured in the cast Leon Eagles, who
became a good friend and, nearly, Peter's best man.

A Merry Death by Nikolai Evreinov has been described as one of the finest plays in the Russian canon. Its comic effect is reinforced by a stylistic mix, including Russian folk drama. It is a short, punchy, comic play and Pierrot is a major part. Leon Eagles directed.

The Drunkard or, The Fallen Saved by WH Smith (not that one) is an American play first performed in 1844. It was extremely popular in the US and led to the beginning of the Temperance Movement's success. The plot follows Edward Middleton, a fine upstanding citizen, who has inherited a large estate. A lawyer has a plan to destroy Edward and take all of his money. Knowing that Edward enjoys an occasional drink, he organises a long night at the bar, turns him into a mad drunk and gets him to sign away his fortune. The family lives in destitution until a recovered alcoholic takes Edward into rehab. Eventually the family is reunited, Edward is sober, the lawyer is arrested and there is a happy, wholesome ending. Dieter's role as second loafer was minor.

As second loafer, centre of the front group, 1951

As the electrician:

November 1947: Music at Night (one of two)
November, December 1947: The Doctor's Dilemma (one of two)
February 1948: The Sacred Flame
April 1948: Our Town
June 1948: Juno and the Paycock
March 1950: Heartbreak House (with Fay Foley on sound effects)
November 1950: Awake and Sing
May 1951: Much Ado About Nothing (with assistant)
October, November 1951: The Way of the World (with assistant)

In charge of lighting:

November 1948: Six Characters in Search of an Author
January 1950: Love for Love

APPENDIX 1

What were my mother's background, upbringing and wartime experiences?

My mother's father was Wilfrid Arthur Foley, born 14 January 1898 in Brixton into a family of glass makers that hailed from Stourbridge. It's believed the family came from Ireland before that. Wilfrid's father came to London and started a business importing materials used in glass making and later opened a factory making glass lampshades. Wilfrid was the ninth child of ten and the seventh boy. Five of the children died in infancy and two brothers were killed in the First World War, such that by 1918, only Wilfrid, his brother Bert and sister May were left alive. My mother, Mavis, knew only his eldest brother, known as Old Uncle Bert because he was twenty-one years older than Wilfrid. His mother, Mavis's grandmother, was 46 when she had Wilfrid and after nine children, she asked Old Uncle Bert, who had recently married, to bring him up so Wilfrid lived with him and his new wife in Catford for his first years. He spent part of his childhood in Eltham, which at that time was a country village, and then came back to the main family home at 24 Vassall Road in Brixton. At the time, Brixton was a desirable area and they had a large house with a live-in maid, as well-to-do people did before the First World War.

Wilfrid's mother was strict and rather volatile. She always carried a stick with her and whacked the children with it if they misbehaved.

Old Uncle Bert was also prone to lose his temper with those around him, including various innocent people such as bus conductors. But despite these two role models, Wilfrid was placid thanks to the influence of his father, who was a band master in the Salvation Army. Wilfrid and his brothers had to learn a brass instrument and join the band. The family was devoted to the Salvation Army, which meant that they were teetotal. Wilfrid's father was a kind and charming man who gave away a lot of his money.

War broke out in August 1914. Everyone was full of patriotic fervour and thought the war would be over by Christmas. In this atmosphere, Wilfrid and his cousin George Trevena lied about their ages to join the army at 16. Wilfrid never talked about what happened next. We know he went into the cavalry and that he saw his best friend killed right next to him and that his own horse was killed in the same incident which led to him having to stay in hospital for a while. Following this he went to fight in Italy and his unit was stranded on a mountainside on the Austrian border and Wilfrid got frostbite in one foot, which never properly recovered. He was in hospital when the armistice was signed and came out in 1919. We can only guess at the emotional trauma he had to overcome.

Wilfrid the boy soldier 1914

Wilfrid had had ambition to become an architect but the war put paid to that. After the war, there were few jobs for the men who had been fighting. He was fortunate to land a job with Rowntree in York, one of the premier manufacturers of sweets and chocolate, and a firm that had a reputation for looking after its employees. He started as a commercial traveller (nowadays called a sales rep) and rose up the ladder to become an Area Sales Manager. One of his claims to fame was a role in the launch of a confectionery brand called Black Magic. The company was robustly advised by market research (he gleefully told me) that the name would never be accepted by the public. That advice was ignored and the brand is still going strong today.

Mavis's mother Doris Ethel Kings was born 3 March 1900, younger sister to Frank and Arthur and older sister to Winnie, Leslie and Vera, the siblings' births spread across fifteen years. Their father was an administrator for the Post Office. They lived in Fordell Road, Catford, in a new house, one of many built in a frenzy of housebuilding, where she stayed for twenty-four years until she married. Every Sunday after church their father led them on a walk to a nearby farm where they fetched milk, as Catford was on the edge of London. Grandma's family were Methodists, which meant a teetotal, puritan outlook and a strict upbringing. On Sundays they weren't allowed to read anything except bible studies and they had to go to church four times. She went to a good school, Haberdashers' Aske's, and won several prizes such as schoolbooks. She trained as a secretary and typist and did well, becoming secretary to the chairman of Eagle Star Insurance. It was a good job but when she married she stopped working, as was the custom.

Doris 1922

Doris and Wilfrid met at a dance at Hither Green Football Club where Wilfrid played at centre-half for the team. She stood out to him with her striking flame-red hair. They were married shortly afterwards in Catford on 12 April 1924. Mavis was born on 13 November 1927 at what was probably a cottage hospital called Millbrook, in Sumner Road, Harrow. Doris used to stress it was North Harrow, which was better than South Harrow. She was called

Mavis because Doris had read that the name's meaning was a song thrush. Mavis's brother Alan arrived almost two years later.

Wilfrid's work for Rowntree meant that the family had a car before that was commonplace. During the days he was calling on sweet shops with orders and

Wilfrid and Doris, wedding 1924

samples and in the evenings he was busy with his paperwork. He stopped playing golf and didn't pursue his painting because it was a solitary hobby, despite being a talented artist, in order to be with his family. Doris was devoted to her children and was close to her sisters Winnie and Vera and at various times each of the sisters lived with her and her family. Her brothers, Arthur and Leslie, were more independent but they were all in close contact.

Arthur had fought in the war and never recovered. He suffered from what was known as shellshock but that covers a multitude of possibilities. The story was that he had been involved in fighting and had passed out or been knocked unconscious and was thrown into a hall set aside to store the heap of dead bodies. He came round, managed to alert someone and was hauled out. Not surprisingly, it affected him for life. Despite his horrific ordeal, Doris and Wilfrid were dismissive and thought Arthur, Doris's own brother, was an idler. It was an attitude encouraged by the older generation who believed shellshock was emotional weakness and that you shouldn't think or talk about what had happened, you should get on with life. After the war, Arthur was only capable of a routine, menial job and held a minor post in the Home Office, receiving a disability pension for the rest of his life. He was a rather unstable personality although mostly charming. He married but never had children of his own and enjoyed games with us boys when we were young. Later in life he practised as a faith healer.

Wilfrid had to move often with his work. At first Mavis lived at Donnybrook, 2 Northumberland Road, Pinner and from age 2 at 17 Woodberry Avenue, Harrow. After six years there, the family moved to 122 Shepherds Lane, Dartford where they stayed for three years. Mavis recalls this was on a corner with the busy A2 and when it was icy, she looked out of the window and watched lorries falling over. The next move was to 52 Princes Avenue in Petts Wood and in 1941 the family moved to the house that backed on to theirs and they were able to move some of their belongings over the shared garden fence at the rear. It was a step up for them, being detached and having four bedrooms and two reception rooms and what were known as mod cons (modern conveniences). This was 12 Greencourt Road where Wilfrid worked hard to create an attractive garden for the family.

The family didn't talk much and Doris could be demanding, perhaps a little depressive. She rarely gave the impression of being happy and wasn't affectionate. Mavis remembers a friend who said she would sit on her mummy's lap in the evenings and have a cuddle. Mavis was incredulous because it never happened in their house. Wilfrid was kind but remote and did not show his emotions, perhaps because he had been deprived of cuddles when he was a child. Doris and Wilfrid were constrained by belonging to a generation that didn't speak about feelings or show affection, and by their own upbringings. Doris used to say to Mavis 'You keep yourself to yourself' or 'Little girls should be seen and not heard.' Despite the slightly repressive atmosphere, Doris and Wilfrid were dedicated to their children, to the extent it became a little suffocating in later years when they wanted to know what time Mavis and Alan came in, who they'd spoken to and so on. Holidays were unambitious although typical of the age. The family would drive year after year to Sandown on the Isle of Wight where they stayed in a boarding house, which Mavis found rather monotonous as she grew older. They had a sort of tent that they erected on the beach which was

Alan and Mavis, September 1936

handy when it rained. The British summers meant that the tent got used a lot.

Mavis and Alan played together when young although Mavis could act the big sister at times, ticking him off because she wanted things done properly and he was more careless. Alan didn't like that. They received 3d a week pocket money which was spent on sweets, such as ha'penny chews, aniseed balls, gobstoppers and mint lumps. In return they were expected to help out around the house by making beds, washing up and laying the table. Mavis played with her dolls, enjoyed jigsaw puzzles and liked reading and was a frequent visitor to the library. She loved to learn about Shirley Temple, the child film actress, and to let her imagination run. She liked the freedom of cycling which was enjoyable as the roads were relatively free of traffic. She swam with friends in the outdoor pools dotted around London. She was disposed to please and sensitive to being told off, unlike Alan, who was boisterous and always getting into scrapes such as shooting people with airguns or whatever was the latest fad. As he got older, Alan became preoccupied with sport, which did not interest his sister, who preferred reading and cycling. They went most weekends to 59 Tivoli Crescent in Brighton to visit their mother's parents. Christmas was a family occasion and they played games, several involving dressing up.

Mavis's first school memory was a dame school in Harrow. These were private elementary schools usually taught by women and often in their home. Mavis and ten or twelve fellow pupils sat round a big kitchen table. They learned to read and write and sang by the piano. She was sick one day and the teacher wheeled her home on her bicycle. Both children then attended a primary school in Dartford, which Mavis enjoyed, apart from when she was called upon by the head teacher to explain Alan's misbehaviour. After Crofton primary school in Petts Wood, Mavis won a scholarship to Bromley County Grammar School and started there in 1938. As a reward for doing well she received her first full-sized bicycle, at the amazing cost of 26 shillings (£2.10p today). She cycled along empty lanes through the countryside which in wartime was largely deserted. She kept that bicycle until 1960. She was never in trouble at school and did all her studies dutifully. Mavis helped her mother with preparing meals and doing the shopping, which involved trekking to the shops with the ration books.

War broke out just before she started her second year. School was suspended at first and on Saturday mornings they went in to collect a week's work to do at home. After a while, tunnels were dug under the netball courts as air raid shelters and some above-ground brick shelters were built so that they could go back to school. As soon as the sirens sounded, they dashed into the shelters where lessons continued as best they could, although they were hampered by some teachers being called up. Mavis and her best friend Pat Ellacott cycled to school because it gave them independence, even though the journey was easy by train. They both loved reading and went to the library most days to read a whole book as there wasn't a great deal else to do. Initially cinemas were closed due to the risk of many people being killed by one bomb but this order was relaxed when it was realised cinemas were important for maintaining public morale and for spreading information. Thereafter everybody went to the cinema at least once a week.

Mavis and Pat were in the Girl Guides and in August 1939 were at a guide camp from where Mavis went straight to the family holiday which was in Cornwall that year. They were on the beach at Bude when somebody came up to say that Hitler had invaded Poland. Wilfrid, like everyone, had believed that what he and his comrades went through had been the war to end all wars and he was aghast that there could be another so soon. He decided that they must get home and they had a terrible journey because the whole country was on alert for air raids and driving with headlights on was forbidden, so Wilfrid had to put black boot polish on his headlights. Even so he kept getting stopped and had to say he had done his best to dim the lights. They limped home in time to hear the announcement of war. At least they made this journey before road signs were removed in order to confuse an invading force and before a twenty miles per hour speed limit was imposed at night, to reduce the numbers of pedestrians being knocked down and killed by unlit cars.

From July to September 1940, the Battle of Britain raged and German forces amassed across the channel. The country wanted to protect children from the threat of invasion and the risk of bombing and therefore developed a scheme to evacuate 24,000 children to Canada, Australia, South Africa and New Zealand. It was planned for the children to return home when conditions permitted. Doris's brother Frank had emigrated to Canada before the First World War, where he had married a woman called Dorothy and had three girls. He came back to fight for Britain and was gassed in battle in Europe, dying within a year of the war ending. His widow came to England in about 1921 with her daughters to meet the family, forming a friendship with Doris, after which they corresponded, Dorothy writing to say she had remarried and moved to Los Angeles. It was decided that Mavis and Alan would go to join her. Mavis was 13 and it seemed like a big adventure. She knew about America from what she'd seen at the cinema, mainly Shirley Temple, and she liked the look of it. They undertook medicals, got their documents and did their packing. They were excited and ready to go.

The first ships left England successfully but within two weeks of each other, two ships carrying evacuee children were torpedoed by German U-boats. The first had left Liverpool with passengers including 320 children bound for Halifax and New York. The passengers and crew abandoned ship and all were rescued by other boats in the convoy. The second ship, SS City of Benares, carrying ninety children bound for Canada, was torpedoed on 17 September

1940. The boat had to be abandoned and sank within thirty minutes. A British destroyer picked up some survivors soon afterwards but forty-two of them were adrift in a lifeboat for eight days before being rescued. Seventy-seven of the children died and in total, 260 of the 407 people on board were lost. The sinking caused such public concern that Winston Churchill cancelled further plans to relocate British children abroad.

Mavis was devastated at the loss of young lives but disappointed that she had to continue to live in drab Petts Wood. They remained at home through the Blitz doing what little they could to help the war effort. Doris feverishly knitted garments for the forces; Wilfrid was in the Home Guard. He said that the glow from the Blitz on central London was so bright that he could read a newspaper in the street at night. They endured a lot of air raids and the tremendous noise of the gun emplacements in the parks around them. Every bit of spare land had a gun on it and there was constant gunfire while the planes were droning overhead. At first Mavis and Alan slept under the stairs, then they got a Morrison shelter in the living room. Every time the air raid siren went they had to dive into it, day and night. The shelters came in kits to be bolted together inside the home. They were about six and a half feet long, four feet wide and two and a half feet high, with a solid steel top and wire mesh sides. They were designed to withstand

A Morrison shelter

the upper floor of a house collapsing and the blurb boasted that a family could use it as a dining table in the daytime. It became part of the routine for Mavis, Alan and their parents to sleep there and Mavis recalls scratching her back crawling in and out. Where they lived, they had grandstand seats for the Battle of Britain. Children stood in the street watching the dogfights and planes being shot down, cheering every time a German plane fell in flames. Mavis and Alan went out in the mornings to collect shrapnel, which was a lovely bright silvery colour, and would rush around in people's gardens picking up the shards before everybody compared their shrapnel collections. The full implications of planes coming down had not dawned on them, even when neighbours were killed in air raids. Mavis had the carefree attitude of youth: 'On the whole, you didn't take the war terribly seriously. It was a bit of a diversion when you're in your teens.'

Once Mavis was woken by knocking on the front door. It was a member of the Home Guard saying 'Come on! It's the invasion!' Wilfrid picked up his gas mask and uniform and ran out of the door. Mavis was petrified at the thought that at any moment German parachutists would be landing on top of them. Her mother came in and said it was an exercise. Mavis was not much comforted by a man coming to the door another time about emergency invasion arrangements and asking if they had hammers, pickaxes and so on: it seemed to her that they planned to defeat the Germans by knocking them on their heads as they landed. She and Pat were thrilled to join the Women's Junior Air Corps at age 14. They wore their uniforms and learned Morse code and she loved feeling part of the war effort. There were parades and marching displays and inter-unit competitions and sports. The sergeant encouraged them to improve their marching by bellowing that they looked worse than a Sunday school picnic outing. This passed as motivation at the time.

As they got older, despite the war grinding on, the craze was dancing. The excitement was going to dances every Saturday night with the air training corps from the boys' school. The fact that clothing was rationed and new clothes were hard to come by didn't deter them. Mavis and Pat wore shoes with wooden soles and argued about whether it was better to have the soles hinged or not, which at the time was about the extent of their fashion choices in footwear.

Mavis, August 1942

The V-1s started to arrive in June 1944. Mavis and her mother stood at the bedroom window and wondered what these things were. They looked like a plane on fire, because they had a tail of flame, then the engine noise stopped and there was a great explosion. They were surprised to discover later that they had no pilots. The intensity of attacks increased and mass evacuation was arranged within weeks, especially for south-east London which was in the path of these flying bombs. There was little time for farewells, only time to pack a gas mask and a small bag. Mavis went with Pat and other friends in a large group to Paddington station. There was an air raid as they waited for their train and they had nowhere to shelter. Mavis stood on the platform and wondered if she would be killed. There was nothing else she could do. By coincidence, her future husband was probably nearby at the time, also terrified, because he lived a few hundred metres from where she was standing.

But the raid ended and the train took them to Plymouth where they were greeted by women with tea and biscuits. The evacuees were divided up and Mavis and friends were on a coach to Mawnan

Smith, a village outside Falmouth. About fifty of them sat in the village hall with their cases and gas masks and it began to resemble a slave market with ladies walking about saying 'I'll have him' or 'She looks all right.' The youngsters were most popular. Mavis and her friends were 17 and less desirable but at last Mavis and Pat were taken off to a smart hotel by a couple of ladies, May and Ethel, who worked there as maids. They seemed old and wizened to the two girls but were probably in their fifties.

Nansidwell Manor was outside the village, a small private hotel with its own beach and extensive grounds. All the guests seemed to have titles, Lady this and Air Commodore that. Mavis and Pat were given a room to share in the servants' quarters above the stables with their own wash basin. In the morning they met kind Mrs Pilgrim who ran the hotel. There was a big kitchen where they had meals with the servants, most of whom were elderly because younger workers had been called up. Largely Mavis and Pat were left to themselves. They had the run of the big and 'really marvellous'

Nansidwell Manor in 2019, now private

gardens from which a path led down to the hotel's private beach, a rocky cove with a small patch of sand, plus there were tennis courts they could use. A battery-powered wireless was their source of entertainment and news although reception in Cornwall was poor, especially at night. Transmitters would be randomly switched off to avoid being used by enemy aircraft for guidance.

The village school taught children aged 5 to 11 in one class which was no good to Mavis and Pat, so their school in Bromley sent them work by post and Mavis had to write home asking for her schoolbooks to be sent. The girls were allowed to do their schoolwork in the hotel lounge which was helpful because their digs above the stables were cramped. Initially it was a huge contrast to the lives they had left behind with little semblance of war, not even blackouts. A number of government regulations were introduced, such as to conserve water everyone had to paint a black line five inches above the plughole of each bath and no one was allowed to fill their bath above the line. Harry Pilgrim, the owner's son, recollects that once a boatload of French refugees arrived at Falmouth and Mrs Pilgrim went to help these tired, hungry and bewildered people, bringing some back and giving them temporary beds. With rationing, the only extra food Mrs Pilgrim could buy for them was oranges. Several of her guests were already grumpy about the rules, the shortages of food and of staff and when these French refugees arrived, there was a near riot.

At first Mavis, from the outskirts of London, was appalled that the village had hardly any shops and that they had to go to Falmouth for most things, using the buses which came only every two hours. Falmouth was four miles away and started to suffer from air raids in response to the gradual amassing of British and US naval forces. Falmouth harbour was full of boats and landing craft and the town was full of Americans. Mrs Pilgrim was friendly with the Commander of the Officers' Mess which was in a hotel in Falmouth.

The young American officers had nobody to take to dances, so Mrs Pilgrim volunteered her evacuees, pitching Mavis and Pat into a heady social whirl of dances at the town hotels. Mrs Pilgrim kept a beady eye on them. She didn't trust sailors, and especially not Americans, so the girls were chaperoned and not allowed to leave the dancefloor. Sneaking off into the garden was unthinkable but if lucky they got a few minutes for a goodnight kiss. Mrs Pilgrim could not be everywhere and soon they were whizzing round the countryside in American jeeps, sitting on the laps of these men and singing American songs. These guys were friendly and exotic and Mavis and Pat had a fantastic time.

Harry Pilgrim was about their age. He was at boarding school but came home in the holidays and Mavis would zoom along the lanes on the back of his motorbike. The hotel had subterranean storage rooms full of tools and supplies where they rushed about chasing each other. Harry had a friend who had a car, which was unusual, and although petrol was severely rationed they managed to get hold of it from farmers. A millionairess was staying at the hotel, who I discovered is recorded online as 'Mrs Arthur Woolley-Hart, famed hostess and socialite of London and Cannes'. The friend used to take Mrs Woolley-Hart for drives and Mavis was allowed to sit in the front seat and enjoyed exploring Cornwall. The old man in the hotel who did the washing up asked 'What would your parents say if they knew what you were getting up to down here?' Mavis rejoiced: 'They're never going to find out!' Her letters home left out all the fun.

Around August Pat returned home as the worst of the V-1 attacks had finished. By this time Doris and Wilfrid were living temporarily near Woking because Wilfrid had been directed to work for the NAAFI based on his experience in the food industry. The house in Petts Wood was empty when it was damaged by a bomb and rendered uninhabitable. So Mavis and Alan couldn't go home and they weren't allowed to go to their grandparents in Brighton because coastal areas were prohibited to people unless they already lived there. Mavis remained at the hotel on her own, quite happy to be independent. She attended Falmouth Grammar School but could not get the education she needed there and had to take physics lessons at a boys' school. She was the only girl studying biology but such was the prudery of the times it was not considered suitable for her to mix with boys for biology and so it was decided that she should be transferred. A lady from the Women's Voluntary Services picked her up and put her on a train.

She arrived at Leicester in November 1944 after an exhausting journey. Trains were slow, often spending long periods in sidings to make way for military traffic, and were always crowded with service personnel. The windows were covered with sticky tape so there was not even the distraction of scenery as she went along. On her first night in Leicester Mavis had to sleep in a school hall before she went to stay with a couple in their forties who made a fuss as if she were a child, coming to tuck her in and say goodnight even though she was 17. Fortunately, this was temporary and she went to stay with the Milner family on Loughborough Road, an elderly couple with two married daughters, one of whom lived at home as her husband was in the forces. Margaret was about 22 and Mavis became friendly with her and they went into Leicester together in the mornings on the bus, Mavis to school and Margaret to work at Halifax Building Society. It would still be dark at 8 o'clock in the morning because Britain was on double summertime, introduced during war years as an energy saving measure. Mavis started off at Loughborough Grammar School For Boys but botany and zoology were not available so she transferred to Leicester College of Technology to study for her Higher School Certificates, as A-Levels were then called.

Alan had spent his time in Allestree, outside Derby. Mavis felt she ought to visit her brother but it turned out to be a strange experience because they were no longer close as siblings. They returned south for Christmas. The house in Petts Wood was not habitable so Doris and Wilfrid had to apply for permission to stay in Brighton with Doris's parents, where the family had a very low-key Christmas. It did not make Mavis feel homesick. She had escaped from the questioning of her parents and did not have parental shows of affection to miss. She was growing away from the restrictions of her parents. The freedom had given her the taste for leaving home.

She was listening to the radio with the Milners when they learned that the war was over. Mavis and some friends went into Leicester and joined the euphoric dancing in the streets. Churchill's address was played over loudspeakers to cheering and jubilation. There was a big bonfire in Birstall, a suburb of Leicester, to celebrate, symbolic because bonfires had been banned during the war. It was a lively evening. She returned in the next days to the now-repaired family home in Petts Wood. Her parents were exhausted by six years of war. The family house had been badly damaged, the back blown in, windows gone and walls and ceilings cracked. The Government paid for repairs but still Wilfrid had a lot of work to do. Mavis had an arduous journey from Leicester, lugging her suitcase through the underground and having to walk from the station uphill to the house carrying her case. She went to the back door which was always open. Alan had already arrived and he and their mother were having a meal. Mavis came in and, to her dismay and disbelief, they carried on their conversation as though nothing had happened. Nobody said 'welcome home' or asked 'how are you?' Mavis was upset after her struggle to get there. A couple of days later she bumped into Alan in the street wearing his cadet uniform but did not recognise him and she realised they had become strangers after so much time apart. Mavis didn't find it easy to slot back into the family.

At least she was in London in time for the victory parade and celebrations. Mavis and Pat went up to town and saw the King and Queen going past in a coach. The crowds were so dense that it was frightening and they got stuck on Westminster Bridge, hemmed in by people, and by the time they made it to Charing Cross, the last train to Petts Wood had departed. They had huge luck in meeting Mavis's cousin who lived in Catford and managed to get there to stay the night.

Within a few weeks Mavis took her Higher School Certificates in zoology, botany, chemistry and physics, passing all subjects with top grades. She was working temporarily for the General Nursing Council near Oxford Street when the war in Japan finished in August. There was more rejoicing, people threw paper out of the windows, like confetti. It was exhilarating. Mavis had filled in forms for university while she was an evacuee and was overjoyed to be accepted at University College London to study biochemistry. She had to apply for a grant which entailed an interview at Kent County Council's headquarters in Maidstone. She sat on a chair in a spartan room facing six people who fired questions, wanting to know all about her. It wasn't easy to get a grant but she was successful. When she told her parents that she had a place at university and a grant, they said that they didn't believe in university education for women, saying there was no point because women would get married and stop work. Her father's income had reduced in the war and they felt spare money had to go towards providing Alan with a good start. They made it sound logical and Mavis was not the sort to argue with her parents despite her bitter disappointment. In Mavis's own words: 'It took me quite a long time to forgive them for stopping me going to university. I regretted that for a long time.' She knew what an opportunity she'd missed, a challenge that she would have relished. I'd say the regret lasted all her life.

She never mentioned it again to her parents and they never imagined the pain they had caused. Doris used to go to a chiropodist

and thought that's what Mavis should do with her interest in
medicine. So that's what Mavis did. It never gave her the intellectual
stimulation she craved but it did give her the opportunity to work
anywhere in the country.

She applied to Chelsea Polytechnic which accepted her and
exempted her from the first term when they saw her exam results.
She often went early into the college to play table tennis before
lectures. In the evenings, she stayed longer than she needed to, glad
to be out of the house. She found her fellow students much more
interesting than her family at home. She even volunteered to help
with sprucing up the dilapidated polytechnic building, staying
behind to wash the walls. She flew through the course and qualified
in less than two years, gaining top marks in her exams. Her first job
was in Catford, working in a practice for a kindly old man who had
emphysema and could no longer perform chiropody. She wore a
plain skirt and blouse (trousers for women were unknown) and a hat.
Everyone wore a hat when out and about. It was an outdated place
that catered to the poorer local people, with cubicles next to each
other and no appointment system. Clients queued in an enormous
waiting room and Mavis had to work as fast as she could along the
line of patients. The charge was 3 shillings for both feet and 2
shillings for one foot (15p and 10p today). She had Wednesdays off,
as well as Sundays. After work, Mavis usually went to a cafe and to an
evening class rather than go straight home. She did courses in drama,
dressmaking, cooking and psychology in Catford and was occupied
most nights. She joined the Women's Junior Air Corps and they did
drills in an old stable yard in Orpington. She went dancing and
acquired a boyfriend who was a good dancer and they danced every
Saturday night at a pub in Chislehurst or at the Daylight Inn in Petts
Wood. There was not much else to spend money on as rationing was
still in place and there were few clothes or luxuries in the shops, so
she saved most of her money in her Post Office Savings Account.

After six months she wanted to see another part of the country and took a job in Weymouth. She found digs right on the harbour wall in spitting distance of the boats. It was a cramped cottage with an elderly lady and her daughter who was about 30. One night Mavis was alarmed by bells going off and lots of running and shouting. It turned out to be the crew manning the lifeboat. She developed a social life by joining the local branch of Young Conservatives which was nearly all young men and she soon had a choice of boyfriends. There was a big naval presence in Portland Harbour and the town teemed with sailors. She got friendly with some crew of a battleship, HMS Anson, and was invited to dinner on the ship. She was taken out on a boat and greeted with full formality before being piped aboard.

After an enjoyable year, she decided to move on. After four days of temporary work in the stationery department of Harrods she took a job in Oxford at a small practice attached to a chemist, the Oxford Drug Company, where there was one other chiropodist, a woman who became a good companion. She took digs on Iffley Road, a pleasant walk from her job in the city centre. It was a cramped, grotty bedsit, the walls were dark green with a little alcove for her clothes, a gas ring to cook on and a bed. There was a basin in the room but she had to go down two flights of stairs to fetch water or use the toilet. When her parents came to visit they struggled to understand why she chose to live there rather than in their smart and spacious house in Petts Wood.

She hardly bothered to cook. She tried cooking meat once but it stank the room out, in which she had to sleep. She got a vegetarian ration book that enabled her to buy plenty of cheese so she didn't need to make proper meals. At Oxford Town Hall there was a British Restaurant where she queued each day for her main meal. These were non-profit communal kitchens set up during the war to help people who had been bombed out of their homes or otherwise needed help, selling a three-course meal for a maximum of 9d (4p today and equivalent to £1.35 in purchasing power). They were supposed to provide diners with at least a third of the day's needs as the Government was concerned about vitamin C intake because fruit consumption was limited by rationing. Cabbage, high in vitamin C, was a staple in these restaurants.

Mavis enjoyed Oxford. She had a boyfriend called Ken who attended the University. Social events were frequent and varied, and she went to the Exeter College Commemoration Ball on 21 June 1949. Dancing commenced at 9pm and the programme of twenty-four dances ran until 6am the next morning. There were three sittings of supper at midnight, 1.15am and at 2.30am. The programme assures people that champagne and wine will be available to buy by the bottle. It was delightful to wear an evening dress after so many years of utility clothing. It was full skirted with a tight waist, part of the 'New Look' from Dior: she kept that dress for a long time. She was elated on the way home as they walked down the high street in their evening clothes in the early morning light. She went to bed at 6.45am and got up an hour later to go to work. Ken graduated and went to work in London as a journalist, and they split up. Mavis decided to return home with the intention of going to work in the north of England, which was unexplored territory.

Around this time Mavis started writing a daily diary. The first entry was in 1948 and the last in 2013 with almost no days missed, resulting in a stupendous quantity of writing in a huge number of volumes that was far too much to digest (although some entries are brief; the day of my birth says: 'Gerald arrived.')

In the meantime she got a job at Scholl's in Regent Street and it was while working here that she acquired the name Fay. In 1948 a radio show launched called 'Take It From Here', written by Frank Muir and Dennis Norden. It is credited with redefining British comedy after the grimness of the war. One of the characters was called Mavis and a man talking to her always said 'Ooooh Mavis', which became a catchphrase. Every time Mavis told someone her name, they retorted 'Ooooh Mavis' and she quickly tired of it. When she started work at Regent Street she was known as Miss Foley and she didn't tell them her name. They started calling her Fairy because she was young and fair and this evolved to Fay. When she met my father and he asked her name, she replied 'It's really Mavis but people call me Fay', which is the name he always used.

APPENDIX 2

What happened to the rest of Georg Hahlo's family?

GEORG'S GRANDPARENTS

Siegfried Salomon Hahlo (27 March 1826 – 27 January 1908) Wilhelmine Löwenstein (12 October 1836 – 6 January 1914)

Siegfried Hahlo was born in Hannoversch Münden, Lower Saxony and moved to Oldenburg in 1841, living first at the home of his uncle, Gottschalk Joseph Ballin. He founded his own business as a clothing merchant and purveyor to the court. His wife Wilhelmine came from the Löwenstein family of Wesermarsch, Lower Saxony. They married on 1 June 1857 and lived above the business premises at Lange Strasse 60. In 1882 they moved around the corner to Gaststrasse 3.

Entries at the National Archives record people with the name Hahlo setting up businesses in the Manchester and Bradford areas, mainly in the 1870s. Siegfried's brother Carl married in Bradford in 1872. His sister Hermine married Philip Goldschmidt who was twice mayor of Manchester.

There is a well-populated strand of family with the surname Barker-Hahlo in the UK. They are descended from Siegfried's brother Georg who married Fanny Barker in Manchester in 1871. There is evidence in the National Archives that some people with this surname changed it to Beauchamp around 1931–34.

Siegfried's father, Herz Hahlo, had married Rosa Ballin in 1823 in Minden. Siegfried's sister Johanna married Moritz Ballin in Oldenburg in 1849. The link between the two families continued when, two generations later, Johanna's granddaughter married her cousin Ernst Ballin in San Francisco. The Ballin family owned the Hamburg-America shipping line and thereby the boat on which Georg escaped to South America.

GEORG'S PARENTS

Wilhelm Hahlo (4 April 1858 – 4 November 1944)
Sofie Helene Wallach (8 October 1868 – 1 August 1950)

Wilhelm and Sofie Hahlo were married on 2 March 1890. They were not of humble origins and their four surviving children all achieved in life. Wilhelm converted to Christianity at the end of the nineteenth century because of antisemitism, changing religion not out of conviction, he was never a churchgoer, but as a business decision.

They emigrated to London around 1 March 1939 helped by their daughter Else and husband Richard, who were already in London, and Wilhelm's sister Helene, who had married William Ruttenau and lived in Manchester for several years, and a relative (possibly her grandson) Charles Ruttenau who acted as guarantor. Wilhelm and Sofie settled in Hendon, living at 62 Vincent Court, Bell Lane, London NW4. Georg's father remained stern and his mother worn by the trauma of leaving Germany in old age.

Wilhelm had a heart attack in 1944 when Dieter was visiting and he had to help him sit on his bed. Dieter's grandfather kept saying 'Now it's all over, now it's all over' in German. He was placed in a nursing home and died soon after. Georg wrote from Bolivia a moving funeral oration that read as though he were at the graveside. After the funeral there was no room in the cars for Dieter so he had a long walk from the cemetery in Golders Green to Finchley in order to get to the important bit – something to eat.

GEORG'S UNCLES AND AUNTS

Wilhelm was one of nine children. Three of the six brothers emigrated from Oldenburg early on. Ernst went to Dallas, Texas and was having children there by 1892. Bernhardt and Karl went to Manchester and some of these Hahlo strands have anglicised their name to Harlow. Philipp married Emmy in Hamburg in 1905 and they arrived in England in April 1939 before making it to America in May 1940.

Helene married William Ruttenau (born in Frankfurt) in Manchester in 1879 where she raised two children. Her son Sidney had children including one named Charles Ruttenau, and it may have been him who was supportive, along with Helene, when guarantors were needed to help Wilhelm, Sofie and Leopold flee from Germany and who provided money for Georg to obtain his visa and ticket for Bolivia. Sisters Anna and Bertha both married and raised children in Germany.

Leopold Max Hahlo (9 September 1868 – 6 June 1954) remained in Oldenburg and was the only one of Georg's uncles and aunts who was a presence in Dieter's life, living close to the family shop. He ran a foods wholesale and distribution business from his place of residence. An advertisement of his from 1907 promoted Solo Margarine: 'tastes like real butter... for almost half the price'. During the First World War, he was made responsible by Duke Friedrich

August for the supply of food to the population of the dukedom.

He arrived in England with Georg's parents around 1 March 1939 as a widower, his wife Auguste (née Roewekamp) having died in 1933. His address in London was also given as 62 Vincent Court and his occupation as wholesale grocer, but with no present work. There is a letter dated 6 January 1947, when Leopold was applying for naturalisation, to confirm that Leopold Max Hahlo is the same person as Leopold Israel Hahlo, the name with which he entered Britain. The name Israel had been imposed on him by Nazi authorities when issuing his passport in 1939. This was routinely done by the Nazis to denote male Jews and must have occurred after Leopold was rounded up during Kristallnacht. The letter is addressed to Ernest Bevin, Secretary of State for Foreign Affairs and came from the Danish Legation in London, because his second wife, Bertha, was Danish. He had met and married her in England.

His registration card, dated 18 January 1940, gives his address as Didsbury, Manchester, in the home of Mrs Buttenan, which is probably a misspelling of Ruttenau. By the time of his naturalisation in July 1948 he is noted as working as a Chief Accountant and married to Bertha. He died in London.

My father claims Leopold came to England with his daughters Helene and Gertrud but there is no evidence of this. Records suggest that Gertrud stayed in Germany and that Helene left in 1933, staying briefly in Italy and then the US before returning to live in Berlin in 1954. Her son, Peter Ries, became a theatre director in Hannover with whom my father later had some contact.

GEORG'S BROTHERS AND SISTERS

Georg had an elder brother and two younger sisters. An older sister, Mathilde, died in January 1895 at the age of 6 months.

Friedrich Wilhelm Max (1 January 1891 – 13 May 1944) was
known as Fritz and was, according to my father, a strange and
unfriendly man. He ran a business in Hamburg that made cardboard
boxes, having trained in Manchester before the First World War. In
order to survive the oppression and to continue his business, he
became a Nazi stormtrooper. My father remembers Fritz turning up
at their home in Hannover in his uniform and his parents being
shocked and horrified.

Fritz married Eva Wiethase who was not Jewish. Masquerading as
a Nazi helped him to survive for a while but his ancestry eventually
came to light, leading to his arrest. He was jailed in 1939 for the
crime of 'racial defilement', referring to sexual relations between
Aryans and non-Aryans. He died in a prison hospital in Hamburg in
May 1944. The factory and the family home were destroyed by
bombing in 1943. Eva survived the war and once came to London to
visit. Life had drained all humour and joy from her and her
comment that she had lost more than Elli did not go down well.

Fritz and Eva had two sons. Gerhard joined the German army
and died in June 1940 at Beaumont and is buried near Sédan. The
other son Werner worked as an office outfitter in Hamburg. He was
sent to a labour camp and, against the odds, survived. The lunacy of
the time is shown in that these two sons with the same mixed blood
were treated in different ways: one asked to fight, the other
imprisoned.

Werner corresponded with my father after the war and they met
once or twice in Germany. He lived in the Alps, at Berchtesgaden,
and later at Garmisch-Partenkirchen where Germany staged the
1936 Winter Olympics. Other than that, it was Christmas greetings
and the odd news update. My father describes him as boring and not
well educated, but pleasant when they met. He had one daughter
called Jutta.

Charlotte Sophie Leonie (21 December 1899 – 3 February 1989), known as Lotte, and her husband Julius Giessel were doctors and paediatricians living in Eichwalde, a well-to-do suburb of Berlin. They had a car, a chauffeur and a maid. As the Nazi policies towards Jews started to grip, and a stormtrooper was stationed outside their home, they got the message and emigrated with their children, Bill and Henry, to Houston, Texas in 1936, sponsored by Lotte's uncle Ernst who had emigrated to Texas in 1891.

When my parents visited America in the early 1980s, they received a charming welcome from Lotte and she invited them to stay with her, Julius having died by then. Bill and Henry, a doctor and a lawyer, were friendly but there was no lasting connection. They never came to England to see family.

Else Paula Wilhelmine (6 April 1903 – 9 June 1985) was a laboratory technician and married Richard Hochfeld, who ran a fruit import and export business based in Hamburg and London. Their children were Wilfried, who was a couple of years older than Dieter, and Ruth. Georg's family and Else's family were close and there are snaps of holidays together.

Richard was Jewish and as events heated up in Germany, they moved to England in 1936. They lived in Finchley and were well-off. They were hospitable and Dieter would sometimes stay with them but relationships cooled due to the bad feeling between them and Elli. Richard died in 1967.

The son, now known as Wilfred, took over his father's business and travelled a great deal, particularly to Chile and other countries in South America from which they imported fruit. My parents used to get parcels from Else at Christmas with fruit and other goodies. In the years after the war, fruit was in short supply and the seasonal gift was a luxurious treat.

Wilfred later changed his name to Hockfield, married and lived in in Barnet. His wife had died when around 2000 he called out of the blue saying he was in the area. My father and he chatted for a long time, having not seen each other for many years. Wilfred was looking to sell the company and retire.

The company is still going, based in Kent. Its blurb says it is 'One of the oldest independent fruit importing business in the UK, formed in 1936. The company pioneered imports from Chile, Greece and India and built its reputation supplying French apples to the major supermarkets and wholesalers.' There is no evidence online that family members with the name Hochfeld or Hockfield are still involved in the business.

Ruth taught gymnastics, married a Swedish man and went to live in Gothenburg. Her daughter Gunna, with whom Fay and Peter used to correspond, lived in Gothenburg and had children of her own, one of whom came to London for a while.

OTHER HAHLOS

HR Hahlo was a distinguished legal scholar with several publications to his name. Professor Herman Robert 'Bobby' Hahlo was born in New York in 1905. He was the stepson of Siegfried Hahlo who was Georg's second cousin. Mother and sons fled to South Africa in 1934 and moved to Canada in 1968. HR Hahlo ended his days in Exeter, near his children, and died in 1985. His son, Ken Hahlo, lives in Bolton.

HR Hahlo rose to eminence as Dean of the Faculty of Law at University of the Witwatersrand (Wits), Johannesburg. He was honoured for having spent over twenty years in the position. He was a formidable lecturer and scholar but believed that the minds of Africans and women were not suited to the study and practise of law.

Nelson Mandela enrolled as the first African law student at Wits in 1943, soon after it opened its doors to students of all races. Mandela failed the final examination three times. On the third occasion, he applied to HR Hahlo to write supplementary examinations in the papers he failed but was denied permission. Mandela recalled in his autobiography that his professor believed that 'Law was a social science and that women and Africans were not disciplined enough to master its intricacies.' On one occasion HR Hahlo reputedly exclaimed at him 'You call this an essay?' Mandela wrote 'I wish that one day he has to write by paraffin light in Orlando.' Mandela's pursuit of his degree is a story of persistence across forty-six years, over twenty-six of which were spent in prison. Arguably one of the factors that drove him was his determination to prove HR Hahlo wrong.

Vernon Brooks, born 1923 in Berlin as Werner Bruck, came to England in March 1939, probably on the Kindertransport. He lived with the Tompsett family in Marden, Kent before emigrating to Toronto, where he was naturalised in 1946. His parents were murdered in concentration camps. His is a distant connection, descended from Georg's great great grandfather making him Dieter's fifth cousin (we think). He prepared a genealogical research document, copies of which are available.

There are strands of the Hahlo family in several locations in the US and Canada, as well as in Australia, Norway and Sweden.

ELLI'S FAMILY

Elli's parents died in Germany before the onset of war. Her father Friedrich Wilhelm Drewin was a likable old man who lived with his daughter in Bad Kreuznach and Hannover. He was placed in an old people's home in Hannover as the family scattered, where he soon died. Her mother Pauline Luise Drewin died in 1919.

Elli and Georg's marriage certificate gives an indecipherable address in Lichterfelde, which is a district in south-west Berlin and presumably where she grew up. She was born a few years after her two brothers, one of whom was a witness at the wedding. She appears to have had little relationship with her brothers, perhaps because they were enthusiastic Nazis (my father's conjecture). Dieter hardly knew them and showed little interest in finding out more about them. His cousin Ellie, daughter of one of the brothers, sometimes came to stay with his family in Germany. She was slightly older than Dieter and lost her husband during the war. She lived in west Berlin after partition. I have not attempted to trace the Drewin side of the family.

ACKNOWLEDGEMENTS AND THANKS

This book could not have been written without the contributions of my grandfather, in completing his journal, and my father and mother who sat and patiently recalled their younger years as best they could over a prolonged period. Thanks to them their stories live on. Many others have not been able to face up to recounting what happened to them.

I am grateful to my brothers Michael and Richard and to my cousin Ian for their support and encouragement.

A special mention goes to Nick Tanner whose intelligent reading of German documents and knowledge of German history has added to the book. Nick also gave valuable feedback on a draft. Lisa Rodrigues helped me to enhance my storytelling and greatly improved the finished text. I thank Lisa and Nick for their time and effort.

My wife Anne has given time and thought to reading drafts, discussing passages and finding solutions to concerns as they occurred. I am grateful for her time and unwavering support.

Sue Cawood and Tracy Wellman helped with the design, layout and production of the book. Both of them stepped in at short notice and swept me away with advice and support that transformed it from a rough draft into a thing of beauty. Their enthusiasm, professionalism and commitment enabled me to get through the daunting final stages with a spring in my step. My eternal gratitude goes to them.

The lovely front and back cover designs are by Robin Cracknell. Robin also agreed to run high quality scans of family photos before he knew the quantity; but he saw the task through and I am extremely grateful to him for all his efforts.

I'd like to thank several welcoming people in Oldenburg. I am indebted to Claus Ahrens at Oldenburg Town Archives who provided several records of the Hahlo family from his office shelves and was hospitable, interested, thoughtful, providing help and insight over more than a year. I am grateful to Sabine Grote, image archivist at Oldenburg Stadtmuseum, for finding many relevant historic photos and for granting permission to reproduce them in the book. The staff at Oldenburg Tourist Office helped, notably Annika Repenning and especially the irrepressibly enthusiastic Bernd Munderloh.

The Wiener Holocaust Library in London is a fantastic resource and provides a programme of events and exhibitions, which have been fascinating. Howard Falksohn, Torsten Jugl and Sonia Bacca deserve a special mention for their helpfulness. Aubrey Pomerance at the Jewish Museum in Berlin gave useful guidance.

Tash Patel and Sarah Coward provided good advice. Thanks to Nick Barlay for his wisdom and to Steve Marsh at The Laughton Press.

Many people have helped with (often fruitless) searches of records. They work for World Jewish Relief, Association of Jewish Refugees or the Arolsen Archives. I received good help and feedback from Dr Clare George at the Research Centre for German and Austrian Exile Studies.

SOURCES

I have plundered many more websites than those listed here. The internet is a warren of possibilities and so many trails were followed that at times I became completely entangled in the web.

The principal place to find information relevant to the Kindertransport is the Wiener Holocaust Library:
   https://wienerholocaustlibrary.org/

Many historical documents concerning members of the family are available for research at the National Archives in London:
   https://www.nationalarchives.gov.uk/

There is a German national archive in which to search for family records:
   https://www.archivportal-d.de/?lang=en

   as well as a commercial offer:

   https://oldgermantranslations.com/translations/page8/page8.html

The excellent Oldenburg Town Archives manages a fascinating collection of historic photos of the town here:
   https://www.alt-oldenburg.de/index.html

Oldenburg Stadtmuseum holds a superb collection of historic exhibits, records and photographs, including photos of the Hahlo family:
   https://www.stadtmuseum-oldenburg.de/

A selection of other sources and relevant organisations:

Jewish Museum, London:
  https://jewishmuseum.org.uk/

Jewish Museum, Berlin:
  https://www.jmberlin.de/en

United States Holocaust Memorial Museum:
  https://www.ushmm.org/

German Federal War Archives:
  https://ersterweltkrieg.bundesarchiv.de/index.html#front-slider

British Newspaper Archive:
  https://www.britishnewspaperarchive.co.uk/

London Metropolitan Archives:
  https://www.cityoflondon.gov.uk/things-to-do/history-and-
  heritage/london-metropolitan-archives

Kindertransport Association:
  https://www.kindertransport.org/

Association of Jewish Refugees:
  https://ajr.org.uk/

Second Generation Network:
  https://secondgeneration.org.uk/

Association of Children of Jewish Refugees:
  http://www.acjr.org.uk/

Generation 2 Generation:
  https://www.generation2generation.org.uk/

World Jewish Relief:
  https://www.worldjewishrelief.org/about-us

JewishGen:
https://www.jewishgen.org/

Library of the Society of Friends:
https://www.quaker.org.uk/resources/library

Holocaust Memorial Day Trust:
https://www.hmd.org.uk/search/node/kindertransport

The Holocaust Explained:
https://www.theholocaustexplained.org/

Leo Baeck Institute:
https://www.lbi.org/

Arolsen Archives:
https://arolsen-archives.org/en/

Association for Oldenburg Landscape:
https://oldenburgische-landschaft.de/

Alemannia Judaica:
http://www.alemannia-judaica.de/oldenburg_synagoge.htm

BBC History WW2 People's War (including a story from Harry Pilgrim):
https://www.bbc.co.uk/history/ww2peopleswar/about/

Austrian Jewish Exile Theatre Collection:
https://norbertmiller.wordpress.com/category/welcome/

Tower Theatre Archive:
https://www.archive.towertheatre.org.uk/archive.htm

Hahlo family on Wikipedia:
https://en.wikipedia.org/wiki/History_of_the_Jews_in_Oldenburg

BIBLIOGRAPHY (SELECT)

The following books have contributed directly and/or have provided inspiration in the writing.

Barlay, Nick, 2013 Scattered Ghosts

Barnett, Ruth, 2010 Person of No Nationality

Baumel-Schwartz, Judith Tydor, 1959 Never Look Back

Boyd, Julia, 2017 Travellers in the Third Reich

Craig-Norton, Jennifer, 2019 The Kindertransport: Contesting Memory

De Waal, Edmund, 2010 The Hare with Amber Eyes

Dove, Richard (contributor), 2007 Out of Austria: The Austrian Centre in London in World War II

Fast, Vera K, 2010 Children's Exodus: A History of the Kindertransport

Freeman, Hadley, 2020 House of Glass

Gershon, Karen, 1966 We Came As Children

Harding, Thomas, 2015 The House by the Lake

Hawes, James, 2017 The Shortest History of Germany

Leverton, Bertha & Lowensohn, Shmuel, 1990 I Came Alone

Lichtenstein, Jonathan, 2020 The Berlin Shadow

Norton, Jennifer, 1976 The Kindertransport: History and Memory (doctoral thesis)

Oldenburg Stadt, 1988 *Die Geschichte der Oldenburger Juden und ihre Vernichtung* (History of Oldenburg Jews and their annihilation)

Oldenburg Stadt, 2001 *Erinnerungsbuch für die jüdischen NS-Opfer aus Oldenburg 1933–1945* (Memory Book for the Residents Affected by Nazi Persecution of the Jews)

Oldenburg Stadt, 1996 *Oldenburger Häuserbuch: Gebäude und Bewohner im inneren Bereich der Stadt Oldenburg* (Buildings and residents in the inner area of the city of Oldenburg)

Oppenheimer, Deborah and Harris, Mark Jonathan, 2000 Into the Arms of Strangers

Rees, Laurence, 2005 Auschwitz

Research Foundation for Jewish Immigration, 1999 *Biographisches Handbuch der deutschsprachigen Emigration nach 1933–1945* (Biographical handbook of German-speaking emigration)

Rosenberg, Sheila, 2019 The Exit Visa

Sebald, WG, 2001 Austerlitz

Seymour, Miranda, 2013 Noble Endeavours

Winton, Barbara, 2014 If It's Not Impossible

Wolff, Marion, 2004 Shedding Skins

The experiences of Kindertransport children and their relatives is a rich seam in literature. You could spend several years reading on the subject and not run short of material. I have other recommended titles should anyone be interested and of course the Wiener Holocaust Library can help with suggestions.

The quote in Chapter 3 is taken from Doctor Faustus by Thomas Mann, Vintage Classics, 1996 and reproduced by kind permission of Thomas Mann International.

PHOTOGRAPHS

Photographs are from the family collection unless otherwise credited below. Photographs are protected by copyright and are not available for public distribution.

The following photos have been reproduced with the kind permission of Oldenburg Stadtmuseum:

Chapter 1: Drawing of Hahlo building
Chapter 1: The last Grand Duke
Chapter 1: Zeppelin crowd and flight
Chapter 1: Portraits of Sofie and Wilhelm and of Leopold
Chapter 2: Building and pupils, Oldenburg Gymnasium
Chapter 2: Golden wedding group photo
Chapter 3: Farewell to the troops and regimental postcard
Chapter 18: The walk of the Jews and the ruined synagogue

The following photos have been reproduced with permission from Wiener Holocaust Library Collections:

Chapter 14: Der Stürmer
Chapter 20: Arrivals inspection
Chapter 21: Dovercourt Bay huts
Chapter 21: Mealtime at Dovercourt
End Note 18: Hampstead Garden Suburb Care Committee index card

The following photos are reproduced with permission from other sources as credited below or are in the public domain:

Chapter 20: Olympic poster: Deutsches Historisches Museum
https://www.dhm.de/fileadmin/medien/lemo/images/ 20023791.jpg
Chapter 22: Beckenham and Penge County School for Boys:
https://www.pengeheritagetrail.org.uk/the-trail-sites/kentwood-school/
Chapter 22: Barrage balloons:
https://commons.wikimedia.org/wiki/File:Barrage_balloons_
over_London_during_World_War_II.jpg
Chapter 23: SS Deutschland:
https://en.wikipedia.org/wiki/SS_Deutschland_(1900)
Chapter 23: Chiropody booths:
https://www.kcl.ac.uk/library/collections/archives
Chapter 25: Otto Tausig with Hansi:
http://www.juedischewieden.at/familie-tausig/
End Note 12: Nuremberg laws:
https://commons.wikimedia.org/wiki/File:Nuremberg_laws_
Racial_Chart.jpg
End Note 17: SS Saarland:
http://www.combinedfleet.com/TeiyoT_t.htm
End Note 22: Das Laterndl programme:
https://london.ac.uk/senate-house-library/our-collections/special-
collection
Appendix 1: Morrison shelter:
http://s00.yaplakal.com/pics/pics_original/4/2/2/12002224.jpg

The following photos are from other sources as listed below and in these cases it has not been possible to trace copyright holders:

Chapter 12: Hanomag: https://www.thairath.co.th/content/680461
Chapter 21: Dovercourt Bay menu:
https://harwichhavenhistory.co.uk/arrival-in-england

Chapter 22: Potato Pete and Doctor Carrot:
https://imgur.com/a/ZjZTx

Chapter 22: Dig for Victory: https://imgur.com/gallery/X2fHP

End Note 5: Iron Cross: https://p1.liveauctioneers.com/1022/
33878/13772394_1_x.jpg?auto=webp&format=pjpg&version=
1350944843&width=512

End Note 24: Helen Clare: http://www.helenclare.com/

Printed in Great Britain
by Amazon

22703094R00209